Nabaṭi Poetry

الشعـر النبطـي

[al-shiʿr al Nabaṭī]

Nabaṭi Poetry

The Oral Poetry of Arabia

Saad Abdullah Sowayan
King Saud University
Riyadh, Saudi Arabia

UNIVERSITY OF CALIFORNIA PRESS
Berkeley Los Angeles London

University of California Press
Berkeley and Los Angeles, California

University of California Press, Ltd.
London, England

Library of Congress Cataloging in Publication Data

Sowayan, Saad Abdullah.
Nabaṭi poetry

Bibliography: p. 217
Includes index.
1. Folk poetry, Arabic—Arabian Peninsula—History and criticism.
2. Arabic
poetry—Arabian Peninsula—History and criticism. I. Title.
PJ8000.S68 1985 398.2'927 84–2480
ISBN 0–520–04882–2

Printed in the United States of America

1 2 3 4 5 6 7 8 9

To my grandfather
Mḥammad as-Slēmān aṣ-Ṣwayyān
with love and respect

CONTENTS

ACKNOWLEDGMENTS

In the time I have been engaged in writing my thesis, I have been through several academic and personal difficulties. Without the support and understanding of my advisors, Professor Alan Dundes and Professor Mounah Khouri, it would have been impossible to finish this work, at least in its present form. Furthermore, Professor Dundes's immense knowledge in the field of folkloristics has always given me invaluable inspiration and help, and I should like to take this opportunity to express my personal gratitude and intellectual indebtedness to him.

Professor Khouri was the first to perceive the value of my work and encourage me to pursue it; I shall always cherish the many hours spent with him in leisurely discussion of my ideas on Nabaṭi poetry and its relevance to the study of classical Arabic poetry. Professor Khouri went beyond the call of duty to provide me with much needed kindness and valuable help, and I shall remain forever grateful to him.

I should also like to thank the other members of my committee for their help and guidance: Professor Hamid Algar, Professor William Hickman, and Professor Amin Sweeney.

I am particularly grateful for the assistance and advice given me by Professor S. A. Bonebakker of the University of California, Los Angeles, Professor T. M. Johnstone of the University of London, and Professor Otto Jastrow, the editor of *Zeitschrift fur arabische Linguistik*. I have benefited from the many discussions I have had with my friends Manṣūr Abu Khamsīn, Joseph Zeidan, Amer Ben Arab, and Larry Michalak.

It is my obligation and pleasure to thank King ʿAbdulaziz University, Jiddah, Saudi Arabia, which provided me with a grant to spend four months (August–December 1978) in Saudi Arabia doing fieldwork on Nabaṭi poetry.

Last but not least, I should like to thank Dr. Julie Meisami, who smoothed my rough English and helped arrange my material in a more polished form, not to mention her excellent and flawless typing.

I

INTRODUCTION

The Aim and Scope of This Work

Nabaṭi poetry is the popular vernacular poetry of Arabia. Due to the great mobility of the Arab tribes, it is not easy to confine this poetic tradition to one particular locality; it is widespread throughout the Arabian Peninsula. The frequent droughts and famines and the political instability of Arabia in the past forced whole tribes and settlements to migrate to the north and east, carrying with them their Nabaṭi poetic tradition. But the indigenous home of Nabaṭi poetry is Najd, the vast territory that includes the central Arabian plateau and the areas around it. All renowned Nabaṭi poets come from Najd, and the diction of this poetry conforms to the colloquial speech of that region. People outside Najd who are familiar with Nabaṭi poetry are people who originally came from that region, where this poetry is most popular and whence it diffused to the periphery.

As is well known by the scholars in the field, the word *nabaṭī* originally referred to the language of the Nabataeans. However, its meaning was eventually extended by the early Arab philologists until it came to be applied loosely to any speech that did not strictly conform to the rules of classical Arabic. It is in this latter sense that the word was applied by learned compilers to the vernacular poetry of Arabia, in order to set it apart from the well-established and highly respected classical tradition. This usage of the word *Nabaṭi,* therefore, is not intended to imply that this poetry is linked in any way to the Nabataeans, but means only that it is composed in vernacular, rather than classical, literary Arabic.

Nabaṭi poets rarely use the term *nabaṭī* in reference to themselves or to their poetry, and many of them do not even know this sense of the word.[1] It is not certain when or by whom the term was first used in this context. Ibn Khaldūn, who was the first to write about this poetry, did not call it *nabaṭī* but reported that it was called *badawī, qaysī, ḥawrānī,* or *aṣmaᶜīyāt* (1967:1125). The first recorded use of the word *nabaṭī* in reference to vernacular poetry is in a poem by Abū Ḥamzih al-ᶜĀmri, a Nabaṭi poet who died over four centuries ago. W. G. Palgrave, who claims to have traversed Arabia in 1862, mentions Nabaṭi poetry three times (1865–1866:I, 169, 281, 335).[2] R. F. Burton (1878:224) also mentions Nabaṭi poetry, but mistakes Nabaṭi for Nabataean. The term now appears in the titles of many printed collections and anthologies.[3]

The Nabaṭi poet may be a town amir, a tribal sheikh, a desert warrior, a daring marauder, a poor farmer, or a member of the urban elite. As in ancient times, the people of premodern Arabia were a nation of poets. Poetic composition was not merely an artistic vocation practiced by professionals exercising their skills in composing panegyrics to wealthy patrons or in entertaining spectators and passive audiences. Poets did not constitute a special class and no formal training or initiation was involved in becoming a poet. But, while anyone could be a poet, there were, of course, different grades and ranks among them.

In premodern Arabia there was considerable reliance on the well-developed and highly stylized idiom of Nabaṭi poetry as a means of communication, especially on solemn or formal occasions. Tribal chiefs and town amirs as well as relatives and friends communicated with one another in poems. Tribal territories, grazing areas, water holes, desert roads and stations; grievances, threats, battles, and other events, large and small—all were recorded and described in poems. Thus, Nabaṭi poetry deals with a variety of topics ranging from the sublime to the most mundane and pertaining to collective as well as personal issues; but it remains, like classical Arabic poetry, predominantly boastful, panegyric, elegiac, and amatory.

Less than a generation ago, Nabaṭi poetry still constituted a vigorous and dynamic tradition; some of its acknowledged masters are still living today. The circumstances of its composition and the manner of its delivery and transmission still survive in the memories of many individuals, some of whom had participated personally in events commemorated by this poetry.

Recent changes in the political organization and socioeconomic structure of Arabia, however, have dealt a severe blow to the vitality and vigor of this poetic tradition; it is disappearing rapidly, and the number of its practitioners is decreasing at an alarming rate. Its popularity is diminishing and its propagation has become restricted to printed anthologies and to a limited number of enthusiasts and old-timers who engage in such activity to pass the time and lament the past. Nabaṭi poets have become silent or turned to such hackneyed themes as unfulfilled love, moral exhortation, and praise of government projects and officials. Their words can no longer arouse the masses and impel them to perform acts of manliness and chivalry. The modern generation can no longer understand the language of this poetry or appreciate its style and imagery. The traditional activities and life-styles which caused Nabaṭi poetry to flourish and from which it drew its material have in recent times become radically altered or have disappeared along with the lore associated with them. The way of life characterized by incessant forays, perpetual feuds, constantly shifting tribal alliances, and the sudden rise and fall of emirates and sheikhdoms, which gave impetus to this poetry, now no longer exists. Raiding is virtually extinct and the establishment of a strong central government has put an end to the expression of tribal feuds and parochial conflicts. The traditional societies of the Arabian Peninsula are rapidly being transformed into modern states whose ties with the past are becoming very brittle. Educational institutions and the modern media of communication have also stripped popular poetry of its social role.

Serious and concentrated effort must be devoted to salvaging and studying this poetry and examining it in its proper social context before the tradition dies out completely and before its diction becomes even more difficult to understand. In addition to its aesthetic appeal, it is a valuable source—often the only one available—of information on the culture and history of premodern Arabia. Furthermore, certain enigmatic questions concerning the composition, transmission, and authenticity of classical Arabic poetry can best be resolved by taking a close look at this vernacular poetry, which is the direct descendant of the classical tradition.

This book is divided into an introduction and three parts. The first part consists of an overview of Nabaṭi poetry in the context of premodern Arabian society and culture. Nabaṭi poetry is so entwined with premodern Arabian life and so filled with allusions to historical events and traditional practices that, in order to perceive its real value and discern its true artistic quality, one must establish familiarity not only with its vernacular diction but, perhaps more importantly, with the way of life that determined its most salient characteristics. The first part of this study is therefore intended to give the reader a glimpse of life in premodern Arabia and to demonstrate that both Nabaṭi poetry and ancient Arabian poetry existed and flourished under essentially the same social and environmental conditions and fulfilled the same social and political functions.

The second part of this work will deal with the composition, transmission, and performance of Nabaṭi poetry. Evidence will be presented to show that composition and transmission in Nabaṭi poetry are separate activities and, consequently, that memory plays a great role in its transmission. The interaction between written and oral modes of transmission will be examined and a distinction will be made between specific and general modes of transmission. In the chapter dealing with performance, I shall discuss the traditional performance context and also touch upon the role of radio and television in altering this traditional context. I shall also give a brief survey of the various occasions for, and manners of, the singing of Nabaṭi poetry.

The third part of this work is comparative. There I shall analyze the prosody of Nabaṭi poetry and examine its formal and historical affinities with classical Arabic poetry in order to demonstrate that the roots of this popular vernacular tradition can be traced back to the classical tradition and that, in fact, it never entirely lost touch with this tradition. The historical relationship of Nabaṭi to classical poetry is supplemented by their literary relationship; evidence will be presented to show that among Nabaṭi poets were some who knew how to read and write and who had direct access to the mainstream of Arabic literature. The topic of literacy in Nabaṭi poetry is of relevance, not only to the discussion of its relationship to the Arabic literary tradition as a whole but also to the examination of its composition and transmission, where it is maintained that the "oral" process and the "written" process coexist and overlap.

The concluding chapter is an examination of the composition and transmission of classical Arabic poetry in the light of its unmistakable kinship with Nabaṭi poetry. In this chapter I shall take issue with some scholars who have attempted to apply oral-formulaic theories—in particular the Parry-Lord theory—to classical Arabic poetry. I shall also attempt to clarify the nature of "orality" in relation to Arabic poetry, in order to demonstrate that the term "oral poetry" should not be considered synonymous with the term "oral-formulaic" poetry.

I must admit that I am more committed to the Nabaṭi poetic tradition itself than to any specific approach or theoretical model in my consideration of it. The object of this work is not to force on the reader a dry and rigid theoretical argument; my principal aim is rather to present a broad perspective of Nabaṭi poetry and to communicate some of the enthusiasm I feel about this tradition. If I can arouse the interest of others in this long-neglected field, I would consider my mission accomplished. With that aim in mind, I shall include many poetic examples and bits of information about famous Nabaṭi poets although, regretfully, much had to be left out.

This work is in no way meant to be the last word on Nabaṭi poetry. The field is too complex and extensive for one individual to master and say everything that can be said about it. The Nabaṭi tradition extends over a vast geographical area and spans a long period of time. The existing scattered treatments and published collections, though admittedly voluminous, barely scratch the surface of this rich field. There are, unfortunately, a very few examples of Nabaṭi poetry in its early stages, and we know little about poets of past generations, except perhaps about some who distinguished themselves in other fields as well, such as politics, trade, or learning. It will take a great deal of diligent research to fill some of the gaps existing in our knowledge of the history and development of Nabaṭi poetry. I therefore regard my own work as more in the nature of a preliminary study which sets forth some of the considerations and problems involved in the investigation of Nabaṭi poetry.

Translation and Transliteration

The difficulties of translating poetry are well known and I need not dwell on them here. Poetic diction is compact and highly specialized. The poetic message is conveyed not only through the denotative meanings of words but also through the images, resonances, connotations, and associations they evoke. The affective properties and suggestive powers of a word are irretrievably lost once it is translated into another language. This makes the exact word-for-word translation of poetry impossible.

The difficulty is compounded when we are dealing with languages, cultures, and poetic traditions that are far apart. Not only are Arabic and English very different but, even more crucial, the aesthetic sensibilities and the world view of a desert Arab are quite different from those of an urban Westerner. There are Arabic words and idioms with no corresponding English equivalents. There are also concepts, images, and metaphors related to the desert environment and nomadic life that cannot be easily rendered for the Western audience. Nabaṭi poetry is, moreover, suffused with popular borrowings, religious allusions, and historical references that an outsider cannot understand without elaborate commentaries. When composing, the Nabaṭi poet assumes that his audience is thoroughly familiar with local traditions, history, and geography as well as with a large repertoire of other poems and lore.

Another difficulty in translating Nabaṭi poetry is best expressed in the words of H. A. R. Gibb in his discussion of the difficulty of translating classical Arabic poetry.

> The general similarity in structure and content of the pre-Islamic odes may give, especially when they are read in translation, an impression of monotony, almost of bareness, mirroring with a certain rude force the uniformity of desert life, its concreteness, realism, absence of shading and of introspection. Where the poet is held almost wholly to specific themes, and his aim is to embellish those themes with all the art at his command, to surpass his predecessors and rivals in beauty, expressiveness, terseness of phrase, in fidelity of description and grasp of reality, then such poetry can never be satisfactorily translated into any other language, just because the thing said varies so little and the whole art lies in the untranslatable manner of saying it. (1963:21–22)

Added to all these difficulties is the fact that the rendition of a poem in one language into a poem in another language is, like poetic composition itself, a skill which, alas, we do not all possess. In belaboring these points, I am not trying to excuse any anticipated shortcomings on my own part, but rather to vindicate the artistic qualities of Nabaṭi poetry in the event that my translations fail to communicate these qualities.

In view of the number of poetic examples presented in this work, it would have been time-consuming and economically impracticable to present transliterations of all of them. Poetry will be transliterated only when necessary, as in the discussions of the prosody and language of Nabaṭi poetry and of the question of literacy. In the main, poetic examples will be given in translated form only, and, if an example is taken from a published source, reference will be given to that source so that anyone interested in the text in its original language can find it.

Names of classical authors and works, classical literary terms, and names of well-known historical figures are transliterated according to the system adopted by the Library of Congress for the transliteration of Arabic. However, colloquial lexical items, the names of tribal poets and less well-known Arabian chiefs and amirs, and the Nabaṭi verses themselves are transliterated according to the system described in chapter 7. The Library of Congress system, which employs a combination of two graphic symbols to represent certain sounds, is inadequate for transliterating vernacular Arabic which, unlike literary Arabic, allows consonant clusters in certain positions. For example, the literary pronunciation of the word meaning "Canopus" is *suhayl,* but in the colloquial pronunciation the vowel of the initial syllable drops and the word becomes *shēl*; thus, according to the conventional system for transliterating literary Arabic, the initial consonant cluster could be interpreted as a combination of two graphic symbols representing one sound only, namely, a voiceless alveopalatal fricative (*š*), and the resulting word (*šēl*) would then not mean Canopus, but "a load," "carrying." Place names will in general be given their most common Western orthography.

Survey of Sources

The first major work on Nabaṭi poetry was the voluminous *Diwan aus Centralarabien* (1900–1901) by Albert Socin. Socin was a diligent scholar and his collection is truly impressive but, as a pioneer, his work shows some serious drawbacks. The collection is based on manuscripts, some of which Socin had bought in Mesopotamia and others of which had been brought from Najd by Charles Huber. In addition, Socin had spent some time in Mesopotamia working with three expatriates: Muḥammad al-Ḥasāwī from al-Hasa whom he characterized as being "terribly inept and in fact stupid" (ibid., 5); Musfir from ʿUnaizah who, says Socin, "had no endurance and finally ran away in anger because he could not take the intellectual work which I demanded from him paying him good money" (ibid., 4); and Muḥammad al-Efendi from Buraidah who is also accused of being inept by Socin, who goes on to say:

> I had much trouble with him and when I exposed him to cross examination in cases which seemed to me problematic, he was impatient and even angry. . . . In time, Muḥammad al-Efendi learned how to explain things properly and understand what I was after. About metrics he understood—we can nearly say luckily—absolutely nothing. (Ibid., 3)

Later, Socin goes so far as to say of his informants: "As far as my informants whom I mentioned in §2–6, and who do have to a degree a certain reputation among their peers as singers, are concerned, none of them had any sense of rhythm. The rhythm did not always come out even when they were singing" (ibid., 55).

Socin presents the poetry in his collection as a linguistic corpus, with little regard for its artistic merits; and although on more than one occasion (ibid., 7, 45) he admits his inability to comprehend thoroughly the poems in his collection, he opens his discussion on the content of the poetry by asserting that it is "fairly valueless and insignificant" (ibid., 46–47). Such a pronouncement has the ring of reflexive reaction rather than reflective judgment. Socin's work suffers from his insensitivity to Nabaṭi poetry and his unfamiliarity with the historical and social conditions of the Arabian Peninsula which this poetry reflects. His analysis is verbose and pedantic, his notes circuitous, and his translations not infrequently far off the mark. He despises his informants and denigrates their insight and intuition, and blames them for his own shortcomings without entertaining the possibility that his manner of conducting research and his technique of soliciting information might be faulty. Because Socin's vision was marred by his racial and literary prejudices, his work turned out to be more a disparagement than a true appraisal of Nabaṭi poetry.

The small collections of G. A. Wallin (1851, 1852) and C. de Landberg (1919) and the sizable collection of Alois Musil (1928) are of a different quality from that of Socin. In translating and annotating the poems in their collections, these three distinguished orientalists put to good use their extensive knowledge of the history and ethnography of the Arabian Peninsula. The collections, however, are still deficient in many ways. In many places the translation is questionable, and in many verses the meter is irregular and some poems are deformed in various ways. Some of these defects can be attributed to oral transmission, and to the fact that these compilers were not sufficiently familiar with the tradition to be able to distinguish competent informants from those who were not, and representative texts from nonrepresentative ones. Moreover, these compilers were generally unaware of the original versions of the poems. (In later chapters, it will be shown that, despite differing oral versions, most Nabaṭi poems have original versions which are in many cases written down during the process of composition or shortly after.) This is not meant to underrate the value of these collections, but only to point to some problems connected with them which make them useful as subsidiary data but not as the sole basis for a serious study of Nabaṭi poetry.

The collections made by H. H. Spoer (1912), Spoer and E. N. Haddad (1929, 1933–1934), C. Bailey (1972), and H. Palva (1976) present other problems. These collections consist of poems and historical narratives collected outside the Arabian Peninsula from informants who were not natives of the Peninsula. Most of these poems and narratives were given by the informants not as representative examples of the poetry and history of their own native land but, the informants maintained, and the investigators agreed, as material originating in the Arabian desert. This is borne out by the general similarity of the poems and narratives to versions collected in the Arabian Peninsula. But the narratives in these collections are badly garbled because the incidents, people, places, and the whole sociocultural milieu with which narratives and poems deal are somewhat foreign to the informants. Furthermore, due to the informants' unfamiliarity with many poetic idioms in the original versions of the poems, and to the difference in pronunciation and syllabic structure between the Peninsular colloquial and their own colloquial dialects, the forms and meters of the poems in these collections are terribly distorted. These distortions cannot be considered simply the result of oral transmission; whatever changes a poem may undergo in this process, it must still retain a reasonably cohesive form and a strictly regular quantitative meter or else it will not be admitted as a poem by the qualified native audience. As for the narratives, we can compare, for example, the garbled narrative recorded by Palva which deals with the rise and strifes of the princely family of al-Rashīd in Ḥāyil with the far more coherent and more accurate versions collected from native informants in the heart of Arabia by Palgrave (1865–1866), Charles Doughty (1921), and Lady A. I. N. Blunt (1881). (See the indices of these works under Rashīd.) Comparison can also be made with the long version dictated to Wadīᶜ al-Bustānī by prince Ḍārī Ibn Fuhayd Ibn ᶜUbayd Ibn Rashīd (Ibn Rashīd 1966) which is accurate enough to be considered a primary source on the history of premodern Arabia. All in all, these collections are valuable as examples illustrating the kinds of changes Nabaṭi poems and the narratives associated with them undergo once they migrate outside the Peninsula and are recited by nonnative informants; but they cannot be considered truly representative of the genuine vernacular poetry of the Arabian Peninsula.

There are many collections of Nabaṭi poetry published in Arabic, but most of them are printed on cheap paper with many orthographic errors and with no commentaries at all. Most collections tend to contain the same poetic texts, but from different sources and with varying degrees of accuracy.

The pioneering collection of Kh. M. al-Faraj (1952) is, however, exemplary. It has a good introduction and copious explanatory notes with brief biographical information on the poets. The collection of A. Kh. al-Ḥātam (1968) is also excellent. He repeats most of the material used by al-Faraj, but adds much more material, especially from earlier periods. The most comprehensive is the collection of M. S. Kamāl (1960–1971). The collection made by M. S. Ibn Sayḥān (1965–1969) is good in that it is not simply a repetition of the same old material.

Later collections are more specialized. M. A. al-Thumayrī (1972) gives us a good selection of short poems that have become popular as folk songs. F. al-Rashīd (1965–1972) gives us a large collection of poems by poets from his home town, al-Rass. A. M. Ibn Raddās (n.d.–1976) devotes his book to the compositions of bedouin poetesses, and explains each poem thoroughly. A. A. al-ᶜUbayyid (1971) appends several poems to his book on the al-ᶜAwāzim tribe by poets of that tribe. F. M. al-Firdaws (n.d.) devotes his anthology to his own poetry and that of kinsmen in his tribe, al-ᶜIjmān, with a few other poets from other tribes.

The collection made by Mandīl al-Fuhayd (1978) is especially interesting. The circumstances of his life brought Mandīl into contact with famous poets and transmitters of poetry from various tribes and settlements. He is an authority not only on Nabaṭi poetry but also on bedouin customs and tribal history. His collection contains the best examples of bedouin poetry, with some information on tribal poets and tribal events. Unfortunately, this collection is badly produced, but that is certainly no fault of the scrupulous but nearly illiterate Mandīl.

Short poems composed by various poets concerning various events are sprinkled throughout F. al-Mārik's four-volume *Min Shiyam al-ᶜArab* (1963–1965). This work is a collection of well-documented anecdotes relating to premodern Arabia which are useful as background information for understanding the sociocultural context of Nabaṭi poetry. Those interested in the true chivalrous poetry of bedouin knights, mostly from the ᶜAnazah tribe, will surely enjoy reading *Abṭāl min al-Ṣahrā*ᵓ by M. A. al-Sudayrī (1968). Besides the poems, al-Sudayrī gives thrilling accounts from the lives of the poet-knights. The resemblance of this collection to the *Ayyām al-ᶜArab* is truly amazing.

The earliest Nabaṭi poet whose memory still survives in people's minds is the half-legendary and half-historical Rāshid al-Khalāwi who is remembered as a great poet and a reliable stargazer. His poems are unusually long; one of them reaches 1,500 lines. A. Ibn Khamīs has written a treatise on al-Khalāwi's life and poetry (1972). Ibn Khamīs has also recently published a collection of poems and anecdotes relating to life in the Arabian desert in the past (1978).

These are the most important collections of Nabaṭi poetry; there are other titles, of lesser importance, listed in the bibliography. Some of these collections are based on oral sources, whereas others are based on written ones. Outside of these collections, there is still much Nabaṭi poetry that needs to be collected from oral and manuscript sources and published.

Although printed collections of Nabaṭi poetry are relatively abundant, native scholars have been generally unwilling to admit this poetry as a proper subject for academic discussion because they believe it fosters religious and political strife. The religious and political status of classical literary Arabic presents both methodological and practical problems in collecting and publishing vernacular materials in the Arab world. Classical Arabic is revered as the language of the Qurʾān, and it is the language of daily prayer, education, the press, public media, and official functions. Though only a few literates achieve proficiency in it, all Arabic speakers are effectively exposed to it through daily prayers and the public media. This classical language unites all speakers of Arabic into one large community. It is believed by many that encouraging vernacular lore is a covert attempt to intensify regional differences and sow political discord and cultural disintegration among the Arab people. Vernacular lore is viewed as a force hostile and destructive to Arab unity. Such attitudes have been effective in hampering research in this area, but not in silencing the people, who continue to recite poetry and lore in their local dialects.

Despite this discouraging intellectual atmosphere, some native scholars have ventured to write on Nabaṭi poetry. Al-Faraj wrote a good introduction to the collection he published in 1952. A. al-ʿUthaymīn wrote a well-researched article (1977) in which he demonstrated the utility of Nabaṭi poetry as a source on the history and society of premodern Arabia.

The best available introduction to the field of Nabaṭi poetry is *al-Adab al-Shaʿbī fī Jazīrat al-ʿArab* (1958) by A. Ibn Khamīs. In this book, Ibn Khamīs gives well-chosen examples with copious notes, and provides short biographical sketches on some poets, a few of whom he knows personally. He discusses the prosodic, stylistic, and thematic features of Nabaṭi poetry and draws parallels between it and classical Arabic poetry. But, like most introductory works, this one lacks methodological rigor and theoretical orientation. Sh. al-Kamālī has also written a similar work entitled *al-Shiʿr ʿinda al-Badw* (1964).

Work in the Field

I have been effectively exposed to Nabaṭi poetry since my childhood. I have heard it quoted or recited almost every day of my life at home or elsewhere. My home town, ᶜUnaizah, is famous for its outstanding Nabaṭi poets, some of whom I know personally. However, I owe my early introduction to Nabaṭi poetry chiefly to my maternal grandfather, Mḥammad as-Slēmān aṣ-Ṣwayyān, an excellent raconteur of anecdotes and a gifted reciter of poetry. His polished style and elegant delivery have fascinated me and captured my imagination since I was a small boy; it was he, more than anyone, who opened my eyes to the rich field of this poetry.

My lifelong exposure to Nabaṭi poetry was supplemented by four months (August–December 1978) of intensive work in the field. This period was divided between Riyadh and ᶜUnaizah. While in Riyadh, I benefited from the few hours I spent with Mandīl al-Fuhayd, the national authority on the authenticity and attribution of Nabaṭi poetry. Until recently, Mandīl was the producer of a program on the Saudi Arabian national radio entitled *Min al-Bādiyah,* which deals with Nabaṭi poetry and bedouin life. The program (which I monitored closely while in Saudi Arabia) is now produced by Brāhīm al-Yūsif, who was kind enough to introduce me to Mandīl al-Fuhayd. To express his encouragement for my research project, al-Yūsif took me with him on two occasions to the recording studios of the radio station in Riyadh to observe the recording session and to meet the poets who came to have their poems recorded and broadcast. At the recording studios I met the poet Fahad al-Firdaws, whom I later visited several times in his home, and who volunteered some interesting information concerning his tribe, al-ᶜIjmān, and explained to me some of the poems composed by Rākān Ibn Falāḥ Ibn Ḥiṯlēn, the famous chief of al-ᶜIjmān, who died at the end of the last century.

In Riyadh I also met several times with Mḥammad al-Ḥamad al-ᶜMiri; I spent many happy hours listening to him reminisce about the famous Nabaṭi poets whom he knew personally. He was very kind to me and very generous with his time and knowledge; he provided me with valuable information on Nabaṭi poetry and allowed me to peruse his manuscripts and copy whatever I wanted.

After I had finished my work in Riyadh and had gone to ᶜUnaizah, I was fortunate to learn that ᶜAbdarriḥmān al-Brāhīm ar-Ribīᶜī, an authority on Nabaṭi poetry and a poet in his own right, had bought a house in our neighborhood into which he moved a few days before my arrival. Almost every day while in ᶜUnaizah, I would meet with ar-Ribīᶜī in the mosque after performing the *ᶜaṣr* (late afternoon) prayer, and he would take me to his house to drink coffee or tea and talk about poetry and poets or read from his manuscripts for about half an hour. Then, we would go to the house of ʿAbdallah as-Slēmān Ibn Ḥasan, where old-timers would get together every day at this time to "chew the cud of the past," as they say. Ibn Ḥasan himself (affectionately nicknamed *al-xāl,* "the grand-uncle") is a well-known poet, and his house is a meeting place for Nabaṭi poets and people interested in Nabaṭi poetry. There, the conversation is always about poetry and old times. Occasionally someone would pick up the written *dīwan* (collection of poetry) of Ibn Ḥasan and recite choice poems from it (Ibn Ḥasan is blind and illiterate and does not memorize his poems, so he could not do the reciting himself). Sometimes a poet would bring a newly composed poem with him. He would read it to the people present and then ask for their opinions, which might vary from approval to sharp criticism. This would go on for about an hour, or until sunset, when it was time for the first evening prayer, which we would perform together. Then, ar-Ribīʿī and I would head back home in my car.

I also had the good fortune to meet several times with the well-known poet Ḥamad al-Mḥammad al-Jābir, who happened to be a good friend of my maternal uncle Ṣālḥ al-Mḥammad aṣ-Ṣwayyān. I would usually go to see him in his house after the last evening prayers, and he would read to me from his poetry or from the poetry of his great-uncle ʿAbdallah Ibn Jābir, who was one of the most outstanding poets of ʿUnaizah at the end of the last century, even though he died very young.

In ʿUnaizah I also met with ʿAlī as-Sālm al-ʿBād and ʿAbdarriḥmān al-ʿAǵīl. Al-ʿBād gave me a small manuscript of Nabaṭi poetry to copy and we had several sessions together which I recorded on cassette tapes. Al-ʿAǵīl is now in the process of collecting and editing an anthology of poets from ʿUnaizah. He put the whole collection at my disposal and, to my delight, he provided me with a few poems composed by my late father, ʿAbdallah al-Brāhīm aṣ-Ṣwayyān. My good friend ʿAbdarriḥmān al-ʿAbdalmiḥsin aḏ-Ḏkēr gave me a most valuable manuscript of Nabaṭi poetry, which was passed on to him by his late father, and also a tape recording of a performance by Ibn Ṣāfī, the outstanding player of the *ribābih*, who died some years ago (the *ribābih* player chants verses of poetry while bowing his fiddlelike instrument).

Most of all, I am grateful to Brāhīm al-Ḥsēn, the amir of aṣ-Ṣbāx hamlet near Buraidah, who supplied me with intimate details concerning the life of the famous poet Mḥammad al-ʿAbdallah al-ʿŌnī who died about 1923, and dictated to me two poems by that poet. Brāhīm al-Ḥsēn knew a great deal about al-ʿŌnī because he is from the al-Mhannā family, who held the amirship of Buraidah until removed by Ibn Saʿud early in the century and who patronized al-ʿŌnī in his early years as the national poet of Buraidah. Much of the information in chapter 4 has been graciously provided by Brāhīm al-Ḥsēn.

In conclusion, I wish to express my deepest appreciation and heartfelt gratitude to all the above-mentioned people for their generous help and encouragement. I must point out that I consider none of them to be merely an informant. They are all my teachers and mentors, and they taught me more about Nabaṭi poetry than anyone else could have.

Part One

SOCIOLOGICAL

II

THE SOCIOCULTURAL SETTING

In describing ancient Arabic poetry, Sir Charles James Lyall wrote:

> The form and spirit of ancient Arabian poetry are very distinct, though it is not easy to bring it within the classes known to European criticism. It is not epic, nor even narrative, except in so far as the description of incident serves to heighten the picture of character. Still less is it dramatic, since the only person and measure known to the speaker are himself and his own ideal. . . . The Arabian ode sets forth before us a series of pictures, drawn with confident skill and first-hand knowledge, of the life its maker lived, of the objects among which he moved, of his horse, his camel, the wild creatures of the wilderness, and of the landscape in the midst of which his life and theirs was set, but all, however loosely they seem to be bound together, are subordinate to one dominant idea, which is the poet's unfolding of himself, his admirations and his hates, his prowess and the freedom of his spirit. . . . No poetry better fulfils Mr. Matthew Arnold's definition of "a criticism of life"; no race has more completely succeeded in drawing itself for all time, in its grandeur and its limitations, its best and its worst. It is in this sense that the poetry of the Pagan Arabs is most truly their history. In it the men of old live their very life, and have found for themselves an expression, the power and faithfulness of which those who understand it best are least able to exaggerate. . . . [W]hat a poet said in his rhymes he had experienced himself; what commended him to his hearers, what commends him to us, is the accuracy and truth with which he drew for them that which he and they knew, and joined their mind and life of every day to the choicest words and noblest form of utterance which their speech permitted. (1885:xviii–xix)

This description of classical Arabic poetry can be applied with equal validity to Nabaṭi poetry. Like the poetry of ancient Arabia, the vernacular poetry of premodern Arabia is a register of social events and a codification of the moral principles and cultural values that made life in the desiccated Arabian wastes, though harsh and weary, meaningful and worthy of pursuit. Nabaṭi poetry is an articulation of the collective sentiment and a cognitive model for the organization of sociocultural realities. When the Nabaṭi poet responds to a given event, whether it is a collective issue or a personal affair, his main concern is not merely to record its concrete manifestation but also, perhaps more importantly, to draw from it general principles which he can relate to the traditional value system of his society. The poet aims at presenting his audience with an emotionally and intellectually satisfying arrangement of the world around them as they traditionally perceive it.

The inner structure and thematic coherence of a Nabaṭi poem are determined by how intelligibly it presents to the audience their physical and social universe. Nabaṭi poetry constantly attempts to order and give meaning to this universe and to bring its various components into harmony with one another. Cognitive and affective bonds are established between these components with similes, images, and metaphors. Appropriate comparisons, apt descriptions, perceptive characterizations, and astute observations are the aesthetic ingredients of an outstanding Nabaṭi poem; these characterizations and observations are blended with moral precepts and maxims of conduct drawn from the life experiences of the poets.

Although it is realistic in outlook and deeply rooted in the life of the people, Nabaṭi poetry is conventional in form and content because it is the product of a traditional society, a society in which the forces of conformity are strong. It is a reflection of a conventional world view and a register of recurring events. Its stock motifs and images are drawn from the social and physical surroundings of those who compose it. In their compositions, Nabaṭi poets try to present their universe using poetic devices which, like any other cultural product of a traditional society, are highly conventionalized. Conformity to convention establishes a continuity between poetry and the cultural tradition of the audience. Moreover, the poet can thus assume a general understanding on the part of his audience based on their full grasp of the cultural and poetic context in which he operates. As his poem unfolds, the poet takes his audience into a poetic ambience created by the connotations and associations of his words and the images and nuances of his verses. By its conventionality and thematic interrelatedness with other poems, each poem reflects back to the members of the audience the whole poetic tradition. Since this poetic tradition mirrors their sociocultural realities, poetic recitation enables the poet and his listeners to come to grips with these realities and gain moral strength to cope with them. The delivery of a poem is in a sense a ritual enactment; with each performance the participants—poet and audience—strengthen their ties with their society and find further confirmation of its fundamental values.

Like the classical poetry of ancient Arabia, Nabaṭi poetry is neither epic nor legendary, but topical and lyrical and chiefly composed in response to happenings in the real world. In order to appreciate its characteristics, one must be intimately acquainted with the sociocultural realities of premodern Arabia, so as to acquire the relevant orientation and develop the appropriate aesthetic framework that enable the native audience of a Nabaṭi poet to enjoy his composition and respond to its message.

Settlers and Nomads

Subsistence patterns and corresponding ecological niches divide the inhabitants of Arabia into two prototypes: settlers and nomads. The settlers, for the most part, till the land, cultivating mainly cereal grains and palm trees. Agricultural settlements are scattered alongside major wadis. The current of a wadi carries with it fertile soil which is deposited on the surface of its banks, while the water seeps through the porous bed of the wadi to collect below on the subsurface rock or clay. Farmers dig deep wells from which they draw irrigation water using a technique called *sawānī*. This technique involves the use of a waterwheel which is placed on top of the well and held there with wooden props and beams. A long rope around the wheel is joined at one end to a large water bucket and at the other end to the saddle of a harnessed camel whose pulling power turns the wheel, bringing up the buckets of water. The arid Arabian climate, however, limits the practice of agriculture severely. Most of the people are nomads who live in portable tents and constantly roam the desert in search of pasture for their camel herds.

Until the recent establishment of the modern Arabian state and the discovery of oil, life in Arabia was a never-ending struggle for bare subsistence. Food and water were permanently scarce and there was a constant fear of war and famine. The subsistence patterns and yearly activities of the entire population were dependent in one way or another on the extreme fluctuations in rainfall, which was never sufficient. A succession of drought years is dreaded by both pastoralists and cultivators. If for one year Allah does not send the dark, water-laden clouds to pour down His mercy on His anguished people, the annual and perennial plants dry up and the water sinks deeper and deeper in the wells. The livestock suffer, the crops wither, and the people are hard hit.

The scarcity of vital resources and the dire lack of material wealth fostered intense intergroup competition over the available means of subsistence and precluded the establishment of a viable and enduring central authority. Not long after the era of the Orthodox Caliphs, the center of power of Arab Muslim civilization shifted away from the Arabian Peninsula, and Arabia again suffered a disintegration of its political structure. Agricultural settlements became fortified hamlets and the nomads reverted to their pre-Islamic habits of raiding and plundering. Peace might reign for a short period when a capable amir or sheikh exerted his authority over the neighboring settlements and forced the nomadic tribes to submit to him. He would impose order and coerce his subjects into paying him taxes and sending him levies as tokens of submission. Petty sheikhdoms and small emirates similar to the pre-Islamic Arab kingdoms thus sprang up at different times in various parts of Arabia. Periods of peace, however, were sporadic and of short duration. Each of the many nomadic tribes and each of the many dispersed hamlets and ephemeral principalities has its own story to tell—usually a labyrinthine tale of internecine conflicts and perpetual feuds.

On the scale of social development, the settlers occupy a slightly higher position than the nomads. Their social organization is a bit more complex, with diverse and specialized occupations. Settled life allows for conveniences and amenities that are not available in the desert. Nomadic life is generally harsher and much more difficult, yet the nomad is proud of his mobility and freedom. He is contemptuous of the settlers who, instead of foraging in the open desert and living by the sword, are bound to their mud houses, toiling continually, like slaves. The martial spirit of the nomad always yearns for raid and booty. In contrast, the settlers long for peace and order so that they can till their land and reap their crops. The amir of every settlement tries his hardest to restrain his subjects from engaging in such acts of aggression as may provide an excuse for others to attack the settlement, destroy its crops, and interrupt its agricultural and commercial activities.

This difference between settlers and nomads has been attributed to the difference in their subsistence patterns. John Bagot Glubb writes:

> The worldly wealth of the nomads consisted of mobile flocks of animals, that of the cultivators of lands, houses and gardens. A nomad, if threatened by a superior enemy, could elude attack by moving hastily away, driving his flocks with him. Indeed, as long as there was still open desert in front of him, he could escape from his persecutors by seeking entirely new pastures, beyond the reach of his adversaries. The cultivator, however, must needs stand his ground and fight it out. If he fled, he became a penniless refugee, abandoning his land and his buildings to the conqueror. War, therefore, to the nomad was never the same grim struggle for survival

> which it represented to the farmer. Indeed to the bedouin, war sometimes seemed little more than a sport, which provided the colour and excitement needed to counteract the monotony of the pastoral life. . . . (1960:30–31)

The following anecdote and poem by Bdāḥ al-ᶜIngrī illustrate some aspects of the settler-nomad relationship and show their attitudes toward each other. The nomads have a low opinion of townsmen, thinking them to be misers and cowards, traits which are anathema to a nomad. The hero in the following episode, however, is a villager who surpasses the nomads in gallantry and proves to them that courage is not the monopoly of nomads. Although the incident celebrated took place in the last century, the poem and the narrative associated with it are still very popular in Arabia. Different versions of poem and narrative appear in Ibn Khamīs (1958:146–150, 1978:127–128), Ibn Raddās (n.d.–1976:I, 316–318), and al-Mārik (1963–1965:III, 95–102).

One summer, a certain tribe camped near Tharmida, a principal village in the district of al-Washim in Najd, traditionally governed by the al-ᶜIngrī family. Bdāḥ al-ᶜIngrī, the son of the then amir, would go to visit the sheikh of the encamped tribe almost daily. Bdāḥ would arm himself and ride his horse, hoping to impress the bedouin ladies, whose hearts were easily won by shows of gallantry. He especially had his eye on the daughter of the sheikh, but she was not at all impressed by him, and whenever he was pointed out to her by her lady friends, she would only say *"xayyal al-ǵrā zēn taṣfīh"* ("the horse-rider from the village is good only for a parade"). Upon hearing what the daughter of the sheikh had to say about him, Bdāḥ wished in his heart that raiders would attack the camp so that he could prove his worth to the maiden. As luck would have it, the camp was surprised one morning by a raiding party from the al-Fḏūl tribe, who stole the herds of the camp after killing several men. Bdāḥ was present in the camp when the raiders launched their surprise attack, but he did not participate in the first round of fighting. He sat on his horse atop a hill watching the action. Only when it became clear that the men of the camp were unable to defend their herds did he spur his mare in hot pursuit of the attackers, who had by now rounded up the herds and driven them off. After knocking down a few of their number, Bdāḥ forced the raiders to abandon the plundered herds and seek safety in flight. He did not capture the mares of the men he had killed, but took only their reins as proof of his deed. The fighting men of the camp noticed that suddenly the battle had turned very much in their favor, but in the confusion of battle they were unable to determine exactly what had happened. They trickled back to the sheikh's tent to refresh themselves and review the situation. A short while later, Bdāḥ walked into the tent, threw down the reins of the horses, picked up the *ribābīh* (a one-stringed, fiddlelike instrument which hangs on the central pole of the tents of many sheikhs) and sang the poem that follows.

It is a custom among the nomads that when a poet begins to recite or sing the women of the tent stop whatever they are doing and lean against the curtain that separates their section from that of the men so that they may better hear the poem. When Bdāḥ was singing his poem, he knew well that the sheikh's daughter was listening to his words. In the poem he talks to her in an admonishing tone but, as he nears the end, he begins to speak to her the words of love. The bedouins do not allow such familiarity on the part of a man to a lady in public unless the man has performed a heroic act, as Bdāḥ has done. Bdāḥ begins his poem by pointing out to the maiden that he is no less valiant than a nomad, for he is a bold man who rides camels and horses and goes on raids. The maiden cannot ask for a more convincing proof of his valor than what he has just done to her enemies.

1 By God, how often have I raided, and returned from a raid. How often have I ridden a fleet mount.
2 Many a time have I climbed into the saddle! Many a time have I ridden in the late afternoon on my way to a raid!
3 Many a time have I handled the Indian sword! Many a time have I shared in the division of herds, herds plundered from men of tenacity!
4 Why then, oh lady with thick lashes, do you scorn me? You say the horseman from the village is good only for a parade!
5 Know that courage is not found among nomads only! It is equally divided among all noble men.
6 Whether nomads or villagers, God has granted them all stoutness of heart.
7 Remember the day al-Fḏūl attacked your camp! They slaughtered your people like butchers.
8 I fought till I broke my spear; then, I unsheathed my sharp sword. I repulsed the enemy. Horses fled with their heads lowered (in fright).
9 Now, pray tell me your true opinion [of me]! Declare the truth or else I will cry out!
10 I will cry like a bereaved mother, or a camel that has strayed from the herd and lost its calf.
11 You are the perfume of a sweet basil growing by the rain pool; wherever the wind blows, it carries your fragrance.
12 You are sweeter than peaches, pomegranates, figs, apples, and apricots from Basrah.
13 Your fair cheeks shine like polished scrolls in the right hand of a

scribe. Oh, the glances of your dark eyes are fatal to those who seek beauty.

14 You are slender-waisted and graceful, of supple figure, like a willow branch swayed by gentle breezes.

Despite their differences, however, nomads and settlers are not sharply demarcated and clearly bounded sociocultural units that can be easily isolated and separated from each other; rather, these two groups are interlinked at various levels of social and economic organization. The very economic specialization that divides the people of Arabia into cultivators and pastoralists brings them together in a symbiotic relationship which revolves around barter and exchange of goods and services. This relationship is formally renewed every summer when each nomadic tribe gathers around the tribal wells near an agricultural settlement, which is usually an ally of the tribe. The nomads take to the village market their clarified butter, dried milk patties, spun wool, and livestock to barter for grain, dates, salt, coffee, tea, sugar, tobacco, clothes, rope, and so forth. During this time nomads and settlers exchange information and renew their connections.

Furthermore, the settler-nomadic classification that is based on subsistence patterns is superimposed upon another which is based on kinship. The settlers and nomads are related to each other as members of various tribes. Members of every tribe, whether settled or nomadic, are presumably related to each other as *bini ᶜamm* who are the descendants of an ancient male ancestor. This kinship puts members of the same tribe, settlers and nomads, under obligation to each other, and the durability of this relationship is maintained through marriage, trade, and political alliance.

In Arabia, settler and nomad are two complementary aspects of the same sociocultural system, although it is dominated by the nomadic outlook. The great majority of settled people can claim nomadic origin. The transformation from pastoralism to cultivation is a continuing process, although it takes place very slowly and in successive stages. Gradually, the settlers develop sedentary habits, which distinguish them from the nomads. They abandon their tribal customs and submit to civil and religious laws. Their tribal loyalties become supplemented by local allegiances. A settler is intensely proud of his tribal affiliation, yet at the same time he is aware of his membership in a local community all members of which are united politically. Nevertheless, the settlers never lose sight of their nomadic past. The nomadic world view persists among the settled people because they continue to live under the same characteristically precarious and turbulent climatic and political conditions.

The constraints and circumstances of settled life make it difficult for the settlers to live up to the nomadic ideals of their brethren in the desert, but they continue to uphold these ideals. The nomadic outlook is more in harmony with and relevant to desert life, where its physical and political determinants are more immediate and their effects more ubiquitous. This outlook persists, nevertheless, among the settled people, who continue to entertain a sense of affiliation with the open desert and the egalitarian nomadic existence.

The conventional images and stock metaphors of Nabaṭi poetry are drawn mostly from the desert. Desert scenes and nomadic ideals serve as inspiration for the poet and as a source of fascination for the audience. To appeal to the aesthetic and moral sensibilities of his audience, a Nabaṭi poet will infuse his composition with strands and colors of desert life. Whether settled or nomad, the poet will most likely mention in his composition the migrating tribe, the departing lady, the deserted encampment, the desert journey, the camel, the horse, the rain, and the wild animals and aromatic plants of the desert. Boastful and panegyric compositions, which constitute the great bulk of Nabaṭi poetry, revolve around such nomadic values as noble birth, liberal hospitality, valor, gallantry, and forbearance.

The settlers' romantic and nostalgic view of nomadic life is reflected in the compositions of settled Nabaṭi poets, some of whom dedicated the major share of their poetry to describing the ways of the nomads and their patterns of migration. The best representative of this school is ʿAbdallah al-Ḥmūd Ibn Sbayyil, whose work is worth noting here.

Ibn Sbayyil died in 1938, at over eighty years of age. His *dīwān* (collection of poetry) was first published in 1952 by Kh. al-Faraj with excellent commentaries. Al-Faraj wrote, "The poetry of Ibn Sbayyil is a register of bedouin life. It contains valuable information concerning the conditions of the nomads in peace and war, their manners and customs and patterns of migration." He went on to say of Ibn Sbayyil's poetry: "Its form is polished, its depictions are realistic and accurate, and its expressions are succinct and harmonious. Therefore, he surpassed many of the ancient and modern [Nabaṭi] poets and his fame spread throughout the desert and the sown" (1952:I, 195).

Ibn Sbayyil was the amir of Nifi, a small village in upper Najd which was also the summer campground of ʿTēbih, a tribe famous for its gallant men and beautiful women. The presence in the village market of throngs of fully armed men and gaily dressed women of ʿTēbih added color and excitement to the otherwise dreary life of the settled folk in Nifi. It was not unusual for the men of the settlement to go out to the nearby bedouin camp to talk to the men of the tribe and to catch glimpses of the bedouin damsels who were freer and more open than the settled women in their interaction with men. Ibn Sbayyil would spend most of the summer in the tents of the desert chiefs and heroes, witnessing their chivalry and lavish hospitality and listening to them relate stories of their forays and bold adventures. This nomadic setting, with all its beauty and romance, inspired Ibn Sbayyil. His poetry is an expression of his fascination with the nomads and their way of life. By the end of the summer, the nomads would pack up and move into the interior of the desert, leaving Ibn Sbayyil behind, like a bird with clipped wings, to lament their departure and to pine for their return in the coming summer.

Al-Faraj rightly points out that Ibn Sbayyil was nomadic in sentiment and outlook, even though he was a settler (ibid., I:194). The treatment of nomadic life in his poetry is generally interwoven with the theme of chaste and unfulfilled love. The object of his love is a beautiful bedouin lass who, though she talks to him sweetly, shuns his advances. In addition to his amorous poems, Ibn Sbayyil exchanged poetic correspondence with some bedouin friends—Ḏᶜār Ibn Mišārī Ibn Rbēᶜān, the chief of ᶜTēbih, and Fēḥān Ibn Zirībān, a famous warrior from the tribe of Mṭēr, among others.

In the following poem, Ibn Sbayyil traces the cycle of nomadic migration. By the end of the summer and the beginning of the rainy season, the nomads become restless and begin preparations to leave their summer camp and move into the interior of the desert. For Ibn Sbayyil, this is the worst time of the year. Therefore, he curses it and prays Allah to strike it with drought. After they settle all their business accounts with the settlers, the nomads disperse into the desert and wander in small groups in search of pasture for their camel herds. Each group goes in a different direction and they lose touch with one another. In their eagerness to reach fresh pasture before it is trodden and consumed by the herds of other tribesmen, the nomads may spend days on the march without pitching camp. In his poem, Ibn Sbayyil does not dwell on this part of the nomadic cycle, but quickly turns to his favorite season, the time when the nomads return to the settled country. He describes how they converge on the water wells, driving away those weaker nomads who raise only sheep. They throng the village market and go to visit old friends in the settlement. At the end of three months, the star Canopus appears in the east at dawn, ushering in the beginning of the rainy season. Riders who had been sent out earlier to scout the desert for pasture come back to tell their tribesmen where the rain has fallen and where herbage is most abundant. This is also the time of the date harvest, so the nomads buy their supply of dates and leave for the interior. After all the hustle and bustle, their camp is now deserted, with naught but wolves howling.

1 May God strike with drought the bustling final days of summer,
when the nomads pry loose the last payment for their butter.

2 This is the time when people in love go different ways, each taking a separate road, following the camel herds.
3 If you should inquire about the whereabouts of anyone, no one could give you an answer. Even camel riders traveling desert roads could not give you a sound report.
4 The tribal chiefs are restless like stud camels in the rutting season, constantly foraging in the desert. A whole week passes in travel, no time to pitch a tent.
5 Each strives to reach the pasture before the other herds arrive and trample it; there they will let graze their camels heavy with sweet milk.
6 Blessed are the summer days, when the nomads crave water, when clouds disappear from the skies and moisture sinks deeper in the ground,
7 When the hot wind begins to blow and the green stalks wither, when milk no longer allays the thirst of the herders.
8 Then the nomads come back to their summer camps, their camel herds covering the hills. The loaded camels are couched, and the pitched tents
9 Are lined up like a chain of black hills. The sheep herders yield up the water wells.
10 The nomads fill the vast plain around the wells of fresh cool water.
11 Some head for the village market to buy and sell; others go to visit old friends.
12 They remain by the wells for ninety days and there is no mention of moving camp.
13 But the cool winds of the rainy season begin to blow and Canopus appears in the east shortly before the morning twilight.
14 And scouts come from the east riding fast camels; they come at the time of the date harvest.
15 Tribesmen swarm in the afternoon market, having made up their minds to move the next day.
16 The next morning the ladies roll up the tents, and the camel herds are watered before they are driven off.
17 The herds spread out in the countryside on their way to a pasture which the scouts have recommended.
18 The camp is left desolate; it has reverted to wilderness, with wolves howling about.
19 I am sad to see the friendly neighbors leave; they have carried my heart off with them.
20 They ride their swift mares. With their spears they have slain many a bold adversary among the nomads.

21 With the season of rain they return to the desert; they follow their leader wherever he takes them.
22 Hardly has this man returned from a raid, when they are off raiding again. Part of the booty they sell and part they brand and add to their herds.
23 After they have bought all they need, without regret they quit the settled country. They go wherever the rain falls.

Nomadic Migration

The nomads are organized into tribes; each tribe has its own territory (*dīrih*) with water wells and pasture areas. The tribe is divided into clans, and every clan has its own sheikh, but these sheikhs are subordinates who answer to the paramount sheikh of the whole tribe. The various clans of the tribe disperse themselves into scattered camps which fluctuate in size according to the time of year. The yearly cycle of the nomadic camp begins when Canopus appears in the east at dawn in September. This is the beginning of the rainy season (*al-wasim*) and the time of the *najᶜih* (when the nomads begin to trickle back to the heart of the desert). Each tribe breaks up its summer camp and splits up into small groups that are continually separating and regrouping as they forage in their tribal territory. Because of the scantness of herbage, these groups are never large and they never linger in one spot for more than a week or ten days.

The disappearance (*al-ćannih*) of the Pleiades (*aṯ-ṯrayyā*) from the night skies signals the beginning of the summer. The hot wind (*al-hēf*) begins to blow, the herbage withers, and the natural water reservoirs dry up. This is the time of *ṭaggt al-ᶜūd* (when the twigs are so dry they crack). The desert becomes gray (*šhaba*) and ash-colored (*misinyih*) with naught but dust (*ġbār*), whirlwinds (*ᶜajāj*), and dazzling mirages (*lāl*). Now the bedouins cannot quench their thirst by drinking camel's milk but must have water every day, and their camels must have it every third day. During this time, the tribes converge around their tribal wells, which are usually located in a low basin (*jaww*) near an agricultural settlement. This summer camp is called *giṭīn, migṭān*. The symbiotic relationship of economic exchange (*msābilih*) between nomads and settlers is reenacted every year at this time.

The moving of camp and the choice of camping ground is decided by the sheikh, who consults with the men of the tribe after receiving the reports of the scouts (*ᶜsūs*) whom he sends to examine the country for pasture, water, and enemies. When the tribe decides to move to new grazing areas, the women strike the tents, roll them up, and load them, along with furniture and provisions, on pack camels (*zamil*). The moving camp is led by the *salaf,* a reconnoitering detachment of daring and experienced warriors who ride ahead of the main party in order to flush out any enemies or raiders who might try to lead away the migrating camel herds. These warriors ride their camel mounts and lead their mares, leaping on them in case of alarm. They carry their long lances on their shoulders and hang their swords and matchlocks behind them on the saddle. The *salaf* is followed by the pack camels and the rest of the tribe. The camel herds are behind, moving at a leisurely pace so they can graze on the march. The moving of one camp is described by Doughty as follows.

> Somewhat more brave is the desert march of the Moahîb than the ráhla of the Fejîr; for these sheykhly housewives ride gaily mounted in saddle-frames *múksir,* with some caparisons of coloured carpets. The creaking múksirs are basket-frames of withy rods, firmly knit and compacted with steeped camel neck-sinews, (which dry, are of an ivory whiteness and hardness,) and with thongs of raw leather. The most are square crates, in which a wife may sit cross-legged, and her young children with her; and overhead is a bowed cross-rod or two, upon which she may cast her mantle, for a tilt, to house them in from the flaming sun. Another litter they have in these parts, and it is perhaps of the Arabian antiquity, for such I have seen in a ráhla of nomads in the little Algerian *Sáhara.* That is a long fantastic wicker frame, like nothing so much as a wind-mill sail, laid overthwart the camel's chine; into this straight cage the maiden creeps, and the swagging creaky arms of her litter, bouncing against tree and cliff, and thrusting upon nigh riders in the ráhla, make it a very uneasy carriage. I have asked how, being in their minds, they could use such faulty furnitures. 'For ornament, Khalîl! and the young women would ride gallantly.' The hareem hang crimson shreds about their litter-frames, and upon the saddle-tree they put a housing with long fluttering tails of leather. So their women's riding makes a brave show, in the fantasy of the Aarab, in their wandering processions. The men pass forth riding, with only their arms, upon the stalking thelûls. In the heat, they mostly march in silence, to speak were to open the mouth to the droughty flaming air which brings thirst: they ride breathing through their kerchiefs, *thorrîb,* of which a lap is drawn up under the girdle of the head (*meyhsub,* or *maasub,* *ʿagâl*), so that of such a masked visage little more is seen than the two robber-like black eyes. (1921:I, 483–484)

Bedouin women and children are tucked in their shady litters, which are mounted on strong male camels. The litters are covered with gazelle skins, colored trappings, and crests of ostrich plumes. They are also studded with shells and mirrors of various shapes and colors which glitter in the distance as the camels rock the litters. Such a tribal procession is described in a famous poem by Rākān Ibn Hiṯlēn, which is worth translating here. The poem is published in al-Ḥātam (1968:II, 198), al-Kamālī (1964:367–360), and al-Firdaws (n.d.:175–176). For the life and poetry of Rākān, see al-Firdaws (ibid., 158–190).

Rākān Ibn Falāḥ Ibn Hiṯlēn (d. 1893) was the paramount chief of al-ʿIjmān tribe. The Ottoman authorities, after occupying the Eastern Province of Arabia in 1870, captured Rākān by a ruse, put him in chains, and sent him to Turkey, where he spent seven years in prison. He was released and sent back home after distinguishing himself in the war between Turkey and Russia.

While in prison, Rākān composed many poems lamenting his fate and expressing his longing for his people and the desert, as in the following poem which is addressed to his friend Saʿūd Ibn Fayṣal Ibn Tirkī al-Saʿūd, nicknamed Abu Halā ("the father of welcome") because of his graciousness and princely hospitality. In the poem, Rākān names several places, all of which are part of his tribal territory. Then he goes on to describe the moving of camp. The second half of the poem describes an imaginary battle between the migrating tribe and some raiders who try to plunder the moving herds. As the migrating tribe decides to pitch camp in the late afternoon, a group of raiders intercepts the moving herds and tries to drive them off. As depicted in lines 18–19, the raiders divide themselves into two groups, one driving off the herds at a fast trot, and the other hiding as *ćimīn* to ambush the tribesmen trying to rescue the camels. The raiders hope to elude the rescuers and hide in the darkness of night. The sentinel of the camping tribe perceives the raiders driving off the herds and shouts to his fellows, who quickly grasp their weapons, unfetter their horses, and ride off after the enemy. The rescuers catch up with the raiders and engage them in a fight. Those who stayed behind to put on their coats of mail join in the melee and the raiders are completely routed. (In the opening line, the "bitter cup" refers to coffee. The desert Arabs make coffee with cardamom and other spices, but they never add cream or sugar to it; hence it is called *ghawat mirr,* "bitter coffee," and a cup of such coffee is called *finjāl mirr,* "bitter cup." On the other hand, a cup of tea is called *finjāl ḥiliw*, "sweet cup," because tea is always made with sugar.

1 The bitter cup I truly miss, the peace of mind and company
2 Of valiant lads and noble men, who are my folk and dearest ones.
3 I wish there were an easy way to make a knave a gentleman.

4 Abu Halā, I am a hawk; an eagle caged, I long to soar.
5 O Gracious Lord, you grant the wish of humble men and help the weak.
6 My anguished heart is filled with awe; my sleepless eyes are filled with tears.
7 Gone are my joy, my glorious days; far am I from my clansmen's might.
8 They move their camp and camel herds to follow the light of rainy clouds.
9 The lightning flashing through the night; the Trēbī's bed has overflowed,
10 From Sāgān basin to coastal lands, from Ridīfih plains to Ḥasnāʾ plateaus
11 And Xṣēfā too, all drenched with rain—the land of those who quench their swords' thirst [for enemy blood].
12 ʿAjmān tribesmen ride their noble mares and graze their herds on verdant steppes.
13 When it is time to change their camp, they strike the tents and move straightway.
14 The cavaliers direct the march; by end of day the marchers halt.
15 Sentinels perched on summits high cry out, "The herds are driven off!"
16 The horses swish their ample tails; disheartened are those who lost the keys [to their mares' fetters].
17 The furious youths charge on their mares to meet the foe and save the herds.
18 The champions shout their battle cries; the battle rages with swords and spears.
19 Thrusts and blows are interchanged; the ambush fights a bloody war.
20 The raiders push the coveted herds; they seek to flee 'neath darkness' veil.
21 Those left behind to don their shields, the coats of mail that David made,
22 Make haste to join the fray; they put to flight the mortal foes.
23 The enemies' blood is flowing free on the bare backs of hastening mares.
24 The dauntless lads of my fierce clan are yearling hawks, the birds of prey.
25 They ride upon their dashing mares with curving swords of shining steel.
26 They fear not death when battles rage; away with those who bow their heads.
27 I pray, my Lord, for peace upon the Prophet's soul, the guided one.

When the tribe decides to camp for an extended period of time, each man chooses a spot for his tent; he sticks his lance in the ground as a sign for his womenfolk to pitch the tent in that spot, while he goes to drink coffee and talk with the men. The tent is divided by a curtain into two sections: *rabᶜih,* where the men sit, and *riffih,* where the women sit. The mare of the tent's owner is fettered nearby and at night his camels couch (*yabirkin*) in front of the tent. The size of the tent is determined by how many poles it takes to prop it up. The largest tent is that of the sheikh, where men gather together to drink coffee and discuss tribal affairs. It is pitched on the most prominent and most dangerous spot in order to repel any sudden attack, and also so as to be the first to receive guests seeking hospitality and fugitives seeking protection.

The arrangement of summer and winter camps is determined by the availability of pasture, and is also subject to considerations of defense and protection of the camel herds. In summer, the tents are all pitched beside the wells in long rows with the ropes of each tent almost touching those of the next one. This mode of encampment is called *nazil.* The tribe must stay near the wells all summer, for the people need water every day. Since no grazing is available near the tents, the camels are sent to graze far away (*yaᶜazbin*), accompanied by a handful of brave youths as guards (*janab*). They come back every third day to drink only. It is at this time that major raids take place, for every tribe knows where its foes are camped and can easily surprise them. Since the herds are attended by a few men only and since they are far away from the main camp, the raiders can surprise the herders, quickly round up the herds, and drive them off. The herders, therefore, must always be on the watch, and the moment they sense danger they call for help while trying in the meantime to stampede the camels and distract the raiders from rounding them up.

In winter, the tribe is continually on the move in search of pasture. The camp is spread over a wide area with the tents scattered in small groups of a few tents each, each group (*firīǵ*) within calling distance of the next. Continual movement and the fact that camels can find sufficient grazing near the tents make surprise assault by enemies almost impossible. But since in winter there is not so much danger from thirst, this is the time when poor nomads traveling in pairs rove the desert on foot to try to steal the camels of the enemy tribe. A nocturnal prowler (*ḥāyif*/*ḥinšūlī*) may crawl into the camp, unfetter one or two of the couched camels and quietly lead them away. To eliminate this danger, each *firīǵ* pitches the tents in a ring (*duwwār*) with the ropes of each tent touching those of the next, and the camels are couched within this hedge of tents and stretched ropes. Under these circumstances, night prowlers cannot lead away any of the camels without causing much commotion, which would wake up the whole *firīǵ.*

The annual cycle of the nomadic camp, with all of its temporal and spatial aspects, has been formalized by poets and condensed into stock motifs which are interwoven with the love theme to constitute a conventional topic of poetic composition. Friendship and love relationships develop between members of the various lineages of the tribe as they occasionally come together in their ceaseless roaming of the tribal territory. But no sooner have these relationships developed than the lineages separate. The pulsating pattern of tribal dispersal and regrouping symbolizes for the poet the separation and reunion of lovers. A poet therefore may begin his poem by picturing himself riding his camel alone in the wilderness, and coming across a deserted encampment which was once the abode of his sweetheart. This sight cheers him up and awakens in his heart sweet memories of love and human companionship. Or the poet may begin his poem differently, by describing his climb to the top of the highest ridge to watch the early departure of his sweetheart with her kinsmen. As this scene vanishes, extreme passion overtakes the poet and he remains in his place till sunset, when he descends, having completed the composition of his poem. The poem describes how the tribal procession goes over hill and dale with the poet's beloved riding in her gaily decorated litter. Heavenly constellations, and rain, with its various manifestations such as clouds and lightning, are incorporated into the poem as metaphors for and direct agents in the separation and reunion of lovers. Several lines will be dedicated to the camel, which is the vehicle for this separation and reunion. The poet may also describe the great distances that separate him from his beloved, and give a list of place names which stand for tribal boundaries, grazing areas, water holes, desert roads and stations, and other places that are the pivots of tribal migration.

The following poem by Swēlim Ibn Twēm ad-Dawwāy of the alᶜAwāzim tribe (al-ᶜUbayyid 1971:124–125) illustrates the use of these topics.

1 Last night I did not close my eyes; my mind was beset by anxieties.
2 Today I stand atop the high ridge like a sentinel walking back and forth on its summit.
3 I climbed atop a high mount strewn with big boulders, watching the moving camp, whither they go.
4 My sweetheart's herds go south, while my people will be moving north.
5 I watch them moving camp with tears in my eyes; now I see them, now they disappear.
6 Confound the Wārih ridge! It is too low; from it I cannot see the moving camp behind the Abrag hills.

7 I descended from it with heavy heart; I was distressed, with no one near to console me.
8 Tears flowed freely from my eyes; may God strike with misfortune any who would admonish my eyes.
9 My eyes shed tears, hot as coffee boiling in the pot; I cried as one bereaved of kin.
10 I cry over my beloved, whose neck shines like lightning from rain-laden clouds,
11 Auspicious lightning, presaging abundant rain that will drench the land and fill the pools.
12 I only looked upon her, I never touched her; for she is a chaste lady whose virtue is without doubt.
13 She is protected by valiant men, supported by strong kinsmen.
14 I shall endure and hope for better days; may the hard times end in joy.

Camels and Horses

Nomadism in Arabia is both necessitated and facilitated by the camel. The nomad is well aware of the importance of camels in his life; hence he calls them *ʿaṭa llah* (the gift of Allah), and derives immense pleasure from talking about them. Camels are an inexhaustible source of bedouin lore, and conversation always leads to this subject. Many a Nabaṭi poem begins with a prelude of several lines enumerating the qualities of a fine riding camel. A thoroughbred camel (*ḏilūl, miṭĭyyih*) is graceful and alert with sharp, glowing eyes, small pointed ears, long arched neck, long limbs, muscular shoulders, wide chest, erect hump, and broad, bulging ribs. It perceives danger quickly and alerts the rider by its movements, but it never growls, for a growling camel can easily attract enemies. It can travel tirelessly over long stretches of waterless desert, and it can graze on the run so that the rider does not lose valuable time.

Going on a long journey in the open desert is a perilous undertaking which may prove fatal to both camel and rider unless they both use their excellent senses and cooperate to avoid danger. These journeys, as the poets point out, are undertaken only by worthy men on worthy camels. The camel starts the journey fat and strong, but by the end of the journey, if it survives, it is emaciated to mere skin and bones. The hump is completely gone and the back is sore and blistered, showing deep marks of the saddle and girths. If the camel dies from exhaustion, the rider may perish with it. An experienced rider never ill-treats his mount, but always looks after its needs, and an intimate bond develops between them.

A riding camel is preferably a barren female because female camels are more docile and enduring than males, especially in winter, the rutting season. Also, a barren camel is stronger and more manageable than a pregnant or suckling camel because the strong attachment of the mother to its calf makes it quite difficult to separate the two. Male camels, however, are much stronger and better able to carry heavy loads; therefore, when the camp moves, the tent, its furniture, and the women and children are loaded onto male camels.

Besides riding camels and common pack camels, every tribe has special camel herds of distinct and uniform color. These herds are, so to speak, the tribal emblem. They are herded under the protection of the bravest youths in the tribe. These honored herds must be defended to the death and the men of the tribe will risk anything to save them, for it is a disgrace to lose them. Glubb writes:

> It is impossible to convey to our unfamiliar minds all the romance and glory attached in the bedouin mind to the idea of camels, in seizing or defending which so many give up their lives. They contain something of the associations which a regiment derives from its colours. Warriors were thus in the habit of calling their flocks by names, which they employed in battle as war cries, in the same manner as the names of women. Men would thus fight, calling out "The horsemen of the Aliya" or "The horsemen of the Gurwa," referring to the titles given to their flocks. (1935:22–23)

The nobility and honor of the tribe is measured by the number of its herds and whether they have ever been taken by enemy tribes. Only strong tribes can defend their herds and fatten them on green pastures, which are usually the most contested spots in the desert.

Next to the camel in importance for the bedouin is his mare. Horses in the desert are symbols of nobility and power. In their boastful poems, desert heroes praise their horses and address their verses to them. The strength and prosperity of the tribe is measured by the number of its horses, which are called *sibāya* (bringers of booty). The horse is indispensable to the nomads who live in a perpetual state of war. The horse and the camel complement each other in the desert—the horse is swift and the camel is enduring. The camel and the horse are not only necessary for the survival of the nomad, but each is necessary for the well-being of the other. Without the horse, the camels cannot be defended against raiders or retrieved when they are plundered. But without the sweet milk of camels, the horse cannot survive in the desert.

Raiding

The nomad's energies are directed toward the welfare and increase of his camel herds. His life, in all its aspects, is adapted to that end. He declines the comfort and ease of settled life to roam the open desert spaces in ceaseless search of pasture for his noble beasts. Camel herding is the most efficient means of exploiting the meager resources of the Arabian desert. Camels, however, are peculiarly vulnerable as a form of capital. They must always have enough pasturage, but this is determined by rainfall. It is unusual for the annual rains to fall over all of Arabia in sufficient quantities. When it does rain, the rain falls over some areas but not others. When seasonal rains fall on tribal territory, the grass sprouts and the shrub comes back to life, blooming with flowers and green with succulent shoots. The desert turns into luxuriant pastures and the camels become fat and overblown with milk. If seasonal rains fail, the tribal territory becomes barren and desiccated. When this happens, the camel herds suffer and may even perish from lack of grazing food. Under such circumstances, the only course left for the unfortunate tribes if they are to improve their lot is to plunder the herds of their more fortunate neighbors or force their way into their pastures.

The swiftness of the camel and its ability to travel for days tirelessly and without food or water make it both means and end of perpetual raids and counter-raids between the various nomadic tribes. Camel riders can carry out distant forays, and by launching a surprise assault they can easily drive off the animals of the enemy and elude pursuers by swiftly retreating into the open desert. As a result of these skirmishes, the political situation in the desert is constantly boiling. Among the tribes, there are always scores to settle and blood to avenge. The desert tracts are continually traversed by raiders on their way to adventure (*mġīrīn*) or returning (*minćfīn*).

Raiding (*ġaziw*) is a mechanism of adaptation to the precarious circumstances of desert life. Throughout the centuries the nomads have developed it into a complex institution with intricate codes and procedures. According to the law of desert warfare, a tribe never engages in hostilities against another tribe before making a formal declaration of war. The most honorable time to attack is in broad daylight, a night attack being considered dishonorable and treacherous (*bōg*). Women, children, old people, the sick, the sleeping, and the unarmed are never molested.

A full-fledged raid is carried out by a sizable group of warriors and takes a long time in preparation. It must have at least one leader (*ʿagīd*) who is responsible for procuring guides and for establishing the availability of water and grazing areas along the way. A raiding expedition may cover hundreds of miles, and it may be months before the raiders are back with the booty (*ćasb*). On these distant excursions, the raiders ride their camels and lead their mares (*yistajinbūn*), which are mounted only at the time of assault (*ġarih*). Each horseman (*xayyāl*) must seek a camel rider (*zammāl*) to carry him and to transport water and provisions for himself and his mare. When the raiders approach the enemy, the cavalry (*xayyālih*) makes the assault while the cameleers (*az-zimāmīl*) remain some distance behind to guard the mounts and provisions and also, if possible, to ambush the sorties (*al-fazᶜih*) and cover the retreat of the horsemen after they have driven off the enemy's herds. The raiders are usually less in number than the men of the attacked camp, so their most effective tactic is a surprise attack. They have the best chance of success when the enemy is moving camp, because the camel herds are already on the move and the tents, along with all the furniture, are already rolled up and loaded on pack camels. If the camp is not moving, the most favorable time for attack is just after sunrise (*aḏ-ḏaha*) when the herds are led to pasture, or a little before sunset (*msayyān*) when they are led back. Other times of the day are not considered good because the herds are so dispersed that rounding them up would be difficult.

It is not always easy for raiders to surprise their enemies. Just before sunrise, the camp sends a sentinel (*riǵībih*) who climbs to the highest hilltop and hides behind a pile of stones (*rijim*) to watch for enemies. The moment he notices anything suspicious he calls out at the top of his voice to warn the camp. Immediately the women unfetter the mares and the men reach for their arms. The men of the attacked camp evaluate the situation and, if they believe they cannot manage a successful defense, they simply withdraw and let the raiders despoil their camp. If the men of the pillaged camp can rally in time, they ride their horses in hot pursuit (*ṭalab*) of the raiders to retrieve their property. If they lose sight of the raiders, they head for the nearest water hole (*mārad*), where the raiders are most likely to halt. When the two parties meet again, a second battle ensues and the pursuers may win back their camels (*yiffikūn ḥalālihum*). On other occasions, the attacked camp may decide that their only course is to wait for a more favorable opportunity to tip the balance in their favor.

When one tribe wants to occupy the pastures of another, the sheikh leads all his people with their herds into the territory they intend to occupy and camps there. The opposing tribes pitch war tents (*byūt al-ḥarb*) and prepare for a major battle (*manāx*). At such times, the tribes use what is called *ᶜiṭfih* (also called *ᶜammārīyah* or *markab*) as a kind of war banner or rallying point for their fighters. This is a richly decorated litter in which sits a sheikhly maiden or other noble and beautiful woman who "warbles the battlenote, with a passionate sweetness, which kindles the manly hearts of the young tribesmen" (Doughty 1921:II, 329). The warriors rally around to defend the lady in the litter who spurs her kinsmen to deeds of valor.

> If it seems as if the enemy would win, the girls, if present, with words and gestures encourage the warriors to persevere. With their

> breasts bared and hair loosened they ride on camels where the greatest danger appears, call to their friends and to those dear to them, and threaten to join the enemy if their own people disappoint them.
>
> Many, especially the younger warriors, then with the left hands raise the hem of their cloaks before their eyes and, with the saber or dagger in the right hand, throw themselves on the enemy. During the fight they shout: "Away! Tremble! At you! at you! O faithless people! Ye shall not escape. We came from afar to get you!" And then the fight changes into a series of duels. Personal bravery, though greatly limited by the use of firearms, may even now be exhibited. (Musil 1928:527–528)

When the fighting becomes fierce, the women tend the wounded and give water to the thirsty. On such occasions, young maidens loosen their hair and bare their breasts and urge their men to fight and defend their honor. This inflames the hearts of the youths who leap into the battle and fight valiantly in the hope of winning the hearts of these beautiful maidens.

Raiding is not only a means of redistributing wealth but also a mechanism of allocating status. "Raiding brings out all that is hard, brave, and skillful in man, so the occupation is honored and encouraged" (Dickson 1949:341). The bedouin warrior is not so much interested in material gain as he is anxious to be known for his hardiness and valor. "War gives him an opportunity of displaying his cunning, endurance, and courage. He neither loves the shedding of blood, nor craves booty, but is allured by danger and delights in the predatory art. The booty itself he will give without thinking much about it—even to the wife of the very man he has just robbed" (Musil 1928:504). Young boys look forward to the day when they are allowed to accompany their elders on raiding expeditions so they can exhibit their gallantry and endurance. Courage on the battlefield is a sure way to gain booty, high social position, and the heart of a young maiden.

Raiding preoccupies the mind of the nomad and colors his whole outlook. It is his only passion and he chooses to look only at the glorious aspects of it. Most bedouin stories and poetic compositions are about fighting and raiding expeditions; as Glubb observed, "Famous raiders acquired great reputations, and the ubiquitous poet was always at hand to celebrate their prowess in sonorous ballads" (1935:22). And Doughty wrote of the bedouins: "All their speech is homely; they tell of bygone forays and of adventures in their desert lives. You may often hear them in their tale quote the rhythms between wisdom and mirth of the *kasasīd* (riming desert poets without letters); the best are often widely current among the tribes" (1921:I, 306).

A desert hero celebrates his bravery in boastful odes in which he also describes the fair cheeks, the fluttering eyelashes, and the long tresses of his sweetheart, who cries out his name and calls after him from her litter to defend her frightened camel mount from attackers. The following is a poem by the famous warrior from Ghaṭān, Nāṣir Ibn ʿAmir Ibn Hādī, which he composed on the occasion when his tribe and the tribe of Mṭēr fought each other at the watering place Amēlāḥ (al-Fuhayd 1978:105).

1 Fortunate are those who were absent the day we were attacked at Amēlāḥ, those who did not witness the uproar of our frightened camel herds.
2 The panicked beasts threw off their loads. My heart was inflamed by the urging shouts of our ladies.
3 When I charged the enemy lines, they met me with lances and spears; but when I fled, the lady with the beautiful eyes cried out after me.
4 After the spear broke I unsheathed Abū Lāḥ, my sword, the only weapon left in my hand.
5 I fought in their midst until I repelled the attacking multitudes. I chased them away like the rutting male camel after she-camels in heat.
6 Slow down, mounted lady with thick eyelashes! I shall defend you as long as my swift mare can run.
7 For the sake of your eyes, I shall run down the foe, and his soul shall leave his body before reaching the ground. I shall leave him for the lame hyenas and spotted vultures to sup on.
8 It is my custom to risk my life on the battlefield while the cowardly run away.
9 These are the words of a fearless man. I am a noble hunting bird.

Valor and Chivalry

Because of the constant struggle against nature and against other men, desert life puts a premium on manly courage and the combative traits of character. Desert knights who are well known for their valor are distinguished by special costumes and badges which they wear on the battlefield; hence they are called *al-malābīs*. A hero among the nomads is also distinguished by his special war cry (*ʿizwih, nxawih*) which he shouts vociferously in the heat of battle. A brave man derives great honor from protecting his camel herds and from defending the honor of his womenfolk; in battle he will use the name of his sister or sweetheart, or the name of his camel herd, as his war cry. Sometimes the war cry is a reference to a previously accomplished act of chivalry.

Before the introduction of firearms, the arms of the bedouins, such as the lance, saber, and coat of mail, along with the horse, allowed full scope for the display of bravery with little loss of life. The bedouins are fond of single combat because it is spectacular and because it gives the individual warrior an opportunity to distinguish himself.

> When two hostile parties of Bedouin cavalry meet, and perceive from afar that they are equal in point of numbers, they halt opposite each other out of the reach of musket-shot; and the battle begins by skirmishes between two men. A horseman leaves his party and gallops off towards the enemy, exclaiming, "O horsemen, O horsemen, let such a one meet me!" If the adversary for whom he calls be present, and not afraid to meet him in combat, he gallops forwards; if absent, his friends reply that he is not amongst them. The challenged horseman in his turn exclaims, "And you upon the grey mare, who are you?" The other answers, "I am * * * the son of * * *." Having thus become acquainted with each other, they begin to fight; none of the by-standers join in this combat, to do so would be reckoned a treacherous action; but if one of the combatants should turn back, and fly towards his friends, the latter hasten to his assistance, and drive back the pursuer, who is in turn protected by his friends. After several of these partial combats between the best men of both parties, the whole corps join in promiscuous combat. If an Arab in battle should meet with a personal friend among the enemy's ranks, he turns his mare to a different side, and cries out, "Keep away! let not thy blood be upon me!"
>
> Should a horseman not be inclined to accept the challenge of an adversary, but choose to remain among the ranks of his friends, the challenger laughs at him with taunts and reproaches, and makes it known, as a boast, during the rest of his life, that such a one * * would not venture to meet such a one * * in battle. (Burckhardt 1831:I, 306–308)

The nomads love the predatory art and live in perpetual conflict with each other. Nonetheless, the martial spirit of the nomad does not stem from an innate or overtly aggressive nature, but is simply a response to the instability and insecurity of desert life. The speech of the nomads abounds with allusions to physical and moral courage as a means to defend tribal honor and protect tribal interests, but the nomads abhor excessive violence and the abuse of power. The objective of tribal warfare is not to annihilate or subjugate opponents, but to plunder their herds or occupy their pastures with a minimum of casualties. In tribal war, only a resisting foe is harmed. It is shameful to kill the wounded or the captive. When a man finds himself cornered on the battlefield in a desperate position, he can always save himself by asking his adversary for pardon.

> He who sees certain death before him asks for pardon in these words: "Give pardon, O rider! *emnaᶜ emnaᶜ jâ ḥajjâl.*"
>
> The man addressed will answer: "Come hither and thou wilt save thy neck. Come hither, Allah lies on thee," or: "Dismount before the face of So-and-So"—naming himself. The suppliant, coming nearer, says: "ᶜ*Aṭni allâh*, give me Allah," or "*Ḥoṭṭ ᶜalejji allâh*, lay on me Allah!" When this is done, the pardoned man says: "ᶜ*Aṭâni allâh w-ᶜaṭejteh allâh ᶜan al-bowḳ*, he assured me by Allah and I assured him by Allah against treachery!"
>
> He then surrenders his arms and most of his clothing, and receives from his captor either a kerchief or head rope, accompanied by the words: "Here, take my kerchief (or my rope) and tell any one who approaches thee that thou hast been pardoned by So-and-So, *hâk kẓâẓṭi* (ᶜ *asâbti*) *w-alli jeğîk ḥabbereh ana manîᶜ flân.*"
>
> His mare or she-camel is taken by the victor, *mâneᶜ eh*, or the latter lets some comrade keep her for him a while and returns to the fight. The pardoned one waves the kerchief or the rope, crying: "I am the *manî* of So-and-So." If both himself and his animal are wounded, his pardoner, *mâneᶜ*, conducts him to his own party where assistance will be given him, or else the *mâneᶜ* will allow him to return home at once. Should he live too far away, he is furnished with a she-camel, water bag, food, and a reliable guide, but must give his word of honor to return everything or to give compensation. (Musil 1928:529)

In desert warfare, fair play and honorable victory are important principles which serve as deterrents to indiscriminate killing. The precariousness of desert life makes the nomad much too aware of the vagaries of fortune to be intoxicated by temporary prosperity or a moment of victory. The victors treat the vanquished as they would wish to be treated should they fall into their opponents' hands.

The nomads have managed to turn the battlefield from a pool of blood into an arena where beaux gestes and glorious deeds are performed. The hero acquires glory not by taking an opponent's life but by giving him a new one; by pardoning him and restoring to him his human dignity. Usually, the combatants are not genuine enemies nor are they total strangers to each other. They know each other personally and treat each other with respect and consideration. There is "a lack of resentment or hatred between the combatants in a war governed by strict rules and a ready generosity to acknowledge the noble acts performed by the heroes of the other side" (Glubb 1937:8). Outside of battle, the warring parties may socialize and exchange courtesies like intimate friends, calling on each other to drink coffee together and to make an appointment for the next round of fighting.

Hospitality

The bedouins respect a daring knight not only for his defense of the tribe and his pursuit of its interests, but for the liberality with which he dispenses booty brought back from distant raids in acts of hospitality. Valor is a quality necessary to attain the more exalted virtue of generosity, which is a basic prerequisite for nobility in the desert. Glubb, who stayed with the bedouins for some time, wrote that "the reckless character of the famous raider often went with equally heedless generosity and hospitality" (1960:31). The reputation (*ḏićir*) and good name (*ṣīt*) of a bedouin is measured by his bounty (*jūd*) and open-handedness (*ṭīb*). When a man slaughters an animal in honor of his guests, he will spray its blood on the necks of their mounts (*rikāyib*). After the guests leave their host and go on their long journey, they meet many people in distant lands who see the blood that was sprayed on their mounts and ask, "Who is the host who slaughtered for you?" The host will thus become famous throughout the desert and stories will be told about his hospitality. Tirkī Ibn Mhēd, the famous knight and chief of the Fedᶜān section of the ᶜAnazah tribes, is nicknamed *mṣawwit b-al-ᶜaša* ("he who calls out for supper") because in lean times he would send his slave to climb on a high knoll in the evening and call forth for anyone hungry to come and eat supper.

Hospitality in the desert is not just the giving of food. It is an intricate web of symbolic acts and rituals that are structurally and functionally interwined with one another and interrelated with the other components of the nomadic value system. The "salt bond" is very sacred among the nomads, and the giving of life is a protection against the taking of life. By sharing his food with a guest, the nomad gives life to the guest (*aḍ-ḍēf*) not only by offering him nourishment but also by granting him protection while he is his guest and for three days after he departs, three days being the length of time it presumably takes the body to digest the last meal the guest shared with his host. It is the *ḥagg aḍ-ḍēf* (right of the guest) to be fed and protected by his host. A man who betrays his guest or fails to provide him with the necessary protection is forever disgraced among the nomads. Of the ᶜAnazah tribe, Burckhardt wrote: "A guest is regarded as sacred; his person is protected, and a violation of hospitality, by the betraying of a guest, has not occurred within memory of man" (1831:I, 176).

The refusal to partake of a man's hospitality is a sign of bad intentions. When a nomad sees a stranger approaching his camp, he will run after him and force him to turn around and stay for supper or at least have some coffee or milk. If the stranger refuses to turn around he is taken for an enemy and may be shot at. When a man goes to see another man on serious business, the visitor will not taste water, coffee, or any food until the host grants him his wish. This in effect means, "Grant me my wish or consider me an enemy."

Preparation and serving of coffee is not just an ingredient of hospitality but its most important and ceremonious part. When a host first perceives his guests, he rushes to meet and welcome them (*yhallī w-yraḥḥib*). After they sit down, he rakes the hearth (*yaḥarṯ al-wjār*), strikes a blazing fire (*yiṭiᶜᶜ an-nār*), and begins to roast the coffee beans. The beans must be roasted slowly and carefully lest they burn. When they turn yellowish brown and start to glisten with sweat, they are cast into a shallow pan (*mbarrad*) to cool off. The husks are then blown off and the roasted beans are pounded with measured strokes, with an occasional rap on the rim of the mortar to give variety to the beat. The rhythmic pounding of the mortar is soothing music to the ears of the weary travelers. The host empties the ground coffee into the first of the two pots used in this process. After a few minutes of boiling, that pot is drawn away from the glowing coals and left for a while to settle (*taṣfī*). The second and smaller coffee pot into which the coffee is now emptied is called *al-mibharih* because it is in this pot that the *bhār* is added to the coffee. The *bhār* consists of one pinch of saffron, a few cloves, and a generous amount of ground cardamom seeds (*hēl*).

The host performs every step in this ritual coffee preparation ceremoniously and with the utmost dignity. With welcoming gestures and pleasantries, he tries to put his guests at ease and let them feel that they have done him a favor by alighting at his tent and honoring him with their presence. He tries to make (*ykayyif*) a truly refreshing cup (*finjāl*) for them which, besides its good taste, looks (in the words of poets) like henna dye (*xḏ̣āb*) on the fair hands of a beautiful bride, a cup that will *yaṭird an-nᶜās* (banish fatigue) and *yiǵiᶜd ar-rās* (clear the head).

The serving of coffee is no less ceremonious than the making of it. When the coffee is ready to serve, the host lifts up the pot to a level almost above his head and pours into the small porcelain cups held in his right hand "a stream of coffee as delicate as a spider's thread. As soon as the bottom of the cup is covered, he hands it to the foremost guest" (Musil 1928:102). The cup must not be filled; "to fill it up to a guest, as in the northern towns, were among the bedouins an injury, and of such bitter meaning, 'this drink thou and depart'" (Doughty 1921:I, 287).

Indeed, the serving of coffee is a ritual act fraught with symbolic significance, as the following quote from Musil illustrates.

> If the attackers learn that there is in the camp to be assailed a fighter feared for his bravery, they prepare to destroy him. The evening before the attack the leader takes a cup of black coffee in his hand and says:
>
> "This cup is filled with the blood of So-and-So. Who will drink it?"
>
> If one of the men present takes the cup and drinks the coffee with the words "I am drinking the blood of So-and-So," he is obliged to meet the aforesaid hero in a duel. During the fight he asks again and again:
>
> "O riders, who of you has seen So-and-So?"
>
> If the hero is not among the fighters on that day, a comrade of his will answer: "O thou son of an honorable family, he is not here. If he were, thou mayst be sure he would not hide from thee. But here is one who will take his place. Only come nearer with her (the mare)! *Jâ walad al-ḥalâl mâ hw ḥâẓer lâ čân ḥâẓer mâ čân ittaḳa ᶜank ḥâẓer min jesedd ᶜanneh mâr zarrebha ǧâj.*"
>
> But if the hero happens to be present, he says: "Oh, who is inquiring for So-and-So? This is he. Thou hast reached him. *Jâ nâšeden ᶜan flân hâḏa hw waṣelt ḥâẓer.*"
>
> The comrades of both warriors then stop fighting, the better to observe the result of the duel, *mulâkaᶜ*. Both duellists first utter the battle cry of their tribe, adding: "Never say: 'He has surprised or tricked me.' *Lâ tḳûl ṛaṭarni w-bâḳni.* Brace up now and defend thyself! *Hôḏ ḥaẓarak w-enfaᶜ ḥâlek.* Oh, how do I frighten heroes! Thou sneerest at me and thy lips are twitching!" (1928:527–8)

Coffee is called *kēf*, "that substance that sets the mood right." Making and serving coffee is a significant theme in Nabaṭi poetry. Many a poet begins his composition with a few lines describing the details of this ritual. The poet speaks of serving the first cup to the worthiest man: he who single-handedly covers the retreat of his comrades, he who drives pursuers away from those comrades whose mares are slow, he who assists (*yiḏhir*) fallen comrades, and above all he whose tent flaps are always dripping with grease and whose ash-mound resembles the dirt heap of a recently dug water well. The poet may conclude his composition by stating that he will not present the cup of coffee to the scoundrel or the slothful who have never gone on a raid and who raise herds to sell in the market instead of slaughtering them for hungry guests. When coffee is served, the hero is always presented with the first cup. But as the cup passes on the right from one man to the next, it bypasses idle men, who are not given coffee until the more respected men have drunk the first round. It is a grave insult to call a man *yā mᶜaggab al-finjāl*, "thou who art bypassed when the cup goes round."

Valor and hospitality are central themes in poems of boasting and panegyric (the great bulk of Nabaṭi poetry), and the two are usually mentioned together. The hero is praised as one who protects the ladies and the camel herds and who dares to pasture his herds on the most coveted, hence most dangerous, spots. His war cry terrifies mares on the battlefield, and his spear always drips with the blood of his enemies. The poet also expands upon the various signs and manifestations of the hero's sumptuous hospitality. These include a many-poled tent pitched on high ground so as to be visible from afar, a brass mortar (*nijir*), the rhythmic pounding of which sends a loud and clear message to men of neighboring tents to assemble for a feast that is in preparation, a blazing bonfire which attracts night travelers, a high mound of ashes, a shallow pan (*miḥmāsih*) for roasting coffee beans, large coffee pots in which coffee is constantly brewing, slaughtered young camels and sheep with fat tails, and huge cauldrons filled with heaps of meat and mounds of boiled rice. The sight, smell, and taste of tallow (*šaḥam*) and fat (*disam*) are rare aesthetic pleasures in the desert. Fat stands for prosperity and a life of ease; thus a year with auspicious seasonal rainfall is called a fat year, *sintin dasmih*. When the nomad squeezes lumps of rice (*ᶜēš*) in his right hand and grease drips from between his fingers, a meal, in his view, can truly be called delicious. After eating with the sheikh, guests wipe off their greasy hands on the front part of the tent, so that the tent flaps of hospitable tribal chiefs are said to be always dripping with grease.

Honor

To cope with the volatile and potentially explosive politics of the desert in the absence of central authority, the nomads devised various codes of honor which served to minimize danger and prevented the breakdown of order. Chivalry in warfare and protection of the guest, which have already been discussed, are constituent elements in a complex system which is instrumental in curbing violence and providing protection for the weak and powerless. This system includes the right of protection to companions, tent-neighbors, and fugitives.

Friends and comrades traveling together are honor-bound to help and protect each other. Like the guest, the traveling companion (*xawiy, rifīǵ*) has the right (*ḥagg*) to be protected. The rights and obligations of comradeship can be extended and applied in a different way. A man traveling alone in the desert is easy prey to marauders from enemy tribes who will attack and rob him. Therefore, a traveler advisedly seeks from every tribe along his route a companion who acts as an escort to see him safely through his tribal territory. This companion pledges to look after the traveler and protect him from his fellow tribesmen. The following anecdote from H. St. John B. Philby illustrates how the tribal escort performs his duties.

> On reaching the western edge we turned aside into a deep hollow and camped for the night. We were now on the fringe of the ᶜAtaiba marches; hitherto from the coast westwards it had never been necessary to take precautions either to conceal our presence or to guard our camps; now it was different; we had turned aside from the road to be out of the way of chance passengers; we had camped in a hollow to conceal our camp-fire; among us were four men of the ᶜAtaiba tribe, who now assumed responsibility for our safety; at intervals they went forth to the surrounding sand-hummocks and proclaimed to the world: 'Look you, O men of the ᶜAtaiba, here am I, Jarman, a man of the Barqa, and I say to you, we are men of Ibn Saᶜud journeying to the Sharif; so let none molest us; and whoso hear my words, let him come to us and share our dinner or drink coffee and welcome; but molest us not or, if you do, say not you knew not who and what we are.' (1922:I, 131)

The tent-neighbor (*jār*) is a stranger who quits his kinsmen and attaches himself to a foreign tribe. He pitches his tent next to that of a strong man in the tribe, thus becoming his tent-neighbor. A nomad considers it a sacred duty to protect his tent-neighbor and look after his interests. A fugitive could also find refuge in the tent of a powerful person, who is obliged by honor to protect him as his *dixīl* (from the verb *daxal*, "to enter the tent"). The *dixīl* is different from the tent-neighbor in that he is a fugitive and he lodges himself inside the tent of his protector. I cannot give a better explanation of this institution than the one given in the following account from Musil.

> One who is oppressed personally has to ask protection of someone more powerful or of a member of an important kin; it is sufficient, however, for him to enter the tent of the one whose protection he desires or even its sacred precincts, *muḥârem*. The precincts begin either at the limits of hearing distance or at a full spear's length from the farthest tent pegs. When a pursued person cries from afar to the tent owner that he is putting himself under his protection and is heard, the latter is bound to protect him. The term for such an occurrence is *ḥaḳḳ aṣ-ṣowt*. On reaching the sacred precincts the pursued man finds himself under the protection of the tent. If

he is unable from exhaustion to proceed any farther and remains lying on the ground inside the precincts, no harm may be done to him, as that would be a violation of the tent, *ʿatab al-bejt*. The owner of the tent, his wife, or child shouts:

"Why dost thou violate my protege? thine eyesight is sharp enough, is it not? *Lêh taʿteb ʿala daḫîli ent ʿajnak žwijje*. With us the precincts of a tent are recognized as sacred by an old custom; no one would dare to violate it; *al-muḥârem ʿendana ʿâdaten sanîjjaten mâ ḥad jaḳṭaʿha*." (1928:441–442)

The codes relating to chivalry and to the protection of the guest, the companion, the tent-neighbor, and the fugitive are basic ingredients of the nomadic outlook, and are universally recognized in the desert. The upholding of these codes is a point of individual honor, and their violation is a treachery that strips the offender of his honor and brings him and his kinsmen everlasting shame.

Among the nomads, an honorable man is one who has the physical and moral courage to keep his pledges and to conduct all his affairs with faith and integrity (*nigā*). He is a benevolent person (*rāʿī mruwwih*) who is always *rāʿī nxawih* (ready to help) and *rāʿī fazʿah* (provide assistance). It is only to this man of honor that the oppressed and powerless turn for help and protection. A refusal to give help "would imply weakness, would blacken one's honor, and the man who refuses would be derided at all camp fires for his lack of manly courage" (Musil 1928:441).

An honorable man would consider an injury to anyone under his protection to be a breach of his covenant and an insult to himself. To cleanse his honor, he must demonstrate his anger and indignation and must punish the culprit severely, even if he is his closest relative, as the following account illustrates.

Certain desert tribes, notably the Dhafir, are particularly proud of the name they have won for protecting their tent-neighbours. They have become famous in this respect, as the following stories will show. . . .

The uncle of Hamud al Suwait, the Shaikh of all the Dhafir tribe, once threatened in public *majlis*, to impale himself upon his sword which he had drawn for the purpose, unless *his own son* were brought before him and slain in his presence, because the son had killed his tent-neighbor in the heat of a foolish quarrel. The various members of the family tried hard to shield the youth, but realizing that the old shaikh was in deadly earnest, Hamud al Suwait (he became shaikh after his uncle's death two years later) himself seized

> the boy and with his own hand cut him down before the eyes of his father. Thus was tribal honour satisfied. This incident happened in 1912. . . .
>
> Shaikh Jadaʿan al Suwait, who succeeded to the Shaikhship of the Dhafir after the death of Hamud, was camped near Athaiba and Ruhail on the Kuwait-Iraq border in 1931. Hearing that one of his own tribesmen had fired at and wounded a Mutairi tribesman who was his *qasír* at the time, even though the Mutair tribe and the Dhafir tribe were open enemies, Shaikh Jadaʿan had the offending tribesman brought before him, and with his own hand slashed him over the head with his sword.
>
> The deed flashed through the Badawin world like lightning at the time, and Jadaʿan's name, as the upholder of Badawin honour, became almost as famous as that of his forebear. Unfortunately the Iraq authorities, with that folly which has frequently characterised them in dealing with the high-spirited tribesmen of the desert, imprisoned Shaikh Jadacan for several weeks, before they saw that they were making a martyr of a desert hero. This act cost them his allegiance. Shortly after, Shaikh Jadaʿan went over to Bin Saʿud, taking half the tribe with him.
>
> Shaikh Jadaʿan told me the story himself, saying that he only acted as he did in order to keep the vital Badawin law clean and untarnished.
>
> So greatly have the Dhafir tribe preserved and guarded their good name in the above respect, that it is said of Mana, another famous Shaikh of the Dhafir, that the immediate cause of his death was the news (which was brought to him as he was riding home from a raid) that a certain well-known guest of the tribe had, in his absence, been attacked and slain. Certain it is that on being told what had happened, his heart seemed to stop beating and he fell forward on his camel's neck and rolled to the ground a dead man. His daughter, whom I met in 1935, told me that the old man had literally died of a broken heart, and her words were vouched for by her husband, Shaikh Hautush al Suwait, cousin of Jadaʿan. (Dickson 1949:129–130)

To solicit the help of a powerful person, a suppliant would appeal to him and ask for his "face" (countenance). The face (*wijh*) of a man is his prestige and standing in the eyes of his fellow tribesmen. An honorable man keeps his face clean and without blemish by leading a noble life of virtue and chivalry. To express approval of a man's conduct one says "May Allah whiten his face," but to express disapproval, "May Allah blacken his face." To demonstrate his gratitude, a suppliant would fly a white flag in honor of his benefactor, showing that the benefactor has performed all his obligations and that his face is white.

Nabaṭi poetry played an influential role in maintaining the various codes of honor and chivalry. Noble and heroic acts were encouraged with poems of praise and blame; honorable men were eulogized and their noble actions immortalized in verses which were handed down from generation to generation, while those who violated the code of honor were vilified by the poets as base men with whom one must avoid intermarriage. Urgent appeals for support and protection were usually submitted in verses extolling the manly courage and honorable reputation of the man from whom assistance was sought. The most rewarding tribute for an act of honor or chivalry was for the beneficiary to compose an ode praising his benefactor as a noble and honorable man.

I shall close this chapter with a story and a short poem which illustrate the seriousness with which a nomad views the violation of his honor (al-Mārik 1963–1965:I, 57–92). Mājid al-Ḥaṯribī and Mfawwiz at-Tajġīf were clansmen of the same section of the famous tribe of Shammar. One morning their clan was attacked by raiders who plundered their herds. Mājid and Mfawwiz, along with the other youths of the clan, followed the raiders in hot pursuit until they caught up with them. As has been pointed out already, it is the custom when a nomad finds himself in a desperate situation on the battlefield to turn to his pursuer, throw down his weapons, put his two thumbs in his mouth, and say to the pursuer, "*ana b-wajhik*" (I put myself under your countenance") or "*ana dixīlik*" ("I put myself under your protection"), in which case the pursuer must spare his life and grant him protection from other members of his (the pursuer's) tribe. Such a protected person is called *minīᶜ*. In the heat of the battle Mājid granted protection to one of the enemy, and to make sure that no one of his own tribe would molest his *minīᶜ*, he gave him his head rope (*ᶜgāl*) as a token. But it so happened that this *minīᶜ* who was granted protection by Mājid was the person who during a previous battle had slain Mfawwiz's father, and Mfawwiz had been looking for him ever since to avenge his father's blood. When Mfawwiz saw this man, he ran him down with his lance and killed him instantly, not realizing that he was the *minīᶜ* of his friend Mājid. After the battle Mājid looked for his *minīᶜ*, but he found him dead and he was told that his friend Mfawwiz had killed him.

When Mājid went back to the camp he found that his mother had struck their tent (to symbolize that the action of Mfawwiz had ruined their house) and threatened to cut her breasts, which had nourished her son Mājid, if he did not avenge his slain *minīᶜ* and wash clean his honor. Mājid sent a messenger to Mfawwiz giving him an ultimatum: he had three days to escape (these three days are called *al-mharrbāt*, from the verb *harab*, "to escape"), after which he would hunt him down and kill him. The killing of his *minīʿ* and breach of his honor caused Mājid such anguish that he became distracted and withdrawn. He refused to eat or even talk to anyone. One of his clansmen by the name of ʿAmir noticed that Mājid's health was deteriorating and kept asking him repeatedly what was the matter with him. In answer, Mājid composed this poem.

1 O valiant ʿAmir who is not afraid to graze herds in the spots of danger, you are the protector of the oppressed person who seeks refuge in you.

2 O brother of Fhēd, [you are] well known for your hospitality; and you throw supper to the vultures hovering over the battlefield.

3 You meet the attacking horsemen and risk your life to protect your people; for days you have pressed me with your ceaseless questioning.

4 Do you not see what state I am in? I am like a little insect, or a wretched man who refuses nourishment.

5 I will not eat though the food might be drenched with butter and fat strips from the camel's hump;

6 Even though it might be grain from al-Balgā and dates from al-Jōf, my soul, overflowing with anger, does not accept it.

7 A slender-waisted maiden clad in her best raiment does not appeal to me, though she might have power over other men's hearts.

8 She does not appeal to me even though we were to meet in a safe place, on a sand dune where there are neither Muslims nor infidels about.

9 I only yearn to meet the noble Mfawwiz, the pick of his peers, their true knight when they give chase to their enemies on the level plain between the soft sands and the rocky mountains.

10 I will advance towards him and cross line upon line of men surrounding him; I will reach him sitting in the innermost part of his tent.

11 Then I will stab him with a sharp saber that will burn his entrails; a new scimitar which has never been mended by blacksmiths.

12 Either his ladies will clap their hands in mourning, or, if he lives, he will never stand upon his feet.

13 He clad me in the black robe of shame; he humiliated me, and I became like a despised coal dealer among settled folks.

14 Once my honor was white as hemp, but he stained it black as wool; [with this threat] he will stay awake at night [from fear of me] while I go to sleep.

In the preceding pages I have attempted to give the reader a glimpse of the social conditions of premodern Arabia, and point out how Nabaṭi poetry, in its world view and thematic makeup, provides a mirror of these conditions. This is an important point to bear in mind, since the native audience of a Nabaṭi poem judge its artistic merit by the degree to which it is a response to, and a reflection of, real life. In this regard, Nabaṭi poetry and classical Arabic poetry share many qualities and, being products of the same social conditions, are highly similar in both content and outlook.

III

POETRY IN THE DESERT

Nabaṭi poetry is the product of a heroic age characterized by political turmoil and intertribal feuds. The incessant raids and forays of the desert Arabs of premodern Arabia were celebrated in poems composed by tribal poets and heroes. Major battles were generally preceded by a period of mobilization during which poems were exchanged by opponents. Such a war of words was part of the sportive attitude generally held by desert Arabs toward fighting. On the way to the battlefield, poets composed verses to challenge the enemy and instill courage in their own party. The circumstances of the fight, the spot where it took place, individual acts of gallantry, the gains and losses of both sides, and other details are recorded and passed on in verse. On the way back from battle, poems were composed to lament fallen heroes, to praise those who fought well, and to taunt cowards. Similarly, on their way back from intertribal raids, driving the booty before them, raiders composed cheerful lyrics praising the galloping of their mares and the stamina of their camel mounts. They described the wild intoxication of the charge, the thrill of the chase, the excitement of the battle, and the narrow escapes from the lances of enemies thirsty to lap up their blood. They also praised their enemies as worthy and gallant men, and expressed apologies for injuries to them and for the looting of their herds, but added that this was an honorable practice that had been undertaken by all noble men since ancient times.

The most stirring are the compositions of nomadic chiefs and desert knights who employed their poetic skills not to amuse or entertain, but to press for a course of action, to reveal a plan, to declare war, to deliver a threat, to challenge a foe, to sue for peace, to appeal for assistance, to celebrate a victory, to document an honorable deed, or to boast about a chivalrous act. Their verses are records of their heroic adventures and the roles they played in shaping the events of their time. Their compositions are characterized by absence of the stylistic embellishments and ornamental devices employed by professional poets. The language they employed is terse, dignified, and to the point. The appeal of their poetry lies in the fact that it faithfully depicts in a rich language a nomadic existence that was heroic, chivalrous, and free.

In addition to the knights and chiefs, each tribe had a host of poets. Just as heroes unsheathed their swords to deal death blows to the men of enemy tribes, the poets unleashed their tongues with verses that flew like sharp arrows to strike enemy tribes and symbolically conquer them. Tribal poets fought their own battles of words, which were fueled by tribal feuds. The tribal poet drew the material for his compositions from tribal life and his role was to record in verse the honorable deeds of his tribe, to sing its praises, and to defend it against antagonist poets. To perform his task most effectively, the tribal poet had to have a thorough knowledge of tribal history and genealogies. In big assemblies, it was the alert and quick-witted poet who cogently and eloquently argued the case of the tribe. He kept in his head any blood debt owed to his tribe by others, and he continuously urged his tribesmen to redress the balance and cleanse their honor by exacting vengeance.

Although nomadic poetry deals mainly with tribal raids and forays, it is not straightforward historical narrative. Poets make only allusions and cryptic references to the incidents celebrated in their poems. Therefore, a poetic recitation usually alternates with a prose narrative which recounts the raids and battles celebrated in the poetry and serves to put the poetry into its proper historical context and to illuminate its allusions. The poetry does, however, serve as an authentic document substantiating the incidents in the narrative and enhancing their circulation and preservation in public memory.

The desert poetry of premodern Arabia resembles the poetry of ancient Arabia in its emphasis on tribal history and the intermixture of poetic recitation with prose narrative.[1] Ignaz Goldziher observed of classical poetry:

> Pagan Arabic poetry truly reflects pre-Islamic tribal life with all its passions and traditional ideology. Its subjects include the petty intertribal feuds resulting from vendetta; the predatory guerrilla warfare (*ghazw*, from which our word 'razzia' is derived though with a modification of meaning); the adventures, both heroic and comic, of the itinerant poets; the praise of some prominent man for his bravery or hospitality, and the vilipending of misers and cowards. Nevertheless, the panegyric (*madḥ*) and the lampoon (*hijâ*) are not confined to individuals for the poet drains to the bottom the repository of their ancestors' traditions, both glorious and unfavorable, and relates the praise or derision of the individual to the history of his tribe. All these subjects are variegated with episodes

> characteristic of the *qaṣîda*. Thus, the poets had excellent opportunities to versify the famous events of intertribal warfare (*ayyâm al-ᶜarab*), the historical details of which are preserved in the prose narratives (*akhbâr al-ᶜarab*) pertaining to the poems.
>
> For these reasons pagan Arabic poetry, leaving apart its artistic value, is the main source of our knowledge of pre-Islâmic social life and institutions as well as tribal history. (1966:12)

Excellent examples of desert poems and narratives are recorded by M. A. al-Sudayrī in his book *Abṭāl min al-Ṣaḥrāᵓ* (1968). This book contains partial biographies of five desert heroes, which are essentially accounts of the roles played by these heroes in tribal wars, along with the poems composed to celebrate these wars. Of course, al-Sudayrī preserves the original vernacular diction of the poems which accompany the biographical narratives, but the narratives themselves are transformed from oral renditions into composite written texts and their language is changed from vernacular to literary. There follows below a freely adapted account drawn from the biography of Siᶜdūn al-ᶜWāji, the paramount chief of the Wild Slēmān section of the ᶜAnazah tribe, who lived in the first half of the nineteenth century. The poems and incidents in this biography were collected from "the mouths of the grey beards of ᶜAnazah" (ibid., 47). In the following account, special attention will be paid to the parts of the biography that deal with the wars between ᶜAnazah and Shammar.

Siᶜdūn al-ᶜWāji was famous for his valor and chivalry and was an outstanding poet who composed many boastful poems. He was obeyed and esteemed by his tribesmen, and even his foes respected him. He had many sons, but only ᶜGāb and Ḥjāb—of the same mother—distinguished themselves. ᶜGāb was counted among the heroes of Najd, and his fame even exceeded that of his father. However, when ᶜGāb and Ḥjāb were still small boys, Siᶜdūn had some disagreement with their mother, who moved away from the territory of Wild Slēmān in Najd to that of her own tribe in the Syrian desert, taking her two small sons along with her. She was from the al-Fidᶜān section of the large ᶜAnazah tribe. Thus ᶜGāb and Ḥjāb were brought up among al-Fidᶜān in the Syrian desert, away from their father. There, they were raised by their maternal uncles, who taught them how to ride horses and how to throw the spear. When they became mature men they distinguished themselves on the battlefield and became the war leaders of the Wild Slēmān tribesmen who had migrated to the Syrian desert and stayed with al-Fidᶜān.

In the meantime, Siᶜdūn continued to be the chief of Wild Slēmān until one of his cousins, by the name of Šāmix, defied his authority and challenged his leadership. Šāmix violated the orders of Siʿdūn and eventually usurped the leadership of Wild Slēmān, stripping Siʿdūn of all power and treating him unjustly. Šāmix pitched himself a large chiefly tent with many poles, and ordered Siʿdūn to live in a small, mean tent which he was obliged to pitch at the farthest edge of the camp. Šāmix also told Siʿdūn that he must never bring his camels to drink till the herds of all other people had had enough. Siʿdūn was thus humiliated and reduced from a venerable chief to a miserable outcast. He composed many poems lamenting his ill fortune, and some of these poems he sent to his two sons, ʿGāb and Ḥjāb, in the Syrian desert. In his poems, Siʿdūn complained to his sons about Šāmix and pleaded for their help. His appeals to ʿGāb, the elder and more valiant of the two, were especially urgent. He implored him to come and help him regain the chieftainship of Wild Slēmān. In the following poem addressed to ʿGāb, Siʿdūn laments the passing of his glorious days and bemoans the reversal of his fortune. In the third line, he pictures misfortune as a horse running after him; in the past he was well ahead of it, but now it tramples upon him with its shod hooves.

1 My heart is set ablaze by anxieties; it simmers as if on glowing embers.
2 Oh, treacherous fate, how quick it turns! My happy days suddenly changed to adversity.
3 I was far ahead of misfortune before, but now it tramples upon me with its shod hooves.
4 I used to wear a badge of distinction, and led the troops astride a noble steed.
5 When enemy horsemen attacked, I was the first to meet them and cover the retreat of my kinsmen.
6 But today, I have no mount on which to carry my baggage. Oh, how shameful! I have been humbled and subdued.
7 Oh, how painful is misfortune! Gone are the glorious days.
8 I have often asked, where is my son, who spills the red blood of the enemy? I have often wondered, where is my beloved son?
9 Enemy horses flee when they hear his thunderous voice; he terrifies the mares on the battlefield.
10 He chases them like an eagle; vultures dine on the flesh of his enemies.

In the second poem, Siʿdūn is more specific in his complaints about Šāmix and his appeals to ʿGāb are more fervent. In line 16 he refers to his sons as the poles and cords he needs to erect the large multipoled tent of chieftainship. In the last line, he appeals to his sons in the name of their sister Nimšah to answer his call.

1 Hail, you rider on a speedy mount, a fleet camel fit to cover desolate wastes;
2 Noble and young, its molar teeth are not all out yet. In a scant two days you reach al-Fiḏīlih,
3 Where you alight near liberal hosts who welcome guests with open arms. After you rest, take leave of the gallant men.
4 Ride your mount and follow the tracks in the wilderness; travel north, keeping the Pole Star before your eyes.
5 Go in safety and carry my verses to ʿGāb and Ḥjāb; when you come to my dear sons, give them my best regards.
6 Give a special salutation to ʿGāb, the valiant lad who protects the weak and the oppressed.
7 Tell him that Šāmix has become a brazen man in his old age; by God, O ʿGāb, he oppresses me so.
8 O ʿGāb, bitter is the taste of defeat; I am forced to stay away from the tribal wells.
9 In the past, I was the champion of the tribal cause, the hero on the battlefield.
10 But now Šāmix owns the noble mares; so long as he is chief, I shall never enjoy the coffee cup.
11 His oppression pains me in the heart, O ʿGāb. For years I have not tasted sweet slumber,
12 As if a guard were standing over me, lest I close my eyes; even food tastes bitter in my mouth.
13 Gone is my glory, O ʿGab; I am a defeated man, a dead man walking among the living.
14 O ʿGāb, O wild eagle, oppression has turned my hair gray; too much suffering has crushed my spirit, and soon I may be driven to distraction.
15 For years I have not enjoyed sleep; I stay awake alone all night, sighing and weeping.
16 A tent cannot be pitched without poles and cords; when will you come, ʿGāb, and build my tent?
17 Alone, I can do nothing but bite on my fingers [in sorrow]; I close my eyes and turn away.
18 I wait for the wind to bring me glad tidings; I hope for the brothers of Nimšah to answer my call.

ʿGāb and Ḥjāb had remained with their maternal uncles in the Syrian desert and did not join their father in Najd after they became grown men because each was receiving a yearly pension of a considerable sum from the Turkish government. At that time, the Turkish government was paying subsidies to notable bedouin chiefs in the Syrian desert in its effort to pacify the nomads and curb their predatory activities, in order to make the desert roads, especially the Ḥajj road, safer for travelers. But upon receiving their father's poems, ʿGāb and Ḥjāb renounced the government subsidies and, in defiance of the Turkish decree, went to Najd to answer their father's call, accompanied by a few faithful friends and servants. Throughout this long journey, ʿGāb gathered information from camel riders concerning his father and the whereabouts of Šāmix.

After thirty days of forced marches, ʿGāb and his company spent the last night of their journey near the wells of al-Ḥēzih, having received information that Šāmix was camping there. At dawn, ʿGāb went alone to look for his father's tent; he knew that Šāmix had obliged his father to pitch a small tent on the outskirts of the camp. When he found the tent, he woke up the herder and ordered him to drive his father's camels to the wells to drink. The herder protested, saying that Šāmix had warned him several times never to take Siʿdūn's camels to the water till midday, after the herds of all the others had drunk their fill. ʿGāb told the herder not to fear Šāmix and insisted that he must take the camels to drink. The herder drove the camels to the wells while ʿGāb hid among them. When Šāmix saw the camels of Siʿdūn driven to the water, he was outraged and ran after the herder with his camel stick, intent on thrashing him. When he came close, ʿGāb, like a furious tiger, came out from among the camels to meet him. Šāmix was so struck by the awesome sight of ʿGāb with drawn sword in hand that he panicked and threw himself into one of the wells. He refused to come out until ʿGāb gave him assurances that his life would be spared. By that time, Ḥjāb had arrived in the camp with the pack camels and the rest of the company. A large, fully furnished, multipoled tent was built for Siʿdūn. Messengers were sent to call out through the camp that every man should come to Siʿdūn's new tent and pay him homage. Thus, Siʿdūn once again became the chief of Wild Slēmān, and Šāmix was soon forgotten.

Siʿdūn was an energetic and capable leader. After regaining the chieftainship of Wild Slēmān, he immediately set out to assert his authority and demonstrate his qualities as a leader. He was supported by his two sons, ʿGāb and Ḥjāb, whose names became known throughout the desert—ʿGāb for his valor and Ḥjāb for his hospitality.

One year, the territory of Wild Slēmān was stricken by drought, so Siʿdūn decided to invade Bēḏ̣ā Niṯīl, a large territory in northern Arabia which is famous for its rich pastures and which then belonged to Shammar. He sent a declaration of war to Miṣliṭ at-Timyāṭ, the paramount chief of the at-Tūmān section of Shammar, in the form of a poem asking him to quit Bēḏā Niṯīl or be evicted by force. The poem, as the opening lines indicate, was sent with a delegation of eight men riding eight identical mounts. According to Musil, "When a chief sends out a mission he takes care that all ride camels of the same color" (1928:319). In the fourth line of the poem, Siᶜdūn boasts that the camels of Wild Slēmān are fat because they graze in the richest and most contested pastures. In the following line, he declares that these camels were not inherited, but were seized by force from other tribes. In the penultimate line, Siᶜdūn states that his tribesmen ride horses of pure breed whose dams were never covered by a nag and whose noble ancestry can be traced back to the time of the Prophet. In this poem, Siᶜdūn does not vilify Miṣliṭ. On the contrary, he praises him as a noble man. Desert knights and poets usually do not disparage their adversaries. Their principle is that a worthy man must fight only with a worthy adversary. For after all, what prestige can a man derive from defeating an unworthy foe?

1 Hail, you rider on a barren mount whose breasts were never suckled by a calf; one of eight identical camels, she is not alone.
2 Their chests are wide, their legs are spotted with white, thoroughbreds of Omani origin.
3 You will alight by the camp of Miṣliṭ, the scion of noble ancestors; tell him to quit his land, we wish to take possession of it.
4 We wish to graze our camel herds there—sweet to the ear is their growling; we fatten them on coveted pastures.
5 We herd them, bearing long lances to protect them against enemy tribes.
6 We did not inherit them from our ancestors; they are the milch camels of our adversaries, which we took by force.
7 They graze protected by ᶜGāb, who carries a sharp spear to guard them from enemy attacks.
8 O riders, tell Miṣliṭ we are marching against him; I challenge him to meet us on the battlefield.
9 For days we march searching for our enemies; we trample upon them with our feet.
10 We ride slender thoroughbred mares whose ancestors we trace to the Prophet's days.
11 We sing on their backs as we deliver death blows; swiftly they retreat, yet more quickly we turn them around.

Having attacked Shammar and driven them out of Bēḏā Niṯīl, Siᶜdūn celebrated his victory over Miṣliṭ at-Timyāṭ in the following poem. He begins by imploring a mounted courier to spread the news in the camps of ᶜAnazah. The speed of the courier's camel mount is compared to that of a terrified ostrich. This is a stock image in Nabaṭi poetry. It is common to compare a fleet camel mount to an ostrich, antelope, or similar hunted animal of the wild. These animals run very fast, especially when terrified by the approach of a hunter or predator. In this poem, Siᶜdūn describes how Miṣliṭ fled the battlefield on a speedy horse, leaving behind his cousin Jrēs, a renowned Shammari warrior, who was slain in Zawāǧīb by the ᶜAnazah horsemen. Siᶜdūn praises his son ᶜGāb and in the last line describes him as young and handsome.

1 Hail, you rider on a speedy mount that runs like a terrified ostrich on level plains,
2 A handsome mount with erect hump and arched neck, a purebred of noble ancestry—
3 Not a common pack animal—it is a wild beast that has never been ridden before.
4 You will alight at the camps of ᶜAnazah, who adorn their sharp spears with gallant deeds.
5 When you join their assemblies in the tents of their chiefs, and my faithful friends among them question you,
6 Tell them, multitudes that cannot be counted attacked us at dawn; the people of the mountain attacked us in the early morning.
7 Praise the Lord, they were vanquished and their stragglers sought refuge in [the distant settlements of] Gfār and Ḥāyīl.
8 Many bodies fell to the ground, their heads severed by our sabers; with our swords we demonstrate our anger at our foes.
9 Many enemy horsemen were thrown down; they fell from their horses and rolled in the dust.
10 Intoxicated by his multitudes [of followers], Miṣliṭ attacked us in the morning, and ᶜGāb, the wild eagle, met him on the field, riding his fiery horse.
11 He [Miṣliṭ] threw down his sword and ran away; he spurred his mare and hid behind the dunes.
12 He left behind [his slain cousin] Jrēs in Zawāǧīb; woe to him, he will bemoan this gallant lad.
13 He [ᶜGāb] sits in the tent, dignified and clad in his war attire; he is still young, but he is already renowned for his glorious deeds.

Miftāḥ al-Ġēṯī, the chief of al-Ġyiṯih, a principal line of the ᶜAbdah section of Shammar, was enraged by the defeat of his kinsmen at the hands of Siᶜdūn. He sent urgent appeals to the various clans of Shammar, inciting them to close their ranks and stand united against Siᶜdūn and his ᶜAnazah tribesmen. Many answered the call of Miftāḥ and a large army of Shammar clansmen marched against Siᶜdūn. The armies of

ʿAnazah and Shammar met by the water wells of Ḏafrih in the lands of Shammar. This time Shammar won the day, and their victory was celebrated by the Shammari poet Ršēd Ibn Ṭōʿān.

The poem opens with the description of the battlefield as a raincloud. This is a stock image in Nabaṭi poetry, which is also reversible: a raincloud may equally be likened to a battlefield. In this image, the smoke from firing guns mixed with the dust raised by galloping horses and trotting camels veils the midday sun like a thick cloud and turns day into night. The flashing of brandished swords and firing guns is lightning, and the sound of galloping and firing is thunder. The bullets are hailstones, and the flowing blood is rain. A mighty tribe is likened to a flash flood raging down from the summit of a lofty mountain to the level plains below. Those who attempt to stand in the way of such a mighty tribe are like a man who tries to stop a torrent with his cloak.

In the poem, Ršēd likens the meeting of the Shammar and ʿAnazah armies on the battlefield to the coming together of rain clouds. The clouds pour rain heavily on Ḏafrih, but it is the rain of death, and the battleground is left strewn as if with mushrooms and grass, with the severed heads of noble mares and the long plaits of slain men. (It is a custom among the desert warriors to grow long plaits.) In line 10, the poet lists the various Shammari clans that fought well. The name Xlēf in line 12 refers to the poet's friend, to whom he addresses his lines. In line 13, the poet lists the names of some settlements and pasturelands of Shammar. The last three lines are dedicated to Rimmān, a Shammari settlement famous for its palm gardens.

1 A white cloud is flashing and thundering, and pouring heavy rains on Ḏafrih.

2 The heads of noble mares [killed on the battlefield] are the mushrooms [growing after the rain], the grass is the long plaits of [slain] gallant men.

3 The sharp curved swords clash and the vultures open their beaks.

4 With long lances, we repulsed the assailants, saying, "Turn back and flee, you hyenas."

5 The men of Shammar loaded their mounts and came in haste from every direction to answer our call.

6 They urged on their fleet camels of the Ṭwāliyyāt breed, traversing the vast plains of hostile lands.

7 ʿAdwān, defender of the oppressed, is the commander of the fierce [Shammari] warriors who adorn their spear shafts with ostrich plumes.

8 I walked among their multitudes to delight my eyes; I gazed at the enemy lines and saw that their heads were low and their eyes aghast.

9 I turned my eyes to my kinsmen's lines and found the men cheerful and the horses at the ready.
10 Worthy are the men of al-ᶜIṣlān and Awlād Abu Sēf; so too are the men of al-ᶜAlyā when the time for vengeance comes.
11 After they ran out of bullets and gunpowder, they grasped the handles of their drawn swords.
12 O Xlēf, with fearless hearts they run to the pool of death, like thirsty camels after water.
13 We do not slacken in defending Salmā, Rimmān, Ajā, and al-ᶜṢāmī, our beloved lands.
14 We shall defend tenaciously the shady palm gardens of Rimmān; many a bold youth we killed in its defense.
15 We spear and are speared in defense of our gardens; we readily give our lives to defend them.
16 From the harvest [of the palm gardens] we feed the hungry guests in lean times when others close their doors and eat their food alone.

Despite the victory of Shammar in this encounter with ᶜAnazah, the latter remained the masters of the field. The Shammaris knew that in order to drive Siᶜdūn out of their rich pastures they must strike down his intrepid son, ᶜGāb. Once, when a large assembly of Shammari warriors was gathered at the tent of one of their chiefs, the chief poured a cup of coffee and declared, "This is the cup of ᶜGāb; whoever drinks it must meet him and slay him on the battlefield." An obscure young man by the name of Aba-l-wgayy sprang up and drank the cup. The next time ᶜAnazah and Shammar met on the field, Aba-l-wgayy challenged ᶜGāb to single combat. ᶜAnazah and Shammar lined up facing each other, the better to watch the fight between ᶜGāb and Aba-l-wgayy. At first, the two champions fought on horseback with spears, but soon they fell to the ground and began to fight with swords. As soon as the two fell to the ground, the horsemen of ᶜAnazah and Shammar charged each other, each side seeking to save its champion. In the confusion of the melee, the valuable sword and noble mare of ᶜGāb went to Aba-l-wgayy, while ᶜGāb walked away with the sword and horse of Aba-l-wgayy. This in itself was a moral victory for Shammar and an honor for Aba-l-wgayy. Siᶜdūn was disheartened by the incident. His friends tried to console him, and promised to obtain a better sword and horse for ᶜGāb as a recompense for the ones he lost to Aba-l-wgayy. Siᶜdūn responded, "It is not the loss of the sword or the horse that saddens me. Rather, I am saddened because they were taken from the hands of my famous son by an unrenowned Shammari youth who is not his equal. I am also afraid that the Shammari poet Mbērīć at-Tbēnāwī will compose a poem about the incident and say, 'We took the sword from the right hand of ᶜGāb, and his noble horse we exchanged for a jade.'" Strangely enough, at-Tbēnāwī did compose a poem about the incident which included this very line. And in the third line of this poem, which is translated below, at-Tbēnāwī points out to Siᶜdūn that it is the ancient custom of Shammar and ᶜAnazah to fight each other. To understand the jest of this line, one must understand that the nomads view human interaction in reciprocal terms. They conceive of their relationships with friends and foes as a form of debt or exchange. An act, whether friendly or hostile, has to be paid back or requited in kind, the sooner the better. The term "son of Wāyil" in line 3 refers to Siᶜdūn, as Wāyil is the ancient ancestor of ᶜAnazah.

1 O fair maidens, paint the hands of Aba-l-wgayy [in recognition of his bravery]; he is truly the son of noble ancestors.
2 We took the sword from the right hand of ᶜGāb, and his noble horse we exchanged for a jade.
3 O dear friends, such is our ancient habit; O son of Wāyil, sweet is fair and swift exchange.
4 I do not belittle ᶜGāb and the likes of him; he is a true hero when he rides his prancing horse.
5 It is well known among all tribes that he meets his assailants courageously on the battlefield.
6 But I have for him specially trained tigers, the stalwart lads of Shammar, on fiery mares.

Hāyis al-Gᶜēṭ, the redoubtable chief of the al-Brēć section of Shammar, once decided to undertake a raid against Wild Slēmān. His plan was to surprise the camel herds of Wild Slēmān in the outlying pastures and drive them off before their herders had time to muster a rescue party. He marched from Mesopotamia to Najd at the head of seventy horsemen of the Zōbaᶜ clan with their *zimāmīl* (cameleers who carry food and water for the horses and their riders). However, it so happened that just in the nick of time Siᶜdūn was informed of the intentions of Hāyis; he called on his sons ᶜGāb and Ḥjāb to lead the troops of Wild Slēmān and proceed to the pastures to protect the herds. They marched all night and reached the pastures at dawn of the same day that Hāyis had chosen for his attack. The small Shammari force was routed by the ᶜAnazah tribesmen. Hāyis and his cavaliers managed to escape, but the cameleers and the provisions were captured. While their kinsmen were dividing the spoils, ᶜGāb and Ḥjāb alone chased the fleeing horsemen. When Hāyis saw that they were pursued by ᶜGāb followed only by his brother,

Ḥjāb, he turned to his horsemen, saying, "O men of Shammar, today is the day of vengeance. Our good fortune has brought ʿGāb to us where we want him. Close your ranks and let us rush upon him as one man." Hāyis also reminded his tribesmen of the famous Shammari knight Hid̲lūl aš-Šwēhrī who had been killed by ʿGāb the previous year. The words of Hāyis filled his comrades with rage and courage. They turned around and charged furiously against ʿGāb and Ḥjāb, killing them both.

The slaying of ʿGāb and Ḥjāb was a great victory for Hāyis, and he became famous throughout the desert. The incident became the topic of conversation throughout the Shammari camps, and it was celebrated by the poets of Shammar as much as it was lamented by the poets of ʿAnazah. The following poem was composed by the famous Shammari poet Ršēd Ibn Ṭōʿān. Ršēd begins his poem by praising Hāyis and comparing him to a wild falcon which soars in the skies in search of its prey. In line 2, the poet says that while still a young man Hāyis had worn out strong rugged camel mounts by his incessant riding and relentless raiding, and that even in his old age he conquered everything in his path till he reached the sea. In the third line, Ršēd begins an account of the raid that Hāyis undertook against Wild Slēmān. He points out that Wild Slēmān had been forewarned of the impending raid and were able to rally in time to defend their camels. The ensuing fight is compared to that between Aba Zēd and D̲yāb, the famous heroes in the *sīrah* of Bani Hilāl. The place where the fight took place is mentioned in line 5, and in line 7 the Shammari warriors are described as resplendent youths whose maternal uncles are noble. (The bedouins believe that the character of a person is equally determined by his maternal and paternal lines; a man who wishes to have distinguished children must marry into an honorable family.) In the second hemistich of the same line, the poet speaks of the warriors of Wild Slēmān as having close ties of kinship and thus as being ready to die for each other. These two hemistichs succinctly draw a picture of the pitched battle between the noble warriors of Shammar on one side and the tenacious, resolute men of ʿAnazah on the other. In line 8, two names are mentioned: Nūt, the wife of ʿGāb, and Hēfā, the mother of Hid̲lūl aš-Šwēhrī, the Shammari knight who had been killed by ʿGāb in the previous year. The ninth line states that it took the search party of Wild Slēmān four days to find the bodies of ʿGāb and Ḥjāb. Ḏ̣bēb, mentioned in line 12, was the cousin of ʿGāb and Ḥjāb, who, upon hearing that they had been killed by the horsemen of Shammar, ordered that all the cameleers who had been captured by Wild Slēmān be put to the sword. The poet rails at Ḏ̣bēb for committing such a shameful act, for it is considered dishonorable to kill a captured foe. In the last line, the poet mildly reproaches Siʿdūn and reminds him (perhaps in apology for the slaying of his sons) that he, Siᶜdūn, should not expect to harry Shammar and yet live in peace himself.

1 A wild falcon took off, followed by horsemen and cameleers, seeking to despoil the enemy and attack him unawares.
2 In his youth he tormented rugged mounts, and in his ripe age he struck the sea with his right hand.
3 The [enemy] camp was alarmed on the night of the attack, and the sorties sallied forth before dawn.
4 They met on the soft sands by the dunes, and the champions fought like Aba Zēd and D̠yāb.
5 Zibār Wrēć was covered by rising dust, and the enemy lances pierced our kinsmen in the back.
6 The battle raged among the valiant men who cover the retreat of their troops and defend those riding on slow mares.
7 Our resplendent youths of noble maternal uncles charged against the dauntless warriors who are close kinsmen.
8 Nūt raised her voice wailing; ᶜGāb we killed to please Hēfā.
9 Four nights had passed before his body was found; he was humbled and his face rolled in the dust.
10 Our women rejoiced and cheered after the wild falcon seized ᶜGāb,
11 But their women wailed and screeched like water wheels; they shuddered at the news brought them by the returning horsemen.
12 O Ḏbēb, you dishonored your house by killing the cameleers; you defiled your tent by killing those who entered it.
13 O al-ᶜWāji, this life is full of adversity; he who rends other people's garments, his garments will be rent.

The Shammari poet Mbērīć at-Tbēnāwī also composed two poems celebrating the victory of Shammar over ᶜAnazah and the slaying of ᶜGāb and Ḥjāb at Zibār Wrēć. Here is one of these poems, in which he adresses ᶜGāb:

1 O ᶜGāb, the eagles of Shammar swooped over you; they snatched your head and another head [that of Ḥjāb].
2 When the mares gave you their backs in retreat, they were not fleeing; they made a sharp turn and charged at you.
3 Beware of the bold [Shammari] stalwarts, riding the slender wiry mares nourished by camels' milk.
4 Hāyis led against you the horsemen of Zōbaᶜ, whose spears drip with enemy blood.
5 When they met you at the western edge of Zibār Wrēć, your body rolled in the dust, headless.

The following is the second poem by at-Tbēnāwī:

1 Last year it was Hēfā who wailed and screamed; but today the wailing of Nūt and the women in her camp fills the heart with pity.
2 ʿGāb was thrown down by the riders of swift mares, and vultures have torn his heart out with their powerful talons.
3 And Ḥjāb, the gallant man in whose tent wayfarers found shade and food; alas for those who mourn him.
4 He was killed instantly by the horsemen of Shammar; he did not return to his loved ones.
5 O dear friends [of ʿAnazah], such are our ancient customs; sweet is the paying of a debt before it is due.

Siʿdūn was grief-stricken by the slaying of his two sons and composed many elegies lamenting their deaths. ʿGāb and Ḥjāb each had a son, so Siʿdūn began to train his grandchildren to be doughty warriors like their slain fathers. He taught them how to ride horses and how to throw the spear. When the two boys became mature men (in the desert, a fifteen-year-old youth is considered mature), Siʿdūn demanded of each that he compose a poem expressing his yearning to avenge his slain father and uncle. Siʿdūn promised Falḥā, the filly of ʿGāb's mare (which was the noblest mare in the desert), to the one who composed the better poem. The son of ʿGāb won the prize for composing the following poem. In line 10, the muzzles of galloping mares are likened to the snouts of wild boars. (Thoroughbred mares breathe through their wide nostrils, never through their mouths. After a gallop, a mare breathes heavily through its nostrils; thus, its muzzle resembles the snout of a wild boar.)

1 I long to ride Falḥā when she is full grown with all her hooves shod.
2 So when raiders attack the moving herds and the pretty virgins glance at me from their litters,
3 I may meet the attacking horsemen of Zōbaʿ, the flashing of whose swords and spears blinds the eyes.
4 With a curved sword of shining steel in my hand, I look for the slayer of my father among the horsemen.
5 If I do not spur my horse to meet the foe, I do not deserve the love of pretty virgins with erect breasts.
6 The day of reckoning will come when we meet on the battlefield to settle our accounts.
7 I must avenge my father, ʿGāb; this is a duty entrusted to me by a venerable man,
8 Siʿdūn, my grandfather, the honorable chief, our commander in peace and war.

9 A debt [is] owed to me by Hāyis, the defender of slow mares on the retreat; I pray to God to bring him to me.
10 If I do not meet the charging horses and repulse their attack—their muzzles like the snouts of wild boars—
11 I do not deserve membership in my noble tribe, nor to be served when the coffee cup goes round in great assemblies.

This poem by the son of ʿGāb was answered by the following poem by a Shammari poet.

1 So what if you ride Falḥā, a full-grown mare? A Shammari youth will meet you on a broad-chested slender steed.
2 Your father was struck by a spear adorned [with ostrich plumes], and fell from his horse, as a bucket is cast into a well.
3 He was felled by a stalwart who does not flee enemy attacks,
4 A fierce fighter on the battlefield. Vultures tore the breast of your father with their powerful beaks.
5 The Zōbaʿ lads are bold warriors who rout their opponents on the battlefield.

Some time later, a major battle took place between ʿAnazah under the leadership of Ġnēm ar-Rubbiḏa and Shammar under the leadership of Hāyis al-Gʿēṭ. The son of ʿGāb joined Ġnēm ar-Rubbiḏa and killed Hāyis on the battlefield, thus avenging his father.

When Fayṣal Ibn Tirkī al-Saʿūd appointed the Shammari prince ʿAbdallāh Ibn ʿAlī Ibn Rashīd as governor of Ḥāyil (see the next chapter), all the sheikhs of the tribes of northern Najd came to pay their respects to Ibn Rashid and present him with gifts of horses. Among them was Ġnēm ar-Rubbiḏa. Upon receiving Ġnēm, Ibn Rashīd presented him to the blind Shammari poet Ršēd Ibn Ṭōʿān, saying, "This is Ġnēm ar-Rubbiḏa; shake hands with him!" The poet replied, "I will not shake hands with him, for there is no peace between him and me." Ršēd extemporized the following two lines to incite Ibn Rashīd against Ġnēm.

1 O Ġnēm, you owe us the blood of Hāyis, the cavalier protecting the troops of Shammar in retreat.
2 If he [Ibn Rashīd] does not repay you with two morning attacks, he is not the progeny of a noble sire.

(Although Hāyis was killed by the son of ʿGāb, the poet here holds Ġnēm responsible, since he was the one who led ʿAnazah tribesmen against Shammar.) Upon hearing these two lines, Ibn Rashīd told Ġnēm, "Take back the horses you offered me as a gift, and go back to your territory and prepare, for I must avenge the blood of Hāyis." Ibn Rashīd did make a raid against Ġnēm, and shed his blood for that of Hāyis.

The aim in presenting this somewhat lengthy biographical sketch of Siᶜdūn al-ᶜWāji and his two sons, ᶜGāb and Ḥjāb, and their tribal wars with Shammar has been to demonstrate the function of Nabaṭi poetry in tribal politics, and the relationship of this poetry to its narrative context. Again, I must emphasize the resemblance of Nabaṭi poetry to classical Arabic poetry in both respects. The above narrative and poems read like a chapter from *Ayyām al-*ᶜArab, "The Days of the Arabs," a popular collection of narratives and poems dealing with tribal wars in Arabia. Such examples illustrate one of the main points I wish to establish—namely, the significant amount of continuity between classical Arabic poetry and Nabaṭi poetry.

IV

POETRY AND REGIONAL POLITICS

In the previous chapter we saw that, among the nomadic tribes, poetry was a vehicle for political action. The poem of a desert warrior was a serious statement, a contemplated utterance made to record a specific event or to demand a specific action. In this chapter, I will discuss the political influence of poets among the settled population and will examine the dynamic role of poetry in the regional politics of premodern Arabia.

In premodern Arabia, central authority was generally weak or absent altogether. The settled regions were divided among themselves, and their relationships with one another oscillated between cooperation and confrontation. The whole of Arabia was torn by regional fragmentation and political disintegration. Each settlement had its own allies as well as adversaries among adjacent settlements and neighboring tribes. Nomadic tribes participated in the parochial rivalries of the settled people as kinsmen and allies. The instability of tribal politics, the subject of the previous chapter, paralleled the instability of regional politics.

This state of political turmoil is reflected and amply documented in Nabaṭi poetry. During the long period of turbulence that preceded the establishment of the modern Arabian states, Nabaṭi poetry flourished as a dynamic political institution. It was employed to mobilize public opinion and promote collective action, since it was the most popular medium of expression and the most effective channel of communication. Each settlement had its own poets who defended its political interests. Outstanding poets occupied prominent social positions and exercised great political influence. Their words had great impact on their audiences, and they possessed the power to rouse the masses as easily as they could calm them down. The people of premodern Arabia were ruled by eloquent persuasion rather than by outright force; therefore, the gift of poetry constituted an essential qualification for effective leadership. Many amirs and princes were accomplished poets who employed their poetic skills to achieve political ends.

ᶜAbdallāh and ᶜUbayd Ibn Rashīd

ᶜAbdallāh Ibn Rashīd and his younger brother ᶜUbayd rank high among princely poets. In addition to their political and military talents, they were gifted poets whose compositions still survive on the lips of the people and in print.[1] Their poetry is mainly an account of their heroic adventures and brilliant successes, as the following sketch will show.

ᶜAbdallāh Ibn Rashīd (of the Jaᶜfar clan of the ᶜAbdih section of the Shammar tribe) founded the Rashidi dynasty about 1835 in Ḥāyil, the capital of Jabal Shammar, after a long and relentless struggle with their antagonist Ṣāliḥ Ibn ᶜAlī. It is doubtful that ᶜAbdallāh would have attained his dream of becoming lord of Ḥāyil and paramount chief of Shammar had it not been for the loyalty and undaunted courage of his redoubtable brother ᶜUbayd (nicknamed "the Wolf"). In their early years, ᶜAbdallāh and ᶜUbayd were very capable and ambitious young men with charismatic personalities and unmistakable qualities of leadership. They even challenged and defied the orders of Ṣāliḥ Ibn ᶜAlī, the then amir of Ḥāyil, who, claiming that war is costly, had refused to allow the people of Ḥāyil to go out and help their tribal confederates, the Shammar, who were constantly harassed in their own tribal territory by their traditional enemies, the ᶜAnazah tribe. ᶜAbdallāh and ᶜUbayd composed exhortative poems admonishing the people of Ḥāyil and urging them to revolt against their weak and ineffectual amir. Because they undermined the amir's authority and constituted a real threat to his leadership, he persecuted them and had them expelled from Ḥāyil with their family. Their expulsion is celebrated in a short ditty composed by their mother (Ibn Raddās n.d.–1976:I, 243). ᶜAbdallāh and ᶜUbayd themselves composed magnificent odes lamenting their sufferings and expressing their intense yearning for eminence and leadership (Musil 1928:300–304; Ibn Raddās n.d.–1976:II, 98; Ibn Sayḥān 1965–1969:II, 45). Here are three lines from a poem by ᶜUbayd addressed to ᶜĪsā, the nephew of amir Ṣāliḥ. In these lines, ᶜUbayd taunts ᶜĪsā for his cowardice and stinginess and suggests that al-ᶜArfijiyyih is more worthy of carrying his weapon (al-ᶜArfijiyyih is a woman from al-ᶜArfaj, a branch of the al-ᶜUlayyan, the princely family of Buraidah, who gained fame after she avenged her son by cutting his killer to pieces with a sword).

1 ᶜĪsā says: War is costly. But I say: Then, why did the smith make the curved sword with a sharp edge?
2 Drench your sword with the blood of your adversary, or send it to al-ᶜArfijiyyih; let her give it blood to drink.
3 If nobility does not run in the blood of a man, he will not act noble when the time comes for noble action.

G. A. Wallin, who visited Ḥāyil in 1845 during the reign of ʿAbdallāh Ibn Rashīd, tells of ʿAbdallāh's early struggle, of how he vanquished his opponents, and of how he celebrated this in his poetic compositions.

> During about ten years, as the inhabitants of Hâil told me, ʿAbd Allah bnu Alrashîd had governed the Shammar tribe. His predecessor, a cousin of his called Sâlih bnu ʿAly, had, out of fear for the great credit and influence ʿAbd Allah possessed among the people, exiled him from the land. ʿAbd Allah resorted to Alriiâd, regarded, after the destruction of Derʿiyé, as the capital of Negd and the residence of the Wahhâby princes of the family of Saʿood, where a prince then reigned called Turky, a son of the hapless Saʿood and father of the present governor of Negd, Feisal. Here ʿAbd Allah joined in a warlike expedition which Feisal made to the environs of Alahsá. While still on the expedition, the report was brought to them that Turky had been killed by his cousin, Almeshârî, who, declaring himself governor of Negd, had taken possession of the palace of the murdered, after having driven away from it his wives and women and other household. Keeping this news secret from their followers, the two leaders hastened their return to Alriiâd, where they, after a short fight, and chiefly by a stratagem, contrived by ʿAbd Allah,[2] made themselves masters of the castle and the person of Almeshârî. The usurper was put to death, and Feisal proclaimed governor of Negd by ʿAbd Allah from the summit of the mosque, and acknowledged by the people in this dignity. Installed in his government, Feisal now declared ʿAbd Allah, to whose prudence and dexterity he chiefly owed his success in the whole affair, sheîkh of the land of Shammar, instead of Sâlih, who was deposed; but as he for the moment had no assistance to offer his friend, not any power to put him in the place he had appointed him to, ʿAbd Allah returned to his native land quite alone, trusting solely to his own personal qualities and the credit he had among his countrymen, for getting the better of his cousin Sâlih. He had many hardships to endure here, part of which he has celebrated in vivid lines of his own composition; during the day he hid himself in the mountains of Agâ, and at night he descended to the villages of Hâil and Kafâr to the houses of some of his friends and adherents, who, in the meantime, roused up the people in his favour. As soon as a sufficient party was brought over to his side, he made head against his adversary and vanquished him. (1854:180–181)

The ex-rulers of Ḥāyil, who were ousted by ʿAbdallāh and his brother ʿUbayd, were given refuge and assistance by the people of Buraidah and

ʿUnaizah, the two principal towns in the district of Qaṣīm, the southern neighbor of Jabal Shammar. This and similar actions on the part of Qaṣīm against Ḥāyil ushered in a long period of rivalry and bitter strife between them, which will engage our attention in this chapter.

The first major clash between these two power centers took place in 1841. It was touched off by an exchange of raids between a section of Shammar and a section of the ʿAnazah tribe, the allies of al-Qaṣīm. The Shammar were given assistance by Ibn Rashīd, and the ʿAnazah were badly beaten. This provoked the amir of Buraidah, ʿAbdallāh Ibn Mḥammad, and the amir of ʿUnaizah, Yaḥyā Ibn Slēm, who were so outraged by the defeat of their allies at the hands of Ibn Rashīd that they vowed to fight the latter in the streets of his capital. They hastily organized a considerable force made up of yeomen from Qaṣīm and tribesmen of ʿAnazah, and they proceeded against Ibn Rashīd. The combined forces of Qaṣīm and the ʿAnazah bedouins penetrated deep into Jabal Shammar until they reached Bagʿa, east of Ḥāyil; there, they were attacked by the forces of ʿAbdallāh and ʿUbayd, who ultimately overcame them. On hearing a report (later proving to be false) that ʿUbayd had been killed in battle, ʿAbdallāh had Yaḥyā killed to avenge his brother's death.

ʿUbayd, who distinguished himself in the battlefield at Bagʿa, celebrated this event in an ode of over thirty verses (Ibn Rashīd 1966:79–85; Kamāl 1960–1971:III, 73–76). Doughty, who visited Ḥāyil in 1877, wrote of ʿUbayd that:

> He was a master of the Arabian warfare, a champion in the eyes of the discomfited Arab. Abeyd, as said, was an excellent kassâd, he indited of all his desert warfare; his boastful rimes, known wide in the wilderness, were ofttimes sung for me, in the nomad booths. The language of the kasasîd is as a language apart from the popular speech; but here I may remember some plain and notable verse of Abeyd, as that which says, "By this hand are fallen of the enemies ninety men. Smitten to death the Kusmân perished before me, until the evening, when my fingers could not be loosed from the handle of the sword; the sleeve of my garment was stiffened with the blood of war." This he made of the repulse of an ill-commanded and worse starred expedition, sent out by the great Kasîm town Aneyza, against Ibn Rashīd. (1921:II, 42)

It is clear that Doughty is referring to the battle of Bagʿa and the poem composed by ʿUbayd on that occasion, but his rendering of the verse "By this hand . . . " is inaccurate.[3] Here are a few lines from the poem ʿUbayd composed following the battle of Bagʿa; the last line is the one Doughty refers to:

1 The covetous enemies attacked our fields and gardens. They boasted that they would fight us in the streets of Gfār and Ḥāyil.
2 Whoever attacks our homeland will be met by prompt and stiff resistance. We are ready to march against our foes in the cold nights and hot days, and we sleep not.
3 We, the settlers and nomads of Jabal Shammar, advance in two columns, encouraged by fair maidens with long black locks.
4 We came to the field in the morning and found the enemy ready for a fight. The smoke of our gunpowder veiled the skies above.
5 We thank our lord, the Almighty, the Just; the Qaṣīmis and the sons of Wāyil [the ʿAnazah tribe] were routed.
6 My gallant comrades quenched the thirst of their sharp swords. The hard ground of Bagʿā flowed with the blood of our enemies.
7 We follow our sheikh Abu Mitʿib; he is the feast of the hungry, the spring of the poor, and the protector of the weak.
8 As for me, ninety of the enemy I slew with the edge of my sword, and I fear not those who yearn to avenge them.

ʿAbdallāh Ibn Slēm, the brother of the slain Yaḥyā, became the amir of ʿUnaizah and vowed to avenge the death of his brother and the defeat of the Qaṣīmis. He started by hiring a jester named Ibn Hādī to assassinate Ibn Rashīd. Ibn Hādī was instructed to go to Ḥāyil and entertain people in the streets with his amusing prancing and astounding handling of the spear. It was hoped that when Ibn Rashīd heard of this new jester, he would have him brought to perform at his court. Once at court, Ibn Hādī was supposed to spring upon Ibn Rashīd and pierce him through the heart with the spear. Ibn Hādī was made to believe that with the right talismans and amulets around his neck no harm would come to him at the hands of Ibn Rashīd's retainers after the assassination. The initial steps of the plan worked perfectly, but when Ibn Hādī was brought to the court he was overcome with fear and could not perform. He was arrested and questioned, but, when it was found that he was a dupe, Ibn Rashīd forgave him and allowed him to reside in Ḥāyil. This incident was celebrated by a poem composed by Ibn Rashīd himself (al-Mārik 1963–1965:I, 174–182). In the poem, Ibn Rashīd contrasts the method of his government with that of Ibn Slēm and portrays himself as a valiant, honorable man who runs the affairs of his domain with a balanced combination of force and diplomacy and who would never stoop to such low devices as the sending of a jester-assassin against an opponent; such is the practice only of cowardly men like Ibn Slēm. Here are a few lines from the poem; in the last, Ibn Rashīd pays tribute to his brother ʿUbayd by uttering his name as a war cry.[4]

1 My country was a place of cold and hunger before I made it secure and prosperous with the cutting edge of the sword.
2 I protect it against those who seek to plunder it. With some enemies I fight and with some I make peace.
3 I run my affairs with intelligence and dexterity, money in one hand and the sharp saber in the other.
4 My heart is bold and in my hand is a sharp sword; it is not like your dancing, O Abu Hādī.
5 I am the brother of ʿUbayd; I advance when the coward scuttles, and I stay awake when the lazy man goes to sleep.

When the assassination plot failed, Ibn Slēm sent out raiding parties to harry the supply routes and outlying settlements of Jabal Shammar. In response to these provocations, ʿUbayd Ibn Rashīd composed several poems addressed to Ibn Slēm, castigating him and reminding him of what had happened at Bagʿā, and threatening him with dire consequences should he continue to meddle in the affairs of Ḥāyil (Kamāl 1960–1971:III, 61–63,68–69). In the following selection, ʿUbayd contrasts the Rashidi military codes and practices with those of Ibn Slēm by saying that the former attack an enemy chief in the public square of his capital in the midst of his people, rather than attacking outlying settlements and defenseless villages, as is the practice of cowards and weak amirs like Ibn Slēm. He urges Ibn Slēm not to be misled by the mischievous amir of Buraidah and advises him to restrict himself to commercial activities and stay at home with his wife, for he is not of the stuff from which warriors and heroes are made.

1 So what, Ibn Slēm, if you attack our outlying settlements? Such bluff and pretense will not be to your advantage.
2 When *we* attack, we slay our enemies by the thousands, and our loot is thoroughbred mares.
3 When we attack, we attack the seat of the chief, and not the outlying villages; our war drums have been sounded in many a sheikhly camp.
4 Were we to hear a cry for help coming from the top of a high knoll, our sorties would come through any mountain pass to give assistance.
5 We drench our swords in enemy blood in defense of our country, riding our shod mares.
6 Do not let the blind amir of Buraidah lead you astray; and do not be deluded by the war dances of butchers in the market of your town.
7 Your brother was thrown from his horse in the battlefield; he was

slain by those who perfume their swords with the blood of their enemies.

8 If you want my advice, keep to your trade, and count your coins and small change.

9 Work for the price of a bed for your pretty wife, and sleep with her; and perfume yourself with the smoke of incense burners.

Ibn Slēm, however, continued to harass the tribes and settlements of Jabal Shammar, and in September 1845 seized some camels and their loads in a raid on a Shammar caravan. In protest, Ibn Rashīd wrote to Fayṣal Ibn Tirkī, the Saudi lord in Riyadh, who was then the nominal suzerain of the whole of Najd, including Qaṣīm and Jabal Shammar. Fayṣal promised action, and sent two agents called Farḥān and Ibn Sbēt with letters to Ibn Slēm upbraiding him and demanding that he restore the booty. After a long stay in ʿUnaizah, the agents failed to achieve restitution; therefore, ʿAbdallāh Ibn Rashīd decided to act on his own.

> Gathering both nomadic and sedentary Shammar tribesmen to the number of some 300, and accompanied by his eldest son Talal, and his brother ʿUbaid, he marched on Qasim. Before the force had gone far, however, ʿUbaid and Talal forced the amir himself to return to Haʾil in order that he not be exposed to unnecessary danger. ʿAbd Allah agreed only with reluctance and after outlining the plan of battle, namely to have a small party attack an outlying flock of ʿUnaizah sheep and then to ambush the retaliatory force which the town was certain to send out in response. The plan worked to perfection. The ʿUnaizites fell into the trap, and several hundred of them were killed. In addition, ʿUbaid took a number of prisoners including ʿAbd Allah Ibn Zamil, the governor. Then ʿUbaid, breaking the traditional desert convention of respect for the person of a prisoner and ensuring the perpetuation of bitter enmity, had the governor and several of his relatives killed. Thus two consecutive governors of ʿUnaizah—and brothers to boot—had been killed by the ruling family of Haʾil. ʿUbaid, who in addition to his other distinctions, was a poet of note, composed an ode on the occasion of his victory. . . .
>
> Faisal was angered by this senseless bloodshed for the sake of camels and similar booty, but, knowing the imam's stern religious nature and anticipating his reaction, ʿAbd Allah Ibn Rashīd had prepared a defense which was unusual if not unique, but which nevertheless worked. Messengers were immediately sent from Haʾil to the imam with a long letter of explanation, in which the *pièce de résistance* was a forty-five-verse ode written by the amir of Jabal Shammar himself. Dari Ibn Rashīd's account of its reception is

> notable: 'When ʿAbd Allah's messengers reached Faisal, he spoke with them and said, "Muslims have been wrongly killed." Then, when the council meeting [*majlis*] broke up, ʿAbd Allah's men gave Faisal the letter containing the ode. At that, he was satisfied and said, "The Qasimis are still unjust and tyrannical people."' One cannot refrain from wondering where, other than in Arabia, a stern and pious ruler would have reversed his opinion on a serious matter because of a poem! (Winder 1965:154–155)

The full text of the poem composed by ʿUbayd on this occasion appears in Kamāl (1960–1971:III, 63–64), and the text of the poem that the amir ʿAbdallāh sent to Fayṣal Ibn Tirkī appears in Ibn Rashīd (1966:94–101) and Ibn Sayḥān (1965–1969:II, 52–54). In his poem, Ibn Rashīd points out to Fayṣal that it was the people of Qaṣīm who started the whole affair; they were the ones who defied their suzerain and refused to abide by the written instructions that were sent with the agents. The following are a few lines from the poem of Ibn Rashīd. In the first line, he refers to the assassination attempt mentioned above, and in the last to the wounds inflicted upon himself when he attempted to subdue Mishārī Ibn Sʿūd who tried to usurp the Saudi throne by treacherously murdering his uncle Tirkī. Ibn Rashīd alludes to this incident in order to mollify Fayṣal Ibn Tirkī and remind him of services previously rendered.

1 After the plot to assassinate me failed, they [the people of Qaṣīm] set ablaze the fire of war in the summer heat.

2 He [Ibn Slēm] refused to return the camels he stole with their loads, although I sent him several messengers [in hope of peaceful reconciliation].

3 He refused to listen to reason, and I became weary of too much complaining [to you, Fayṣal] and pleading with him.

4 Seeing that he did not read the letters you had sent him, we went and taught him a good lesson in obedience; we slew him as we had slain his forebears.

5 This is the punishment he brought upon himself for not heeding your commands; he refused to follow the orders you sent with Farḥān and Ibn Sbēt.

6 O sheikh, we committed no treachery; we attacked them in broad daylight on swift mares.

7 ʿUbayd—I pray to the lord that I may never lose him—God sent him against them like a shooting star or an earthquake.

8 When one of our people is attacked by an enemy, we give our souls and all else we possess in his defense.

9 It is our custom to protect our neighbor and we are quick to help whoever seeks our protection against a stronger foe.

10 We give food to the guests when their mounts kneel at our door, and whoever comes seeking our bounty goes back home with his hands full of gifts.
11 With gentle words I try to dispel malice from the heart of an opponent, but I accept evil from no one.
12 It is to punish the recalcitrant that the smith made the sharp curved sword; with it, we force those who go astray back to the right path.
13 When the time comes for war, I find joy on the battlefield.
14 I endure bravely like the mighty mountain which does not give way under the steps of treading multitudes.
15 The evidence is on my body, the marks of wounds the like of which I inflicted upon my opponent. People can tell genuine nobility from pretense.

Mḥammad al-ᶜAbdallāh al-ᶜŌni

Al-ᶜŌni is called the poet of strife and contention because his poetry is a reflection of the political turmoil of his time, and its content is inextricably linked to the turbulent events in the history of Arabia at the end of the nineteenth and beginning of the twentieth centuries.[5] Although he was born into a humble family, al-ᶜŌni attained social eminence due to the popular appeal of his poetry and the powerful influence it exercised on the masses. In describing the effects of his poetry, he once said: "It is of no real consequence to lead an army. What is of real consequence is to be a poet like me. Here I sit peacefully by my hearth and coffee pots, yet with my words I can raise multitudes up in arms against each other for any cause I choose" (Ibn Khamīs 1958:14).

According to Fahad al-Mārik (1963–1965:III, 280), al-ᶜŌni was born about 1870 in ar-Rbēᶜiyyih, a hamlet near Buraidah. By that time, the political structure of Arabia was undergoing major shifts. Fayṣal Ibn Tirkī, the nominal suzerain of Arabia at the time, had already demoted al-ᶜLayyān, the traditional ruling house of Buraidah, and given the amirship of the town instead to the family of Ab-al-Xēl. After the death of Fayṣal in 1865, a civil war broke out between his two sons, ᶜAbdallāh and Saᶜūd, which led eventually to the disintegration and collapse of the Saudi dynasty. The total eclipse of the Saudi dynasty was brought about by its former vassal, the Rashidi dynasty, before the end of the nineteenth century. After Fayṣal Ibn Tirkī had passed away, the administration of the Saudi realm became the responsibility of his eldest son, ᶜAbdallāh, who, despite his military prowess, was an inept politician. Among his political mistakes was his attempt to wrest the amirship of Buraidah from the family of Ab-al-Xēl and give it back to al-ᶜLayyān, who promised to give more sincere allegiance to Riyadh. Instead of achieving this political objective, ᶜAbdallāh Ibn Fayṣal ended up losing Buraidah and eventually the whole district of Qaṣīm to the new rising star of Arabia, Mḥammad Ibn Rashīd, the scion of ᶜAbdallāh Ibn Rashīd, founder of the Rashidi dynasty. To protect himself from the plot hatched against him in Riyadh, the amir of Buraidah, Ḥasan al-Mhannā Ab-al-Xēl, adroitly sought the friendship of Ḥāyil by marrying his sister to the amir Mḥammad Ibn Rashīd, and his daughter to Ḥmūd al-ᶜUbayd, the cousin of the amir.

The keen and observant Mḥammad al-ᶜŌni was a witness to all these political developments. Shortly after he was born, his family moved to Buraidah, where there was more demand for the services of his father, who "worked with mud" (i.e., was a master at building mud houses). The young al-ᶜŌni impressed people by his alert mind and quick intelligence. The amir of Buraidah, Ḥasan al-Mhannā, decided to sponsor this exceptional youth and took him into his household and raised him with his own children; in the words of Brāhīm al-Ḥsēn, "he ate with them and dressed like them, they gave him weapons and they taught him horseback riding." In other words, al-ᶜŌni was raised in a princely house frequented by dignitaries of various towns and chiefs of various tribes, a house in which history and politics were the usual topics of conversation. Thus, he assimilated a great deal of information concerning the history and genealogies of Arabia, and he also observed how political actions are conceived and executed.

This rich background, coupled with his exceptional intelligence and handsome appearance, made of al-ᶜŌni not only a captivating poet but also a charismatic personality and a wise counselor, whose advice and friendship were sought by such giants in local politics as Mbārak aṣ-Ṣabāḥ, ᶜAbdalᶜazīz Ibn Saᶜūd, ᶜJēmī as-Siᶜdūn of the al-Mintifig tribe, and Saᶜūd Ibn ᶜAbdalᶜazīz Ibn Mitᶜib Ibn ᶜAbdallāh Ibn Rashīd. His poetic genius and thorough knowledge of Arabian affairs enabled him to manipulate various genealogical and historical facts in such a way that he was able to influence the minds of the masses and play on their sentiments with his poetry.

In his early years, al-ᶜŌni was totally dedicated to the cause of the house of Ab-al-Xēl. He composed poems eulogizing leading members of this family and defending the political interests of Buraidah. But since there was at that time a political alliance between Buraidah and Ḥāyil, as well as an affinal relationship between the two houses of Ab-al-Xēl and Ibn Rashīd, al-ᶜŌni composed poems eulogizing Mḥammad Ibn Rashīd and his wazir and cousin Ḥmūd al-ᶜUbayd.

The friendship between Ḥāyil and Buraidah did not last long. ᶜAbdallāh and Saᶜūd, the two sons (of different mothers) of Fayṣal Ibn Tirkī, were rapidly dissipating the vast dominion passed on to them by their illustrious father. The diminishing influence of the weakened Saudi government left central Arabia a power vacuum which was gradually and quietly filled by Mḥammad Ibn Rashīd, the enterprising amir of Ḥāyil. As the Saudi government became weaker, local amirs would seek the assistance of Mḥammad Ibn Rashīd, who was always ready to give it, as if he were totally disinterested and simply responding to his sense of Arab chivalry; although later he would annex to his realm those very territories he had come to liberate. The people of al-Qaṣīm became suspicious of Ibn Rashīd's annexation policy. Therefore, the amir of Buraidah, Ḥasan al-Mhannā, and the amir of ᶜUnaizah, Zāmil as-Slēm, both capable men, reconciled their differences and united in preparation for a show of strength against Ibn Rashīd, their northern neighbor. These developments caused the pendulum of al-Qaṣīm to swing back to the south. The confederates of al-Qaṣīm made common cause with ᶜAbdarrạhmān Ibn Fayṣal Ibn Tirkī (who became the governor of Riyadh after the death of his two older brothers) in order to stop the southern march of Ibn Rashīd. But by then the Saudi strength was completely sapped and Riyadh was no match for Ḥāyil. The final showdown between al-Qaṣim and Ḥāyil came in 1891.

The Qaṣīmis, led by Zāmil, began mobilizing in late December of 1890; Ibn Rashīd, realizing that the struggle must this time be decisive, mustered as many troops as he could from Shammar and allied tribes and marched to a plain called al-Mulaida, twenty miles west of Buraidah, to meet and fight with al-Qaṣīm. The fight was lengthy, lasting perhaps a month, with many ups and downs, and seemed at first to go in favor of al-Qaṣīm.

> The decisive point in the engagement came in January 1891 when Muhammad Ibn Rashīd decided on the classic Nejdi military manoeuvre of the feigned retreat coupled with a surprise counter-attack. He headed toward Dalfaᶜah, a town some eighteen miles due west of Buraidah. The Qaṣīmis followed as Ibn Rashīd had planned, and he counter-attacked. But the counter-attack was a spectacular one. Ibn Rashīd massed several thousand camels in the centre and stampeded them forward against Zamil's oncoming forces by setting fire to the bundles of brush which had been tied to those in the rear. The infantry followed close behind the camels, and cavalry and camelry simultaneously attacked the flanks. The Qaṣīmi army was destroyed and scattered with casualties between 600 and 1,200 killed—including Zamil himself, his son, and others of his House. Hasan Ibn Muhannaᶜ of Buraidah lost his hand and was interned in Haᶜil for the rest of his life. Of those who were spared, many fled as far as Kuwait, Iraq or Syria. The triumphant Shammar ruler followed his brilliant military success with political consolidation. He appointed Salim Ibn Subhan governor of Buraidah

> and still another of the Zamil clan to the comparable post in ᶜUnaizah. Indisputably the master of Nejd, Muhammad returned home to Haᶜil, which for more than a decade to come was to eclipse its southern rival. (Winder 1965:277)

Al-ᶜŌnī composed many poems eulogizing his patron and personal friend ᶜAbdalᶜazīz Ibn ᶜAbdallāh al-Mhannā Ab-al-Xēl, who fell in the battle of al-Mulaida. After the death of ᶜAbdalᶜazīz, al-ᶜŌnī attached himself to his brother Mḥammad Ibn ᶜAbdallāh al-Mhannā and fled with him to Kuwait to escape the wrath of Ibn Rashīd. It is no accident that Ab-al-Xēl, as-Slēm, and other leading families of al-Qaṣīm, along with al-Saᶜūd, sought refuge with Mbārak Ibn Ṣabāḥ of Kuwait. Ibn Ṣabāḥ was becoming more and more concerned about the expansionist designs of Ibn Rashīd, especially since the latter coveted Kuwait as a seaport and perhaps a naval base for the growing Rashidi empire. Therefore, Ibn Ṣabāḥ welcomed all dissident elements of Najd, knowing that one day he could make use of them against Ibn Rashīd.

That day was not too far off. Mḥammad Ibn Rashīd was a shrewd man; he knew that, although Kuwait was a small country, its amir Mbārak could easily enlist the help of the Ottomans or the British against him. Therefore, he made no overt advances. Ibn Ṣabāḥ himself was a master politician, and knew how to save his small country by creating tension and strife among his opponents. For ᶜAbdalᶜazīz Ibn Saᶜūd, the young son of ᶜAbdarriḥmān Ibn Fayṣal Ibn Tirkī who was destined to regain the right of his ancestors to the kingship of Arabia at the very beginning of this century, attending the court of Ibn Ṣabāḥ was a valuable lesson in diplomacy and international politics, especially since Kuwait was an international port open to the world and teeming with foreign visitors and political agents.

The clash between Ḥāyil and Kuwait did not come until after the death of Mḥammad Ibn Rashīd. On his death bed, Ibn Rashīd (who was childless) warned his nephew and heir, ᶜAbdalᶜazīz Ibn Mitᶜib Ibn ᶜAbdallāh Ibn Rashīd, never to provoke Ibn Ṣabāḥ. The young ᶜAbdalᶜazīz, however, was not a skillful politician but a reckless desert warrior. He soon forgot his uncle's advice and began to make excursions against Kuwait and the eastern tribes. These hostilities precipitated the major battle of aṣ-Ṣarīf, which was fought on the soil of al-Qaṣīm between the forces of ᶜAbdalᶜazīz Ibn Rashīd and Mbārak Ibn Ṣabāḥ. Before discussing this battle, we must review the condition of the Najdi fugitives in Kuwait and the role of al-ᶜŌnī in all of this. The following account is a paraphrase of one published by Fahad al-Mārik (1963–1965:III, 280–291) as it was related to him by the late ᶜAbdalᶜazīz Ibn Zayd, once the Saudi ambassador to Syria and Lebanon, who was a close friend of al-ᶜŌnī.

As Kuwait and Ḥāyil were in a state of war, the Najdi fugitives under the leadership of ʿAbdarriḥmān Ibn Fayṣal Āl-Saʿūd made of Kuwait not only a refuge but also a base from which they undertook raiding expeditions against Ibn Rashīd, in the hope of one day liberating their homeland. During one of these expeditions, a few days after Ibn Saʿūd and his followers had quit Kuwait to raid the tribe of Ghaṭān in Najd, Ibn Ṣabāh sent a messenger to Ibn Saʿūd telling him that Kuwait and Ḥāyil had just concluded a peace agreement in which each promised to cease immediately all hostilities against the other; therefore, Ibn Saʿūd and his followers must abandon their expedition. Ibn Saʿūd sought the council of the leading men in his party. Al-ʿŌnī, who happened to accompany Ibn Saʿūd on this expedition, vehemently opposed abandoning it and proposed a stratagem to foil the peace agreement. The following is a paraphrase of what al-ʿŌnī told Ibn Saʿūd.

"Our primary concern is not necessarily to please Ibn Ṣabāḥ or to seek his approval. We seek to liberate our homeland from the Rashidi tyrant and recover our legitimate positions among our people; therefore, we must not lose sight of our objective. In fact, because of the peace agreement between Kuwait and Ḥāyil, we can no longer count on the help of Ibn Ṣabāḥ in our effort to liberate our land. To renew tensions between Ḥāyil and Kuwait, we must go on with our expedition, plunder some camel herds from the subjects of Ibn Rashīd, and sell them in the market of Kuwait. Certainly this will anger Ibn Ṣabāḥ, but we can tell him that we had left on this expedition before the signing of the peace agreement; therefore, the expedition is not covered by the agreement. With the money we earn from the plundered camels, we can buy provisions and leave Kuwait to escape the wrath of Ibn Ṣabāḥ, and to make further raids against Ibn Rashīd. As for Ibn Rashīd, once we carry out this raid, he will hear of it long before Ibn Ṣabāḥ has time to send him a letter of explanation and apology, and he will understand this to be a violation of the peace agreement. After we leave Kuwait for the second time and make our second raid in Najd, Ibn Rashīd will be led to conclude that Ibn Ṣabāḥ is deceiving him and that his apology for the first raid was only a ruse. This will certainly lead to the deterioration of relations between Kuwait and Ḥāyil and the resumption of hostilities between them. Thus, even if Ibn Ṣabāḥ drives us out of Kuwait, in the end he will plead with us to come back and join him against Ibn Rashīd."

ʿAbdarriḥmān Ibn Saʿūd followed the advice of al-ʿŌnī and, indeed, everything went according to plan. Ḥāyil and Kuwait resumed hostilities and Ibn Ṣabāḥ prepared to attack Ibn Rashīd in the latter's territory. While Ibn Rashīd was camped in the desert south of Iraq, "he received news that Mubarak al Sabah, with a strong force including Saʿdun Pasha and his Muntafiq tribesmen and a contingent of the Dhafir tribe, as well as the Saᶜudi princes, to whose call the ᶜAjman and Mutair tribes had rallied in strength, had left Kuwait for the Shauki valley beyond the Dahna sands whence it had reached Buraida, the capital of Qasim" (Philby 1955:258).

The forces of Ibn Ṣabāḥ and Ibn Rashīd met in a vast plain lying some distance north of Buraidah between aṣ-Ṣirīf and aṭ-Ṭirfiyyih (hence the battle, which was fought at the close of the nineteenth century, is called the battle of aṣ-Ṣirīf by some and the battle of aṭ-Ṭirfiyyih by others). Here is how Philby describes the battle.

> Ibn Rashīd—ᶜAbdul ᶜAziz Ibn Mitᶜab, the successor of the great Muhammad—lay camped at Sarif, some distance back in the *Nafud*, with his Shammar and a loyal contingent from Buraida which had revolted from his allegiance and closed its gates. Mubarak Ibn Subah lay at Tarafiya with his allies—Saᶜdun of the great Muntafik tribe of ᶜIraq; ᶜAbdulrahman, father of the present *Wahhabi* ruler, with a *Najdi* contingent and a contingent from Buraida. Ibn Rashīd sent out a small cavalry patrol to reconnoitre the enemy and a brisk fire was opened on it by a similar force operating from Tarafiya. On hearing the sounds of firing Ibn Rashīd gave the order to advance, and Ibn Subah doing the same, the battle took place on the first slope of the *Nafud* and on part of the Tarafiya plain. Ibn Subah was decisively defeated and the enemy occupied his camp, while he and his allies took to flight and were only saved from the attentions of parties sent out in pursuit by the victor by a timely and very heavy fall of rain. The slaughter had been heavy during the encounter itself and the flood, they say, ran bloodred, carrying before it the corpses of the slain and depositing them in rows on the edge of the wide *Sabkha* depression along the east side of the Tarafiya basin. ᶜAbdul ᶜAziz Ibn Saᶜud, still a mere boy, was simultaneously laying siege to Riyadh, but raised it as soon as he received news of the defeat and withdrew to Kuwait. Meanwhile Ibn Subah fled *via* Zilfi, and the *Najdis* were remorselessly pursued as far as the confines of ᶜAridh, many villages being sacked and burned by the pursuers. Ibn Rashīd himself marched straight on Buraida, whose gates were opened to him by treachery, and taught its people the dreadful consequences of rebellion by executing 180 of its citizens and exacting enormous fines from the rest. . . . But the harsh and vindictive treatment of the vanquished by the victor had made the name of ᶜAbdul ᶜAziz Ibn Rashīd hated throughout Najd, and ᶜAbdulrahman, safely arrived at Kuwait, had foretold that Najd would soon return to its rightful rulers —a prediction whose fulfil-

> ment began in the following year at the hands of a son, for whom destiny had so much in store. (1928:321–322)

Following the battle of aṣ-Ṣirīf, al-ᶜŌnī composed an apologetic poem in which he explained that the defeat of the Kuwaiti forces was due not to lack of courage on the part of Mbārak aṣ-Ṣabāḥ, but rather to lack of wise counsel. He pointed out that the prophet Muḥammad himself was defeated in the battle of Uḥud; therefore, defeat is not a sign of God's wrath, just as victory is not a sign of His pleasure. Al-ᶜŌnī argued in his poem that there is no shame in defeat; shame lies in submission and in neglecting to avenge defeat. The poem ends with various threats in the name of Ibn Ṣabāḥ against Ibn Rashīd (al-Ḥātam 1968:II, 241–243).

Unlike his uncle Mḥammad, who managed to annex the whole of Najd to his dominion after the battle of al-Mulaida, ᶜAbdalᶜazīz Ibn Rashīd was unable to follow up his spectacular military victory at aṣ-Ṣirīf with any political gains. On the contrary, his cruel treatment of the conquered populations prepared the way for a general uprising against him and in favor of ᶜAbdalᶜazīz Ibn Saᶜūd, who was able to recapture Riyadh in 1901 as an initial step toward the reestablishment of Saudi rule and the complete extinction of the Rashidi dynasty.

To protect himself and to avenge his humiliating defeat at aṣ-Ṣirīf, Ibn Ṣabāḥ appealed to Great Britain for help, and at the same time gave full material and political support to ᶜAbdalᶜazīz Ibn ᶜAbdarriḥmān Ibn Saᶜūd, who was able, in a bold and heroic adventure, to recover Riyadh after killing the Rashidi governor, ᶜAjlān Ibn Mḥammad. After establishing Saudi authority in ᶜĀridh and the southern district, Ibn Saᶜūd sent for the Qaṣīmī fugitives in Kuwait, including members of the families of Ab-al-Xēl and as-Slēm, the legitimate rulers of Buraidah and ᶜUnaizah. In the meantime, Ibn Ṣabāḥ suggested to al-ᶜŌnī, who was still a refugee in Kuwait, that he compose a poem urging the people of al-Qaṣīm who had sought refuge in Kuwait, Mesopotamia, and Syria, to unite and rally behind Ibn Saᶜūd, in order to oust the Rashidi tyrant and liberate their homeland. Al-ᶜŌnī composed such a poem, in which he addressed the people of al-Qaṣīm by their war cry, *Awlād ᶜAlī*. It is related that when the poem was recited in al-Mēdān, the quarter in Damascus where the people of al-Qaṣīm had established themselves, the Qaṣīmīs were so moved by it that they sold all their possessions, bought all the guns and horses available in Damascus, and sallied forth to liberate their homeland. Some of them are even supposed to have left their shops and homes open and unattended in their haste to join the others. The poem was called *al-xalūj* because its prelude was inspired by a *xalūj* (a camel bereaved of its newly born calf) which al-ᶜŌnī heard crying throughout the night at the palace of Ibn Ṣabāḥ. He began this poem, which has over seventy lines, by admonishing the wailing camel for crying so over such a trivial loss; he then recounts his own losses and urges the Qaṣīmīs to rise up against Ibn Rashīd (Kamāl 1960–1971:V, 30–38).

1 But, O camel, I cannot count my losses—there is no remedy for my grief, and I find no relief in complaining.
2 Were I to find solace in crying, O camel, I would cry every white day and every night.
3 If crying would bring back the lost ones, I would shed tears till my eyes became parched.
4 I would cry over the events that are tormenting my soul; I would cry over the humiliation of the openhanded valiant ones.
5 I would cry over my dear ones whenever the wind blows; I would cry all my life till my soul was seized by death.
6 I would cry over the homeland where we grew up, bordered on the north by lofty escarpments,
7 And bordered on the east by the sand dunes of al-Arāxim; it is situated between al-Lwā and as-Sirr. I remember those sand dunes—oh, how beautiful they are.
8 A homeland in Najd that was once a haven, a refuge sought by those burdened by hard times.
9 She resembles a fair chaste maiden; in her beauty my homeland outshines all fair maidens.
10 The covetous lower their eyes when they pass by her; they fear the gallant youths who grew up in her courts.
11 She is our mother—oh how sweet was her flowing milk; she nourished us, she raised us, we are her children.
12 She is kind to us; no mother is so devoted to her children as she is to us; she is loving, but we are ungrateful.
13 We wear silk and satin while she is naked; she wails and cries, but none takes pity on her.
14 No one expressed indignation when she was stripped of her clothing; and no one cares what befell her after that.
15 Oh, I sigh and say, "How disheartening!" Woe to us; how can we bear to watch our mother being violated before our eyes?
16 Hail! rider on a fine mount which steals distances with its swift pace; a spirited wild beast, it is startled by its own shadow.
17 An eight-year-old barren camel, never suckled by a calf, and never couched to carry loads.
18 Now that an urgent matter has come up, saddle it, but hold tight to the rein lest it jerk away.

19 Pay no mind to the saddlebag, there is no time for fancy trappings; just carry a waterskin and balance it with your provisions.
20 Hearken, O messenger! you must travel day and night, and must not let your eyes taste sweet slumber.
21 After traveling for ten and five days due west, you will reach al-Mēdān. Then, let your mount graze loose.
22 When you come to the afternoon market, you will meet sturdy lads who tread on flowing silken garments with their leather sandals.
23 They will ask you, "O good man, let us have your tidings—the land of Najd, what happened to it after we left?"
24 Tell them that the men of al-Qaṣīm and other regions rose up to liberate their homelands from tyranny,
25 Except for your homeland which you fled, leaving her crying for revenge. She pines for past generations [who were more gallant than you]; I feel sorry for her.
26 She is terrorized by strangers—shame upon you—and your fair ladies are scattered, homeless, with none to protect their honor.
27 Your grandsires are also beaten for no reason; they were revered in the past, but today, in their old age, the hair is plucked from their honorable beards.
28 O Awlād ᶜAlī, the time has come to show your mettle; may he who wastes his life seeking material gain be deprived of the Lord's mercy.
29 O Awlād ᶜAlī, know that life is short, and that only a man's praiseworthy deeds will survive him.
30 This is a perilous venture that only an exceptional man can undertake. O Awlād ᶜAlī, which of you says, I am for it?
31 Know that wrestling with danger is the only way to eminence; to achieve your noble goals you must persevere.
32 Rise up and with the help of God pay your debts; you are not base men, you are noble.

At first, al-ᶜŌnī was committed to the cause of Ibn Saᶜūd; and in two exceedingly long poems, one consisting of ninety-six lines (Kamāl 1960–1971:V,7–14) and the other of one hundred and eighty-four lines (ibid., V,15–29), al-ᶜŌnī, who had accompanied his patron and personal friend Mḥammad al-ᶜAbdallah al-Mhannā Ab-al-Xēl back to Buraidah, gives a detailed and accurate historical account of the campaign of Ibn Saᶜūd against Ibn Rashīd from the time he left Kuwait until the time he captured al-Qaṣīm.

Al-ᶜŌnī at first enthusiastically supported the cause of Ibn Saᶜūd, but later sided with Ibn Rashīd. Al-Faraj (1952:II,264) and al-Ḥātam (1968:II,234) explain this change of position as the result of vacillation and caprice on the part of al-ᶜŌnī and his propensity for creating tension. In my opinion, however, this is not a satisfactory explanation, because it overlooks the political realities that made al-ᶜŌnī change his position, which I shall now discuss.

After Ibn Rashīd was driven out of al-Qaṣīm, Ibn Saᶜūd gave the amirship of Buraidah to Ṣāliḥ al-Ḥasan al-Mhannā Ab-al-Xēl. This angered Mḥammad al-ᶜAbdallah al-Mhannā, Ṣāliḥ's cousin; he went back to Kuwait accompanied by his friend al-ᶜŌnī. Later, Mḥammad made peace with his cousin and came back to Buraidah, but al-ᶜŌnī, who was never to set foot in Buraidah again, remained with the paramount chief of the al-Mintifig tribe, Siᶜdūn as-Siᶜdūn, and his son ᶜJēmī. In the meantime, Ṣāliḥ al-Ḥasan seems to have misunderstood the intentions of Ibn Saᶜūd to reimpose Saudi hegemony over al-Qaṣīm, and thought that once al-Qaṣīm was liberated from Ibn Rashīd, its affairs should be left completely in the hands of its native amirs. In his dealings with Ḥāyil and the Turks, he exhibited a degree of autonomy that did not please Ibn Saᶜūd, who killed him and appointed his cousin Mḥammad al-ᶜAbdallah in his place. Mḥammad, however, continued to pursue Ṣāliḥ's secessionist policy and began secret correspondence with Ḥāyil. This brought upon him the wrath of Ibn Saᶜūd, who banished him to Iraq and took the amirship of Buraidah away from the family of Ab-al-Xēl. Thus Buraidah's prospects of independence were crushed forever, and Ab-al-Xēl lost all hope of a political comeback.

While these developments were taking place, al-ᶜŌnī was staying with Ibn Siᶜdūn, the paramount chief of the al-Mintifig tribe. It must be understood that al-ᶜŌnī devoted all his sympathies and loyalty to the cause of Buraidah, and to the house of Ab-al-Xēl, who had raised him. When he saw the tragic end of this house at the hands of Ibn Saᶜūd, al-ᶜŌnī became disillusioned with him and crossed over to the Rashidi side. His move might have been encouraged by his host, Ibn Siᶜdūn, who himself had switched to the side of Ibn Rashīd. Now, we must review the political situation in Ḥāyil from the time that al-Qaṣīm fell into the hands of Ibn Saᶜūd to the time that al-ᶜŌnī left the al-Mintifig tribe to join the court of Ibn Rashīd.

By the end of 1904, virtually the whole of al-Qaṣīm had come under the control of Ibn Saᶜūd, and at dawn, on April 13, 1906, ᶜAbdalᶜazīz al-Mitᶜib Ibn Rashīd was killed in battle at a place called Roḏat Mhannā. By this time, the Rashidi dominion had shrunk considerably and had become confined to the Jabal Shammar district. After his death, ᶜAbdalᶜazīz was succeeded by his son Mitᶜib, but soon the affairs of Jabal Shammar fell into disarray. Mitᶜib and two of his three brothers were assassinated, while the youngest brother, Saᶜūd, was smuggled to the safety of Madinah by the as-Sabhān, his maternal uncles. The murderers were Sulṭān, Saʿūd, and Fayṣal, the sons of Ḥmūd Ibn ʿUbayd Ibn Rashīd. Sulṭān became the ruler of Ḥayil, but in less than a year he himself was murdered by his brothers Saʿūd and Fayṣal. Saʿūd Ibn Ḥmūd then became ruler of Ḥāyil. Soon, however, the as-Sabhān brought Saʿūd Ibn ʿAbdalʿazīz al-Mitʿib Ibn Rashīd back to Ḥāyil, and made him amir, after they murdered Saʿūd al-Ḥmūd.

At about this time, al-ʿŌnī arrived in Ḥāyil and immediately became actively engaged in the politics of Jabal Shammar, employing his poetry in the service of the Rashidi cause. He composed long poems eulogizing the young Rashidi amir, Saʿūd ibn ʿAbdalʿazīz, and his regent, Ibn Sabhān. He also composed several poems on the war between Ibn Rashīd and Ibn Shaʿlān, chief of the Rwalah bedouins.

The reign of Saʿūd Ibn Rashīd was a relatively stable period in the turbulent history of Ḥāyil, and lasted for about ten years. But, as in the case of most Rashidi amirs, a tragic end was in store for him; he was shot dead by his distant cousin ʿAbdallāh Ibn Ṭalāl. Al-ʿŌnī played an important role in this palace affair. Because Saʿūd Ibn Rashīd had ascended the throne of Ḥāyil when he was only ten years old, several factions emerged in the palace, which included those of the mother of the young amir, members of the as-Sabhān family, and the palace slaves and retainers. At the same time, members of the rival branch of the Rashidi family were stripped of all political power in order to stifle any ambitions they might have of usurping the throne from the young amir. ʿAbdallāh Ibn Ṭalāl Ibn Rashīd and his brother Mḥammad were not pleased with this arrangement, and with time they became more and more discontent. Al-ʿŌnī also became disenchanted with the policies of Saʿūd and went over to the side of the sons of Ṭalāl, ʿAbdallah and Mḥammad. Along with some other men, al-ʿŌnī began to meet regularly in the house of ʿAbdallah and Mḥammad Ibn Ṭalāl (which was in a quarter of the town called Lubdih) to discuss the affairs of Ḥayil and the situation in the palace. Saʿūd as-Ṣāliḥ as-Sabhān heard of this; he went to the amir and told him that the sons of Ṭalāl and the people of Lubdih were holding regular meetings and were most likely conspiring against the throne. The amir sent his chief slave, named Dirʿān, to order those assembled to break up their meeting and never meet again. That the amir should send a slave carrying his sword to enter the house of noble men and princes and order them not to meet or to express their concern for the welfare of their town was too much to bear. ʿAbdallāh and Mḥammad Ibn Ṭalāl decided to take the matter into their own hands; they were encouraged by a poem composed by al-ʿŌnī on this occasion in which he urged them not to accept humiliation from the slaves of the palace. Their plan was to assassinate the amir. This was done by ʿAbdallāh Ibn Ṭalāl, who was himself immediately cut down by his victim's slaves, while his brother Mḥammad was thrown in jail. The throne of Ḥāyil passed to ʿAbdallāh Ibn Mitʿib, the nephew of the slain amir, who was then only thirteen years old.

Al-ʿŌnī composed several poems elegizing ʿAbdallāh Ibn Ṭalāl and expressing the hope that the latter's brother Mḥammad would be freed and that the star of the Ṭalāl branch of the Rashidi family would soon rise above that of all others. He exerted a great deal of energy and employed much cunning to obtain the release of Mḥammad Ibn Ṭalāl (al-Mārik 1953–1955:III, 292–298). Before long, Mḥammad Ibn Ṭalāl was set free and appointed governor of al-Jōf, north of Ḥāyil. However, under the indecisive leadership of ʿAbdallāh Ibn Mitʿib the political organization of Jabal Shammar soon began to disintegrate, and Ḥāyil was besieged by the forces of Ibn Saʿūd. Mḥammad Ibn Ṭalāl hastened from al-Jōf to Ḥāyil, not so much to usurp the amirship of Jabal Shammar as to somehow rectify the worsening situation. This move was enough to terrify the amir and to drive him to the camp of Ibn Saʿūd, the enemy of Ḥāyil, to seek refuge. Unlike ʿAbdallāh Ibn Mitʿib, Mḥammad Ibn Ṭalāl was a man of courage and initiative. He made a serious attempt to restore the glory of Ḥāyil, but the odds against him were overwhelming. Beside him was al-ʿŌnī, who was composing poems in his name or, as the Arabs say, "*ʿalā lsān ibn Rišīd*" ("on the tongue of Ibn Rashīd"), urging the various sections of the Shammar tribe, in the name of their tribal honor, to rally behind their amir to protect their capital. These poems are as stirring and powerful as *al-xalūj*, the poem discussed above, but they did not have the same effect. At that point in time in the long history of Arabia, the heroic age was fading, to be replaced by a new political order which ultimately undermined the effectiveness of the Nabaṭi poets. Instead of responding to the appeals of Ibn Rashīd as they were communicated through the poems of al-ʿŌnī, the various sections of the Shammar tribe crossed over to the side of Ibn Saʿūd. In 1921 the citizens of Ḥāyil opened the gates of their town to his armies. The amir Mḥammad, al-ʿŌnī, and a few others locked themselves inside the castle and refused to come out until Ibn Saʿūd gave them pledges of safe-conduct.

After the capitulation of Ḥāyil, Ibn Saʿūd took Ibn Rashīd and al-ʿŌnī with him to Riyadh along with others whom he wanted to keep under close watch. They were given strict orders never to be seen together at any time in any place for any reason. A few months later, al-ʿŌnī accompanied some of ar-Rashīd to attend the funeral of a Rashidi child. On the way back from the funeral, the men stopped by al-ʿŌnī's house. They were talking about the past and lamenting the good old days when they were surprised by the men of Ibn Saʿūd, who had come to break up their meeting. Al-ʿŌnī, in view of the topic of conversation at the time and the warnings of Ibn Saʿūd, became seized with fright and tried to hide. This aroused the suspicions of the police, who arrested him; and Ibn Saᶜūd send him to Ibn Jalawī to be imprisoned in a miserable dungeon in the city of Hufūf. In prison, al-ᶜŌnī composed poems apologizing to Ibn Saᶜūd and asking various members of the family of Ibn Jalawī, as well as other men of weight like Ibn Haḏḏāl, the supreme chief of the al-ᶜAmārāt tribe, to intercede on his behalf and persuade Ibn Saᶜūd to release him. In these poems, al-ᶜŌnī describes the dreadful conditions of the underground prison, which lacked sunshine and fresh air. His legs were locked permanently in a wooden contraption resembling stocks, which prevented any movement and caused open sores to fester on his legs. He complains that he was constantly tearing rags off his garment to wrap around these bleeding wounds. His pleas for pardon fell upon deaf ears. As a result, he lost all faith in humanity, and in his total despair he turned to God and composed his famous poem entitled *at-tōbih*, his last poem. In this poem he expressed his bitterness and disappointment with his friends, who had failed to secure his release. He also talked about penitence, death, the hereafter, and the mercy of God. At last al-ᶜŌnī was set free, only to die soon after, in 1923, of tuberculosis.

When people talk about al-ᶜŌnī, they call him "the poet of Najd, the famous one." His poetry is the poetry of action and exemplifies the power of words and the important function of poetry in Arabian society. It is related that the poet Brāhīm Ibn Jᶜēṯin once warned al-ᶜŌnī, "Your poetry will bring death upon you"; but he died the death of a hero and his name will never be forgotten. Al-ᶜŌnī, the last poet of the heroic age in Arabia, was the victim of change in the political order. The emergence of statehood in Arabia rang the death knell for Nabaṭi poetry as a viable political institution.

Part Two

LITERARY

V

COMPOSITION: THE POET'S VIEWPOINT

Nabaṭi poets delight in versifying their views and conceptions concerning the processes of composition and transmission. Indeed, it is an established tradition to comment, in the opening verses of a poem, on the arduous task of poetizing, and perhaps mention how the finished work is to be communicated to the audience. Occasionally these views are given direct expression, but in most instances they are obliquely stated in figurative language and encoded in stock motifs which are worked into the prelude of the poem.

The prelude forms an integral component of the poem's artistic identity and contributes to its compositional intricacy. Aside from its aesthetic function, however, the prelude can be analyzed as a metapoem—a poetic commentary upon poetizing (see Dundes 1966) which, upon close inspection, can provide us with a revealing inside view of the accepted methods and common practices of composition in Nabaṭi poetry—and, perhaps more importantly, tell us how poets themselves conceive of the poetic process. I shall examine in the following pages the poet's view of inspiration and composition as expressed in the prelude to the poem, supplementing my discussion with material from my field experience as well as that gleaned from various written sources.

The Nabaṭi poet considers his words as a mirror reflecting his private feelings and inner emotions, or what is variously called *sadd, ćinīn,* and *ʿazā*. In composing, the poet *ybayyiḥ sadduh, ybayyiḥ ćinīnuh, ybayyiḥ ʿazāuh*, that is to say, he exposes himself to the public eye and divulges to all his innermost and most deeply guarded secrets. Despite his oft repeated vows to hold his tongue and remain silent, there are times when he is so overwhelmed by the poetic urge that he can no longer restrain himself, hard as he may try to resist the temptation.

Even in his old age, the poet finds it impossible to disregard the poetic call. This is because the poet is characteristically a compassionate person who is very sensitive to the pathos and the difficult conditions of human existence. His keen mind is constantly preoccupied (*mšaggā, mʿanna*) with the vicissitudes of life. The poet is also a man of passion (*rāʿī hawa*).

His impulsive heart (*galb al-xaṭā*) is easily enamored (*miġram, mwallaᶜ*) by scenes, actions, and qualities that strike his fancy and appeal to his imagination. He is readily moved by such sights and sounds as the deserted encampment, the departure of the tribes after summer camping, the procession of a migrating tribe, the rumbling of thunder, the flashing of lightning, the sad groaning of a mother camel over her lost calf, the cooing of a dove, the passing figure of a shapely woman, and so on. It is scenes like this that enflame the heart of the poet, stir (*yhayyiḏ*) his passions, and tear the scab off his emotional wounds (*ynaggiḏ jrūḥuh*).

This outlook is illustrated by the following popular anecdote concerning Baṣri al-Wḏēḥi, a famous poet from the Shammar tribe (al-Thumayrī 1972:147–148; Ibn Khamīs 1978:152–154). In his old age, Baṣri vowed to dissociate himself from poetry and the pursuit of pleasure; he undertook to perform the religious duty of *ḥajj*, hoping to please God and ask for His forgiveness. While at Mecca performing the rites of *ḥajj*, Baṣri was approached by one of his friends who, to tease him and test his faith, said: "O Baṣri, there is a rare piece of *silᶜih* (merchandise) exhibited in the marketplace; I would like to buy it, but I thought I should get your expert opinion first." Baṣri took his friend's words at face value and followed him into the marketplace, until the latter stopped at a crowded corner where a famous bedouin beauty was doing her shopping. She was the daughter of Šaᶜāᶜ Ibn Rbēᶜān, one of the principal chiefs of the mighty ᶜTēbah tribe. When his eyes caught sight of the bedouin princess wearing her colorful garments and riding in her decorated litter which was surrounded by onlookers, Baṣri realized what the words of his friend had really meant, but it was too late. He became transfixed and could not take his eyes off the princess. He gazed at her for a long time, and then gave a detailed description of her beauties in a poem, which later became very popular; the opening line of the poem is: "Confounded be the one who led me here and renewed my wounds; oh, pity me, I am a frail old man!"

The poetic genius of an outstanding poet is conceived of as always being near at hand, lying dormant like smoldering embers to be set ablaze at the moment of inspiration. When the poet is inspired (*mtahayyiḏ*), the door of his heart opens and it becomes possible for him to travel the difficult path of poetry. Some poets claim that at the moment of inspiration they become delirious, as if they were intoxicated. During this trancelike state, the heart of the poet begins to bubble (*yijīš*) with emotions like a boiling cauldron (*mirjal*). Notions seeking articulation invade his mind like a swarm of locusts. His breast overflows (*yajhaš, yifīḏ*) with words pouring forth like a stream flowing from a spring (*ᶜidd*). This poetic surge is compared to *darr* (abundant milk flowing from the udder) or *jamm* (abundant water collecting at the bottom of a deep well). A poet may boast that his poetic *darr* would fill every vessel to the brim, or that his *jamm* is so abundant that waterwheels working day and night could not dry it up. Others may make more exaggerated claims and compare their poetic flow to an ocean that would drown everything, or to a torrent that would sweep away anything in its path. This wild poetic surge, however, must be controlled and turned into well-ordered verses. Order must be imposed on the formless poetic mass of vaguely connected words, images, and ideas that flood the poet's mind. Here are a few lines from the prelude of a poem by Mḥammad al-ʿAbdallah al-ʿŌnī which convey these ideas (Kamāl 1960–1971:V, 73–77).

1 [My verses are] gems and pearls reaped from an overflowing ocean of ideas,
2 Which I subdue and fetter lest it [the ocean] deluge the world in less time than it would take to swallow a sip of coffee.
3 When I am inundated with the surging ocean of reflection, and its foaming waves begin to press against my body, I confine it with heavy chains and a thousand locks.
4 Were it not for such constraints, my words would stream forth like tumultuous seas where giant ships voyage.
5 Turbulent passions stirring inside my breast have chased slumber away from my eyes, so that I remained sleepless all night.

Although poetry is inspired by passions, composition remains a deliberate and reflective process. The diction of the poem must be evocative and musical; therefore the words must be chosen with extreme care. Musil writes that the nomads "hold that the words used in a poem must be out of the ordinary, not those heard in common everyday life. The more unusual words the Bedouin can put into his composition, the better he thinks it. The poet therefore revises every verse most painstakingly, repeats it many times, substitutes some words for others, and asks the opinion of his friends before producing his poem" (1928:284). Of one particular poet, Musil observes: "When I found that he depicted me in his poem as sitting upon a *heǧîn* (mount camel) I demurred, saying that I rode a *d̲elûl*, that the Rwala do not say *heǧîn*, but *d̲elûl*. The poet acknowledged this, but said he could not employ such a common word as *d̲elûl* in his poem, for in a poem one has to use the word that is more graceful even if less familiar" (1927:237).

The strict rules of rhyme and meter in Nabaṭi poetry make versification a slow and difficult process. A Nabaṭi poem ranges in length from a few to more than a hundred verses. But whether it is a short ditty or a long ode, all the verses of a poem must be of the same meter. They must have the same number of long and short syllables combined in exactly the same order. The verse is divided into two hemistichs which are metrically identical, but each of which has a different rhyme. The first hemistichs of all verses must rhyme with each other, as must the second hemistichs, no matter how long the poem may be. Due to the importance of rhyming in Nabaṭi poetry, a poem is often called *gāf* or *gīfān* (rhymes). To make all the verses of a poem fit this grid of rhyme and meter, each verse must be carefully polished (*mḥakkak*). The labor involved in such a painstaking process is reflected in the various terms that poets use to refer to it, such as *ywallif* (to harmonise), *yᶜaddil* (to straighten), *yāzin* (to measure), *yanḥat* (to sculpt), *yṣaxxir* (to hew), *yᶜasif* (to tame, break).

There is a close link in the minds of Nabaṭi poets between poetry and love. Regardless of the principal subject of his composition, a poet is likely to pay tribute to a charming woman who is the source of his poetic inspiration. It is *ṭard al-hawā* (the passionate pursuit of exquisite beauty and amorous affairs) that impels poets to undergo the pains and agonies of composition. This search for ultimate beauty and ultimate joy inspires the poet to seek aesthetic perfection for his composition, regardless of the difficulties and hardships he brings upon himself in executing this demanding task. The poet may stay up all night carefully polishing his words and revising his verses, as expressed in these lines from the prelude of a poem by ᶜAbdarriḥmān al-Brāhīm ar-Ribīᶜī (Ibn Sayḥān 1965–1969:II, 198).

1 I was still awake when the Pleiades descended in the western horizon as if driven by my ever-watchful eyes; thoughts swarmed in my mind and I was unable to close my eyes.
2 The ship of my passions sailed in the deep ocean of reflection and plunged into a vast chasm whose bottom is frightful.
3 Its waves push against each other painfully inside my breast; I am burdened by the calamities of fate.
4 From this ocean of ideas I harvest what strikes my fancy, gems of verses which I string intricately.

Poetic inspiration is likened by poets to the blowing of the wind, but the difficult process of composition is likened to the laborious operation of winnowing (separating the grain from the chaff) or, more commonly, to sailing. Poetic reflection is viewed as a mental journey in a turbulent sea of passion (*baḥr al-hawā, baḥr al-ġarām*) whose waves are frightful and whose depths are full of terror. The probing for words and images is like diving for pearls. Only bold and worthy men can dive deeply in the sea or delve deeply into poetic reflection. These ideas are expressed in the following verses from a long poem by Rāshid al-Khalāwī (Ibn Khamīs 1972:247).

1 My verses are precious pearls selected by my discerning mind; like pure gems they appeal to men of sound judgment.
2 I picked them from the abyss of a deep ocean; whoever dives in it other than me, [who am] experienced, will drown in its bottomless depths.
3 Others tried it before me, but they lost the shore; many a ship was overturned, its captain flung into the dark chasm,
4 Ocean depths which only Rāšid can sail and dive into without the help of ropes and haulers.
5 My tongue pulled them [the verses] from the bottom of my heart to fashion them into a splendid form.

Naturally, a Nabaṭi poem is more than a collection of verses that share the same rhyme and meter. The artistic unity of the poem is achieved by the skillful interweaving of its thematic components. The conventional themes, stock motifs, topics, and formulas of the Nabaṭi poetic tradition are compared by poets to flowers in a meadow, fruits in a garden, or gems and pearls. The poet picks those things he fancies (*yixtār, ytanaggā, yajni, yagṭif*), sorts them out, and weaves them into an intricate and harmonious composition of his own.

In its thematic development, the Nabaṭi poet follows very closely the structural principles employed by the ancient Arab poets. A long poem usually consists of several themes strung together and studded throughout with similes and images, all of which are conventional, but each of which is given a slight semantic turn or a new artistic twist. The goal of the poet is to strike a balance between the familiar and the unique. In his composition, the poet does not touch upon all the themes at his disposal, nor does he necessarily arrange the themes he chooses in a set and rigid order. Themes in the same poem are not treated at the same length or according to a fixed proportion. The poet has a wide range of options with which to start his poem and develop it to a successful completion. He works within a modular structure in which themes are components that can be augmented, truncated, added, deleted, and shifted around for artistic effect. The poet tries as skillfully as possible to relate the thematic components of his poem to each other and coordinate them gracefully in one harmonious whole. This is achieved by the intricate interlacing of themes and by the smooth transition from one theme to the next so that all converge together to form a poem that is at once traditional and original.

Nabaṭi poets are well aware that the verses of a poem must exhibit an artistic unity—a structure—beyond that of rhyme and meter. They employ visual images to convey their conception of poetic order and they metaphorically represent the intellectual process of composition as a visually intricate handicraft. The various compositional methods a poet may follow in developing his poem are compared to desert roads that crisscross each other, going up and down over soft sands and hard rocks. Only an expert poet can extricate himself and steer safely through this poetic maze. One poet, Zēd as-Salāmih al-Xwēr, boasts in the opening line of one of his poems that his verses are *riyām w-mawālīf*, that is to say, they follow each other closely and in perfect harmony like the file of mother camels followed closely by their suckling calves on their way back from pasture. The most common word used to refer to composition is *naḏm*, which also refers to the threading of beads. To praise the intricacy and beauty of his composition, a Nabaṭi poet would most likely appeal to the visual sense of his audience, and compare its verses to gems and pearls of variegated colors and sizes strung together into a resplendent necklace. Other words used in reference to composition are *yabni* (to build) and *yšayyid* (to construct). The word for verse is *bēt* (a house, a structure, an edifice), and the beginning of the poem is called *sās* (foundation).

Poetic cogitation is not only compared to manual labor (e.g., carving, hewing, building, weaving, threading,) but in some instances it is accompanied by physical activity such as the making of coffee. When the poet feels the spark of inspiration stirring inside him, he fixes himself a cup of coffee to clear his head and help him compose. Coffee making is as elaborate and absorbing a ritual as composition. The way a man makes his coffee is his *nūmās*, since it reflects his nimbleness, alertness, composure, tact, and taste. A man takes as much pride in his coffee making as he does in his poetic composition. Coffee making involves building the fire, washing the cups and pots, boiling the water, slowly roasting the coffee beans, pounding the roasted beans rhythmically in a brass mortar, throwing the ground coffee into the boiling pot, letting it boil for a few minutes, drawing it away from the fire and letting it settle, crushing the cardamom seeds, casting the right amount of crushed cardamom into a fresh pot, pouring the coffee that was left to settle into this fresh pot, letting it just come to a boil with the cardamom, withdrawing the pot from the embers, and leaving it for a while to settle and become clear. In other words, coffee making and composition are both patterned activities, except that one is manual whereas the other is purely mental. It is this resemblance in one way and difference in another that makes these two activities go together so nicely; each is in some way a mimesis of the other. While the poet makes his coffee he also makes his poem, deciding its rhyme, meter, and opening line, which is called *mišadd*, from the verb *šadd* (to saddle a camel mount), because the other verses of the poem ride upon the first line; that is, they depend on it, in rhyme and meter. By the time the coffee is ready, the poem is well on its way. As he sips his coffee, the poet reviews his poem, revises its verses, and adds some finishing touches. Finally the poet, having finished his coffee, closes his poem with a line of prayer for peace upon the soul of the Prophet.

We see, then, that composition is generally viewed as a mimesis of physical activity and is in fact at times accompanied by such activity. It is of equal interest to note that the mental operation of poetic composition is for some poets associated with a vigorous and restless body motion. This physical motion is a visible sign that the poet is emotionally moved—that he is in a state of poetic labor. When the poet is inspired (*mtahayyiḏ*), he feels agitated and burdened and he cannot rest until he unloads the heavy burden of passion (*ḥiml al-ġayy, ḥiml al-hawā, ḥiml al-ġarām*), that is, until he finishes his composition. The poet paces around (*yisūj*), roams about (*yihjil*), and runs (*yihrif*), as the poets say, like a mad man, a wild beast, or a thirsty camel separated from the herd and lost in the empty desert wastes. Because the poet is always on the run, poetic composition is compared to hunting. Actually, many famous poets were also famous hunters—like Srūr al-Aṭraš, who composed while walking alone in the wilderness stalking wild game. Like hunting, poetic composition is an obsession (*wilᶜih*) which is toilsome yet enjoyable. The hunters pursue *ṣēd* (wild game) such as *ḏbā, rīm,* and *ġizlān* (all species of gazelle), while the poets woo beautiful virgins who are also called *ṣēd, ḏbā, rīm,* and *ġizlān*. In pondering over his poem and in searching for the right words and images, the poet undergoes all sorts of hardships, just like a hunter in pursuit of the quarry. Some poets elaborate this metaphor by describing the sad lot of the hunter: his body is weary from ceaseless running, his skin is shriveled and darkened from overexposure to the burning sun, his back is aching from frequent stooping and stalking, and his bare feet are bleeding from stepping over thorny bushes and sharp rocks.

In addition to the visible sign of body motion, composition is also associated with emotional turbulence and excitement. The heart of the poet is set ablaze by passions burning inside him, and hot tears flow down his cheeks like the splashing of water buckets drawn from the bottom of the well by four strong, fast-moving camels. He sobs (*ytaᶜabbar*), wails (*yinūḥ*), moans (*yagnib*) and howls (*yaᶜwī*) like a bereaved mother, a camel who has lost her calf, a man whose leg has been broken on the battlefield, or a hungry wolf. Many poets prefer to be alone while composing, because they do not want to be seen in such a distressed state. They seek solitude in the empty desert or on the forlorn summits of lofty cliffs away from people. The following four brief examples—by Riḍa ibn Ṭārif of Shammar, Srūr al-Aṭraš, Mḥammad Ibn Aḥmad as-Sdērī (Ibn Sayḥān 1965–1969:II, 137), and Zabn Ibn ᶜMēr (ibid., 226), respectively—illustrate the poet's state while composing.

1 When passions fill my breast I say: bring forth my graceful mount, put on her saddle and her trappings.
2 Put on her saddle and grant me leave [to go]; I must seek relief on the desert roads.

* * *

1 I spent all day yesterday on the ledge of a lofty cliff; I did not come down till darkness fell.
2 There, I was sobbing; my tears were streaming like the copious rain of the clouds.
3 I was moved by the memory of my love; she is as beautiful as the wild doe grazing peacefully with the flock.

* * *

1 These are the verses of the one who leaped over the forlorn summit of a lofty escarpment which only eagles can reach,
2 A high heap of boulders which is difficult to climb but whose top I seek when passions overrun my heart.
3 There, I sit alone and my mind sinks into the abyss of reflection.
4 There, I sit and muse, so puzzling is the change of times.

* * *

1 Leave me, leave me, dear friends, leave me. Leave me, do not reproach me; I can no longer hold back my tears.
2 I wish to be left alone in the empty space to cry and relieve my heart; I do not want others to hear me.

As these examples show, composition is accompanied by emotional outbursts and loud vocalization. Generally speaking, a Nabaṭi poet does not compose in silence. Rather, he sings out his verses (*yiṣibb aṣ-ṣōt, yazʿaj aṣ-ṣōt*). Even when there are people present, the poet cannot control himself, but keeps murmuring aloud his yet unfinished verses. Here are the opening lines of a poem sent by Tirkī Ibn ʿAbdallah Āl Saʿūd to his cousin Mishārī, then a prisoner in Egypt (al-Ḥātam 1968:II, 9).

1 I was alarmed by a serious matter that chased sweet slumber away from my eyes.
2 Secrets that I have been striving to conceal are leaking out of my breast; the people around me are startled by my loud mumbling.

3 My heart is inflamed by the sad news I received from a noble man [Mishārī] complaining of hardship and ill fortune.
4 Go on, pen! Write a most tender greeting to my cousin, Mishārī.
5 He gallantly walks the dangerous path of glory, the scion of valiant ancestors who in boldness are like hungry wolves.

That composition is accompanied by singing and loud vocalization is also attested to by this interesting observation recorded by Musil.

> Our omnivorous poet Miz^cel aḫu Za^cêla was composing a poem in my honor. Since a roving versifier must earn his living by his art, he apparently thought I would pay him well for a poem I liked. It was interesting to watch his procedure. He would ponder for several minutes and then recite two verses twenty or thirty times, substituting for some of the expressions new and better ones—*azjan*, as he called them. Then he would bid Ṭâreš pay attention and remember these verses. After Ṭâreš had learned them, Miz^cel would be absorbed and silent again, and after a while would sing the first two verses and add the third to them. Having sung them to Ṭâreš innumerable times in his shrill voice, he would ask me to write them down while he composed the rest. (1927:236–237)

Singing and loud vocalization are not only signs of an emotional outburst; they also help the poet to measure the rhythm of his verses. It has already been mentioned that the verses of a poem must all be identical in the number of their long and short syllables and in the manner in which these syllables are concatenated. Syllabic scansion, however, is a scholarly procedure with which Nabaṭi poets are not acquainted. For Nabaṭi poets, "meter" translates into "rhythm," and "scansion" into "singing" or "chanting." The word *meter* (*baḥr* in literary Arabic) is unknown to Nabaṭi poets, except perhaps for the few literate poets among them. Instead, they use the two words *ṭarg* and *šēlih*, both of which refer to the way a verse is sung or chanted. The word *ṭarg* is related to *ṭirīg* (a beaten track) and it means beat or rhythm. The word *šēlih* comes from the verb *šāl* (to raise one's voice in singing). As will be discussed in a later chapter, the Nabaṭi poet views his meters musically, and determines whether or not their scansion is correct by singing them. The relation of singing to composition is indicated by the expression *y^caddil lḥūn*, which refers to the act of composition and which means "to harmonize some tunes" or "to straighten some rhythms." A poet may call his composition *miḥkam al-fann*, meaning that its verses are of a perfectly measured rhythm. Sometimes the rhythm of the poem is guided by loud pounding which beats rhythmically (*yidikk, yarjis*) against the poet's ribcage (*aḏ-ḏlūᶜ al-maġālīġ*).

In concluding this chapter, it is perhaps advisable to remind the reader that we cannot always impose a literal interpretation on everything the poets say about composition. The poet may very well mean it literally when he says that he stayed up all night composing his poem, or that he composed while running or climbing the ledge of a lofty cliff, or that he was inspired by a passing beauty—he may also simply be employing these stock motifs as part of the conventional prelude. Yet the evidence, internal as well as external, which we have examined in the preceding pages unequivocally demonstrates that in Nabaṭi poetry composition is a difficult labor and a slow process which is independent from, and prior to, transmission and performance.

VI

TRANSMISSION

Written Transmission

This distinction between oral and written modes of composition and transmission is blurred in Nabaṭi poetry, where the two modes coexist and overlap. Not only do some Nabaṭi poets know how to read and write, but the two processes of composition and transmission are two independent activities, one preceding the other, just as in a written literary tradition. Whether literate or illiterate, a Nabaṭi poet will polish his composition and review it several times, and may even seek the opinion of a trusted friend to whom he recites the finished work before delivering it to a public audience. With regard to transmission, the illiteracy of the poet does not rule out the transmission of his work in writing, nor does the poet's literacy preclude the transmission of his work orally.

As we shall see in more detail in a later chapter, mention of writing and writing implements constitutes a stock theme of Nabaṭi poetry which has been thoroughly assimilated into the conventional prelude. It is not uncommon even for an illiterate poet to open his poem by imploring a scribe to take down his verses, as in the following examples, the first by Zēd as-Salāmih al-Xwēr (al-Ḥātam 1968:I, 214) and the second by ʿAbdallah al-Wirʿ (Ibn Sayḥān 1965–1969:II, 58).

1 I can no longer restrain my passions, O scribe! Bring forth sheets of Syrian paper, white as a crane.
2 Bring forth a flask of ink and a reed stem whose end is split with the sharp edge of the blade.
3 O scribe, in straight lines arrange the verses I dictate to you while the door of my heart is wide open.

* * *

1 Help me, O friend; passions have unlocked the door of my heart; bring forth a flask of ink and Syrian paper
2 Along with a discerning and diligent scribe, a connoisseur who is skilled in writing and who fathoms the meaning of my beautiful verses.

A literate Nabaṭi poet would usually collect poems in a *dīwān* which he would inscribe in his own hand. Illiterate poets might also have some of their poems committed to writing in order that they might be sent to a distant relative, friend, patron, antagonist, or to whomever the poem might be addressed. Often, illiterate town amirs and tribal chiefs had their scribes write down their poems and the poems composed in their honor. Furthermore, there have always been some concerned individuals whose appreciation of Nabaṭi poetry has prompted them to seek it out from oral and written sources and to organize their collections into handwritten *dīwāns*.

ᶜAbdarriḥmān al-Brāhīm ar-Ribīᶜī, who resides in ᶜUnaizah, is an outstanding example of a devoted collector of Nabaṭi poetry. He has spent most of his ninety years assiduously collecting this poetry to augment the collection passed on to him by his father, himself an avid collector of Nabaṭi verse. Before he lost his sight a few years ago, ar-Ribīᶜī maintained a steady correspondence with Nabaṭi poets and transmitters of Nabaṭi poetry all over the Arabian Peninsula. He made his living by composing panegyric poems, selling copybooks of Nabaṭi poetry, and entertaining people by going to their homes in the evening to chant their favorite poems. Ar-Ribīᶜī is considered an authority on the authenticity and attribution of Nabaṭi poems, and disputes regarding these issues are usually referred to him.

Mḥammad al-Ḥamad al-ᶜMirī, who resides in Riyadh, is another ardent collector of Nabaṭi poetry. For decades, al-ᶜMirī has been energetically collecting texts of Nabaṭi poems, and he has his collection organized into separate *dīwāns*, one for each poet. In addition, he has in his possession old manuscripts and rare printed *dīwāns* which he has managed to procure from different sources throughout the years. Recently, he sold part of his collection to the library of the University of Riyadh—a welcome sign that academic circles in Saudi Arabia are beginning to realize the importance of this poetry.

I have seen many manuscripts of Nabaṭi poetry in ᶜUnaizah and in Riyadh. I was told by some people that such manuscripts abound in the towns of Najd, al-Ḥasā, Kuwait, Bahrain, Qatar, and Abu Dhabi. Some of these manuscripts have found their way to the Western world. Albert Socin (1900–1901:III, 9–27) mentions three manuscripts that were brought from Najd by Charles Huber, and Socin himself bought one manuscript in Sūq aš-Šyūx in southern Mesopotamia and saw in Ḥawrān, Syria, a written collection of the poems of Nimr ibn ᶜAdwān, the chief of the ᶜAdwān tribe. G. A. Wallin (1852:193) asserts that Nimr ibn ᶜAdwān was literate; therefore, it is likely that he wrote down his poems in his own hand. One of the three informants from whom Socin collected

A sample page from a handwritten *dīwān* of Nabaṭi poetry.

A poem by Mḥammad al-ʿAbdallah al-Gāḏī in his own handwriting.

the poetic texts for his *Diwan aus Centralarabien* carried a manuscript to refresh his memory.

The writing down of a composition does not necessarily confine it to the written page, nor does it prevent it from circulating orally. Many popular Nabaṭi poems originated in writing. For example, love lyrics by al-Hazzānī, Ibn Liʿbūn, and other literate poets are quite popular among the urban masses in Arabia. Two of the most popular poems in the town of ʿUnaizah are by the learned poet Mḥammad al-ʿAbdallah al-Gāḏī; one is about coffee preparation and the other, on death and the hereafter, he composed on his death bed.

Thus a Nabaṭi poem might originate as a written text and later become popular, circulating orally and becoming subject to the variations so common to the oral mode of transmission. Undoubtedly, such a poem will acquire many oral versions as time passes, but its original version is fixed in writing. The written original ensures the survival of the poem, and also serves to check the oral versions from diverging too widely from the original. If a poem is not written down during or immediately after composition, its precise original version may become lost, and the written versions that might be collected later from oral sources would most likely exhibit noticeable divergences (Socin 1900–1901:III, 5–7).

Oral Transmission: General and Specific

Before the spread of literacy in Arabia (which came about within the last few decades), the vast majority of Nabaṭi poets were illiterate, and the great bulk of Nabaṭi poetry was transmitted exclusively by oral means. While the poet is slowly composing his poem, he is at the same time commiting it to memory. When composition is finished, transmission begins. In Nabaṭi poetry we have to distinguish between two modes of transmission: the specific act of transmission from the poet to the particular individual to whom it is addressed, and the general process of transmission, which is the passage of the composition from mouth to mouth and its diffusion through space and time. I shall first discuss this general type of transmission.

The emphasis placed by Nabaṭi poets on vocalization and singing at the time of composition, which we discussed at the end of the previous chapter, underscores the orality of Nabaṭi poetry. It shows that Nabaṭi poets are predominantly oral poets who view poetry as spoken discourse, as a voice. For them, the transmission chain goes from mouth to ear, carried through the air or by the wind, not from hand to eye through the written page. The words of the poem must taste sweet on the tongues of reciters, so they will recite it more often; they must also sound pleasant to the ears of the listeners, so they will demand to hear the poem more often. To praise the beauty of his poem, the poet appeals to the audience's sense of taste and hearing. He praises the crisp rhythm and cadence of his measured rhymes and compares their pleasant sound to the cheerful ringing of pure silver coins in the hand of a man who is in extreme need. He compares the taste of his verses on the lips and tongues of reciters to the sweetness of honey and ripe dates, or to the milk of a camel which nips at the fragrant flowers and succulent shoots in lush desert pastures. A poet of distinction will boast that his poems are spread in all directions by desert travelers who sing them to dispel fatigue or to urge on their camel mounts, and by men who stay up all night by the fire reciting them again and again to fathom their meaning and enjoy their music. He will compare the rapid dispersal of his verses to the blowing of the wind, the flight of arrows, or the fleeing of frightened wild beasts. The verses of an oral poet must spread fast and wide if he is to achieve fame. The very survival of his poetry depends on its popularity, and the effectiveness of his verses, being mostly panegyric, boastful, and propagandistic, is measured by their diffusion.

In addition to the general transmission there is also the specific act of transmission of the poem to its intended recipient. It is not unusual for a Nabaṭi poet to address his poem to, or compose it in honor of, a particular person who may be separated from the poet by a great distance. How the poem is to be transmitted from its composer to its intended recipient is generally spelled out in the poem itself, and integrated into it as a part of its overall thematic structure. The poet may write down his poem and send it with a courier or a traveling party. In many cases, the poet may traverse the intervening distance to deliver the poem himself; or he may teach it to a deputy (*nidīb*) whom he entrusts to deliver the poem verbatim to the person for whom it is intended. This deputy is chosen with great care; he is described by the poet as an intelligent, alert, bold, and articulate man who traverses desert wastes on a noble camel mount. The deputy never closes his eyes—he might forget the poem if he fell asleep—and he continually urges on his mount by singing the verses of the poem, going over them again and again lest he forget any of them. After describing the deputy, his mount, and the desert road, the poet turns to the main topic of his composition by addressing the deputy thus: "And when you alight by so-and-so [i.e., the intended recipient of the poem], tell him that . . ." In the remaining verses, the poet spells out the poetic message and praises or vilifies the intended recipient, depending on the occasion and the circumstances. In other words, before revealing the message of his poem, the poet has shed considerable light on the process of its transmission.

When the deputy arrives at the place of the person for whom the poem is intended, he is given water, coffee, and food to allay his thirst and hunger. After this routine hospitality, his fatigue dispelled, the deputy is besieged with questions by the hosts and the assembled guests who are always curious to hear fresh news. At this point, after an appropriate introduction, the deputy begins to recite the poem to the attentive assembly, exactly as he learned it from the poet. The deputy will remain with the host for several days and will have many occasions to repeat the poem in the presence of the host, who may have to prepare a suitable poetic response in the same meter and rhyme to send back with the deputy.

We have already seen how poetic correspondence between desert chiefs for the purpose of delivering a threat or declaring war was transmitted in a formal manner. A deputation of well-mounted, gallant riders, whose mounts were of the same breed and exotic color, was dispatched with the poetic message. At other times, a poet addressed his composition not to a particular individual but to a whole group. An example is the poem entitled *al-xalūj,* which al-ʿŌnī composed to exhort the people of al-Qaṣīm to revolt against Ibn Rashīd. In such cases, the transmitter must be an eloquent orator and a gifted reciter so that he can drive home the poem's message and influence public opinion. He moves from hearth to hearth and from one assembly to another in order to spread the poem swiftly and extensively.

To illustrate how the manner of transmission is integrated into the poem as part of its thematic structure, here are two short poems by two bedouin poetesses. The first was composed by Mwēḏi al-Brāziyyih, from al-Birzān section of the Mṭēr tribe; it was sent by her to Abu Šwērbāt, the chief of al-Birzān, after his leg was broken in a battle between al-Birzān and al-ʿAmārāt tribe under the leadership of their chief, Ibn Haḏḏāl (Ibn Raddās n.d.–1976:I, 130–132).

1 Hail, rider traveling through gray mirages on a fawn camel not weakened by a rear rider:
2 She started cantering sprightly in the early morning; by the end of the day she began to shed her fat.
3 Beautiful are her saddle trappings and the small water bag newly made by the cobbler.
4 You [rider] will alight by the chief's tent, large as a black hill, dismount, and loose your camel to graze.
5 Before you are questioned, you will be offered a cup of coffee to refresh you, and a fat sheep will be slaughtered for you.
6 Say to the chief: How is your leg? O defender of the retreating horsemen when the battle rages,
7 As on the day when you and Ibn Haḏḏāl fought like eagles in the sky, while cowards scurried like rabbits to their burrows.
8 Would that your wound were inflicted upon worthless braggarts, so that you might arise and your pains go away.

The second poem was composed by Ḏićir, the daughter of al-ʿWājī, the Chief of the Wild Slēmān section of the ʿAnazah tribe. She sent it to her brother, Frēḥ, after she heard that he had abandoned the noble practice of raiding to live on a government pension. (This was in the second half of the nineteenth century, when the Ottoman government was paying subsidies to notable bedouin chiefs in an effort to pacify the nomads and curb their predatory activities.) (Ibid., I:199–201).

1 So soothing to my soul is the smooth riding on a fine camel; singing in the saddle relieves my mind.
2 Hail, riders on the swift coursing mounts, those graceful thoroughbreds with fancy saddles.

3 When you leave at early dawn, take with you my fervent verses.
4 Your stout mounts are not weakened by your distant journeying; they are spirited wild beasts which were startled by their own shadows.
5 Beautiful are the girth marks on their flanks; they rest only when they halt to drink from wells on the way.
6 Their hooves scarcely touch the rugged road; they run like ostriches frightened by the sight of hunters.
7 They will bring you to a noble man who welcomes hungry guests to lavish feasts.
8 Oh my brother, you are the spring season to weary riders whose mounts are jaded from long journeys; you give them sweet sustenance.
9 Your coffee pots are black as ravens; they are constantly boiling beside your blazing hearth.
10 What keeps you away, O brother, from the verdant pastures? Only base men live on subsidies.
11 Noble men live by the sword; your thunderous voice chasing enemy mares still rings sweet in my ears.

In addition to friendly poetic correspondence and poems of defiance, exhortation, and incitement, we must also consider eulogies. Among Nabaṭi poets, there are some professionals who make their livings or supplement their sources of livelihood by composing panegyric odes in honor of tribal chiefs, town amirs, or any wealthy patron willing to pay for their laudatory verses. A panegyrist may confine himself to one patron, or he may be an itinerant poet who wanders from camp to camp or from town to town in order to deliver his odes himself and receive the rewards for them. He journeys to the court of the amir or the tent of the chief and asks permission to deliver his poem. After permission is granted he declaims his verses in a loud voice or, if he has a pleasant voice, he may chant them. In the opening verses, the poet describes his jaded camel, the difficult journey, and the vast, waterless desert wastes that he had to traverse to come to the patron. He does this in order to arouse the sympathies of the patron and evoke his generosity. The poet concludes with a line or two in which he asks the patron for a gift.

To illustrate how an itinerant panegyrist delivers his poems and receives his rewards, I shall relate the following two anecdotes (the poems will be omitted) which I recorded as my grandfather related them to me. The first concerns Ibn Hḏēl, a farmer from the settlement of Ṣbēḥ who lived in the second half of the nineteenth century. One year, the camels he used to draw irrigation water from the well died from a camel sickness called *as-slāg*. As a result, his crops withered and died. This double loss drove Ibn Hḏēl into extreme poverty, and his creditors made life unpleasant for him. Since he was a poet of repute, he decided to try his luck at panegyrizing chiefs and princes in the hope of receiving generous rewards from them.

First, he went north to the tribal territory of al-ʿAmārāt to praise their chief, Ibn Haḏḏāl. Ṣbēḥ is separated from the territory of al-ʿAmārāt by a very great distance; therefore Ibn Hḏēl sought a man of the Ḥarb tribe to carry him to Ibn Haḏḏāl and to serve as his guide (*dilīlih*) and road companion (*xawiy*). Having reached the camp of Ibn Haḏḏāl, Ibn Hḏēl delivered his panegyric ode to the chief. After the poem was finished, Ibn Haḏḏāl took off a tattered vest he was wearing and tossed it to Ibn Hḏēl as his reward. Ibn Hḏēl was shocked by the uncharacteristic stinginess of this nomadic chief and said: "What can I do with a tattered vest full of lice? I can hardly carry the clothes I already have on! But see this man of Ḥarb whom I hired for ten riyals to bring me to you; give him his fee, and as for me I shall seek the bounty of another chief."

Ibn Hḏēl then went to Ḥāyil to deliver a panegyric ode to Muḥammad Ibn Rashīd, who rewarded him with a thoroughbred camel mount. On his way back to Ṣbēḥ, Ibn Hḏēl came across a camp of Ḥarb tribesmen, so he composed a panegyric ode in honor of their chief, Niga aš-Šṭēr. At the end of this poem Ibn Hḏēl praised ar-Ribāʿēn, the chiefly family of the ʿTēbih tribe who were the kin of the wife of Niga aš-Šṭēr (it is common for a poet praising a nomadic chief to praise also the family of the chief's wife; the implication is that the chief is a noble man who marries only into noble families, and that his offspring will be of noble blood on both sides). While Ibn Hḏēl was reciting his poem, the wife of Niga aš-Šṭēr was leaning against the pole separating the men's section of the tent from the women's, listening to his words, and she heard his praise of her family. After he finished his poem, Niga aš-Šṭēr told him: "The ʿIggar herd is couched over there; go and pick the camel you like." (The ʿIggar is a herd of black thoroughbred camels owned exclusively by the Ḥarb tribe which has never been seized by other tribes.) Upon hearing her husband's words, the wife shouted from the women's section of the tent: "Were the horsemen of the Bani Ṣaxar tribe to charge at the ʿIggar herd they would not be able to lead one camel away from its companions, so let the man take two camels." Thus Ibn Hḏēl received two camels. The poem he composed in honor of Niga aš-Šṭēr is so exquisite that when it was recited by a transmitter to Ibn Rashīd, he said: "Had he composed this poem in my honor, I would have made him rich for the rest of his life."

The second story, which deals with the encounter of Ṣāliḥ ibn ʿAwaḏ, a poet from al-Shinānah, with Ibn Saʿūd, was told to my grandfather by the poet himself. In the initial phases of his campaign against Ibn Rashīd in al-Qaṣīm, Ibn Saʿūd once camped in al-ʿĀžli, a plain near al-Shinānah;

Ibn ʿAwaḏ went to see him and deliver a poem he had composed in his honor, hoping to receive a camel mount as a reward. Ibn ʿAwaḏ greeted Ibn Saʿūd and said, "May your life be long, give me permission to recite to you a few words I composed in your honor." Ibn Saʿūd replied, "This is not the appropriate time for panegyrics. As you see, every three of my men share a mount, and we cannot spare any camels to reward you." Ibn ʿAwaḏ said, "But these few verses which I have brought with me are intended for you. I shall deliver them to you and depart in peace." Ibn ʿAwaḏ delivered his verses and Ibn Saʿūd promised him a camel.

Some time later, Ibn Saʿūd raided the encampment of Fayṣal al-Dawīsh, the paramount chief of Mṭēr, and won tremendous booty. On his way back from this raid he camped at al-Malḥa. Ibn ʿAwaḏ came to see him again with a second panegyric ode, at the end of which he reminded him of his earlier promise. After Ibn ʿAwaḏ had delivered his poem, Ibn Saʿūd said, "Our mounts are couched over there; go and choose one and bring it here and I shall have my men saddle it for you." Ibn ʿAwaḏ went and picked out the very mount which Ibn Saʿūd himself was riding. The guards tried to drive him away from it, but he said, "Ibn Saʿūd told me to choose the one I liked, and this is the one that struck my fancy." Ibn Saʿūd told his men, "Leave him alone. I told him to choose what he liked, and I cannot go back on my word." The camel was fitted with a new saddle, new saddlebags, new saddle cushions, and even a halter and a rattan cane for driving it.

Panegyric poems are not only composed by professional poets seeking material reward. When a desert chief performs a chivalrous act, he becomes the object of praise by the recipient of his magnanimous deed, though he may be his tribal enemy, and by the poets of his own tribe, who praise his deed as an honor to the tribe. A panegyric poem of this sort is usually transmitted by the poet himself, who journeys to the camp of the chief to pay his respects and give his poem as a sort of public declaration of appreciation and admiration for the chief. The chief's tent is always thronged with guests, including tribal heroes and notables as well as dignitaries and chiefs of other tribes. When the poet stands up and praises the chief in front of this large assembly of noble men, this is the most eloquent expression of gratitude. The chief will be respected the more by his tribal equals, the foreign visitors will carry the poem back with them to their tribes, and thus will the poem become popular and the chief famous.

The Role of Memory in Oral Transmission

Although a great deal of Nabaṭi poetry is composed and transmitted orally, the orality of this poetic tradition is distinctly different from that of the oral epics of Yugoslavia described by Albert Lord in *The Singer of Tales*. Each Nabaṭi poem has an original version by an original composer. For some time after it is composed, a poem will remain fresh in the poet's mind, and will circulate among his friends and associates. The poet will have many occasions to spread his poem and recite it in public and to his close friends. A newly born poem usually arouses public interest, and the poet's friends are always eager to learn his compositions from his own mouth. Musil wrote that among the nomads "A poem is but rarely written down. As a rule the poet's friends learn it by heart, and others learn from them" (1928:283). A popular poet will most likely have his entourage of admirers who memorize his poems and spread them in distant territories. In this way, a poem passes from mouth to mouth and spreads very quickly over a wide area. This is especially true with respect to the nomads, with their patterns of migration and constant movement.

A newly born poem goes through an active stage of transmission during which the poetic text rarely changes. Whether the reciter is the poet himself or someone else, recitation of the poem is never a recomposition but an attempt to reproduce a memorized original faithfully. It is important to keep this fact in mind—that both poets and transmitters have a conception that there is an existing and correct, original version of each poem; hence, the emphasis is on memorization of the poem word by word, rather than on recomposing it as is the case with the Yugoslav epics. The brevity of the Nabaṭi poem and the strict pattern of its rhyme and meter facilitate its memorization and, hence, its preservation and stabilization for an appreciable period of time. There is always a demand by the audience and an attempt on the part of the reciter to recall and reproduce the original word for word. When the reciter is caught or catches himself making a mistake, such as forgetting a verse or replacing an original word with a different one, he will always stand corrected. The original composer will not tolerate any tampering with his poem, and the audience, some of whom may already know the whole poem by heart, will challenge any gross departure from the original. The transmitter of the poem may be the poet himself or some other person, in which case he tells the audience who the original composer is. Attributing the poem to its original composer is an essential part of the transmission process, and the audience is always eager to know the name of the author of a new poem (see Musil 1928:283).

By observing closely the transmission process of Nabaṭi poetry, the unmistakable signs of rote memorization, such as pausing, hesitation, and attempt to recall, will immediately become apparent. It is common for a reciter to admit that he has forgotten this hemistich or that verse, or to say that the poem is long and he can remember only a few verses.

Even poets sometimes forget their own compositions (see Musil 1928:283–284). Because of such lapses of human memory, an orally transmitted poem is bound to become subject to various changes and may eventually be heard in various versions. The length of the poem as well as its composer, subject, importance, exquisiteness, and originality are all factors that affect the survival and stability of the poem. Poems of sufficient interest and exceptional beauty not only gain wide distribution and long life but often remain true to the original composition.

Nabaṭi poets are painfully aware that oral transmission can alter, even destroy, a beautiful poem. The poets are especially contemptuous of incompetent reciters. In one anonymous but very famous verse, a Nabaṭi poet declares that he keeps many beautiful verses jealously hidden in his breast undivulged to the public lest they be ruined by careless and ignorant reciters. A poet's concern for the correct recitation of his poems and his abhorrence of careless and incompetent reciters ruining his compositions is expressed in the following anecdote told about Rākān Ibn Falāḥ Ibn Hiṯlēn, the paramount chief of the al-ʿIjmān tribe. Rākān once heard one of his poems on the lips of a shepherd who mangled its verses and changed their order. This perturbed him so much that he gave this incompetent reciter a gift and asked him to pledge never to recite a poem unless he knew it well (al-Firdaws n.d.:185). On this occasion Rākān composed these lines:

1 When I make an exquisite ode, I do it as a gift for discerning men, to sing it and pass the time.
2 But then indiscriminate churls begin to meddle with it, shortsighted men who do not understand the true value of words.

A transmitter other than the poet himself may learn his version either directly from the poet or through a chain of transmitters. To give his version more credence, the reciter-transmitter will explain to the audience how and by whom the poem was passed on to him. Needless to say, there are transmitters who are more gifted than others and who have better memories. The qualifications and authority of some transmitters are publicly recognized. Disputes between qualified transmitters concerning the authenticity and wording of a particular poem are common. Musil writes:

> As we sat there together, the Prince recited many ditties and poems to us, which Ǧwâd and I jotted down. I was much interested in the manner in which he defended the originality of particular words and refused to concede that Ǧwâd's version might be better; for the latter also knew many poems and songs but frequently differed

with the Prince as to the position of the words in sentences and as to the phraseology.

"Even if that word does fit better there, still it does not belong there," the Prince would declare. "As I say it, thus I have learned it, and I do not wish that anything be changed." (1927:191–192)

A Poem by Swēlim al-ᶜAlī an-Nwēṣir as-Sahali: A Close Look at Transmission

Swēlim is an illiterate Nabaṭi poet who is counted among the best and most representative of contemporary Nabaṭi poets. Five of his poems are published in Ibn Sayḥān (1965–1969:II, 208–214). Among these is one of thirty-six verses which begins with the line *yā-xūy ṭāb al-kēf lih w-at-taᶜālīl//ṣadrih wisīᶜ w-la tijīh al-hmūmī.* The form and content of this poem testify to the richness and complexity of the Nabaṭi poem and demonstrate the close affinity of Nabaṭi poetry to ancient Arabian poetry. The topic of the poem is the departure of the lady with whom the poet is in love. It opens with two lines in which the poet compares his state of mind with that of his brother. The brother is in a good mood because the lady he loves is nearby and he can see her and send her messages. The poet, on the other hand, is distressed because his lady has departed with her tribe to a distant land that messengers cannot reach. The poet describes the tribal procession of his lady, which appears and disappears in the distance as it goes over the hills and through the valleys. He goes on to speak of love and its effect, and curses whoever might blame him for feeling the way he does. In the rest of the poem, the poet laments the departure of his lady, and describes his grief in two extended metaphors, one drawn from nomadic life and one from settled life.

The extended metaphor is a well-established compositional device in Arabic poetry which allows the poet to expand any of the themes in his poems through the suspension of the thematic development and the embedding of a short narrative or descriptive episode in the poem. This technique was employed frequently by the classical poets (see Gibb 1968:17), and it has been preserved and further developed in Nabaṭi poetry. The extended metaphor can be expanded and embellished in various ways. In some cases it forms only a small segment of the poem; but in other cases, as in this poem by Swēlim, it is elaborated on and makes up the major portion of the poem.

To illustrate the gravity of his situation, Swēlim first compares his grief to the grief of a noble and well-to-do nomad reduced to poverty and humiliation following the plundering of his camel herd by a raiding party of the al-ᶜIjmān tribe. The battle between the raiders and the nomad is described in detail; the nomad loses, not because he lacks courage, but because his horse is shot dead. The raid leaves him so destitute that he can no longer continue his honorable practice of entertaining guests; in the desert, failure to entertain guests is a shameful act that strips a man of his honor and plunges him into social disgrace that passes on to his children and his children's children.

This metaphor closes with a verse that serves to link it masterfully to the second extended metaphor, in which the poet compares his grief to that of a farmer who plants seed on his land and works hard to irrigate it, using two shifts of four strong camels to draw water all day long and a good part of the night. The farmer works hard and his expectations are high; but just before harvest time, his crop is totally destroyed by a hailstorm. Such a catastrophe would put an Arabian farmer at the mercy of the landlord who owned the land and shared the yield with the farmer, and the creditor who lent him money to hire help and to buy farm animals and seed. This extended metaphor closes with the farmer bewailing his fortune as he stands watching his crop being carried off by the current.

1 My brother, you are merry and joyful; your contented heart is not beset by grief.
2 You may rejoice, for you can see your love and send her messages; but woe to me, mine has gone to a distant land that messengers cannot reach.
3 Her people are striking camp; intent on moving, they rush around with fluttering sleeves
4 To load their luggage on sturdy pack-camels; some have already started to move, while some are still loading.
5 The loaded camels travel fast, going up and down the distant hills and slowly disappearing behind the ridges.
6 I watch them go from the lofty peak of a forlorn cliff.
7 I watch the ladies in their litters move west; she moves with them, the beautiful one.
8 I may never again behold her lovely eyes; I may never see her undulating figure again.
9 Woe to my heart should she stay away from me for long; I shall run around aimlessly all day long, every day.
10 Like a lonely camel lost from the herd on a dark night, the herd that was driven to distant water.
11 Love is calamity, it pains the heart and causes madness; were it not for shame, I would rend my garment and run naked.
12 May God inflict whosoever blames me with misfortune; O wretched blamer, may you be struck by misery and bad luck.
13 May you live in poverty and in the hereafter may you be cast into hellfire.

14 My grief over my departed lady is like the grieving of a noble man, the owner of a camel herd grazing in the lush pastures:

15 A herd of fat camels, some pregnant and some with calves; he guards them astride his noble horse.

16 The herd was spied by well-mounted raiders of the al-ʿIjmān tribe; the backs of their mounts are bald [from the saddles] and their sharp eyes are the size of lemons.

17 The raiders are fearless youths who have proven their valor many times before. They covet the herd and they are not to be blamed for seeking booty.

18 They charged the herd riding their swift horses, and were met by the owner of his fiery horse.

19 He gallops his horse to meet the raiders. He is a tenacious man, the progeny of noble ancestors.

20 He sees them drive off his herd but will not let them despoil the wealth that is rightfully his own.

21 He charges against them and his horse in enveloped by dust; the thick dust raised by the galloping horses and camels resembles the clouds.

22 He is concerned lest he be accused of cowardice, so he fights valiantly, dispelling any doubt about his courage.

23 [But] a sharpshooter aims and shoots at his horse, and it falls on its back, its shod hooves up in the air shining like stars.

24 He turns around, humbled, fleeing across the soft sands and rubbing his hands against each other, with the bitter taste of defeat filling his stomach.

25 After a life of glory and good fortune with plenty of coffee beans and cardamom and fat sheep to be slaughtered for guests,

26 Now he stays up the long nights, alone and silent, with his heart full of sadness.

27 This is my grief, the grief of the owner of a camel herd: the herd was broken up, the raiders having divided it amongst themselves.—

28 Or the grief of the farmer who employs four waterwheels. He starts to work at early dawn,

29 Irrigating four hundred *sāʿ* of pure red seeds of wheat with the help of strong camels,

30 Four camels with another four to relieve them, all muscular and robust, drawing water in large buckets.

31 When the wheat is fully grown and the grain in the ears is ripe, a dark cloud gathers and begins to rain hailstones as large as the heads of baby lambs.

32 The cloud rains gently on the desert pastures, but on parts of the settled country it rains large hailstones.

33 What is left standing of the wheat stalks is swept away by the current, the ears of the wheat floating with the debris like old rags.
34 The farmer is left wailing and sobbing; he has been deprived of the toil of his hands.
35 May Allah protect us from the evil of rainstorms and grant us only the benefits of rain, for He is beneficent.
36 Thus end the verses I composed for the sake of a lady, charming, virtuous, and no gossip she.

This poem first came to my attention in the fall of 1977 when a good friend of mine who works at the radio station in Riyadh and who had access to the station's archives taped several Nabaṭi poems on a one-hour cassette tape which he sent to me here in the United States. The poems on the tape were culled from taped segments of the popular radio program *Min al-Bādiyah*, which were stored in the archives of the radio station. Among the recorded poems was this one by Swēlim, which he had recorded in his own voice. He delivers from memory this poem of thirty-six verses, plus four verses repeated for dramatic effect, in three minutes and twenty seconds; each verse consists of twenty-four syllables (six short and eighteen long), nearly five syllables per second. In this recorded version Swēlim gives a superb performance. The delivery is effective and dramatic. It gives power to the words and life to the images. The smooth thematic progression and compositional development are accentuated by subtle changes in intonation and voice quality.

While I was doing field work in Saudi Arabia in the fall of 1978, I tried to get in touch with Swēlim but was unable to do so. However, Muḥammad Abū Salīm was generous enough to allow me to tape from his private archives six poems by Swēlim in his own voice, including the one under discussion. These poems had been recorded by Abū Salīm to be broadcast on his popular radio program, *Alwān Shaᶜbīyah* which, like *Min al-Bādiyah*, is broadcast from the National Radio station in Riyadh. In other words, this poem by Swēlim exists in at least one written version, published in Ibn Sayḥān, and two oral versions, one recorded for *Min al-Bādiyah* and one for *Alwān Shaᶜbīyah*. The three versions are nearly identical in content, but the two oral versions are different in performance, even though both are recorded by the poet himself. In the version I recorded from Abū Salīm, the performance is not very inspiring. There is an obvious attempt to recall. There is also one clear instance of hesitation and one case of error where the poet has to repeat the hemistich and correct himself. The delivery on the second recording was slow and took nearly four minutes, with five instances of verse repetition.

In terms of content, the two oral versions are identical, word for word, and the written version contains one instance of obvious scribal error and two instances where a word common to the two oral versions is replaced by a different word which gives the same meaning and has the same syllabic structure. Despite my repeated inquiries, I was unable to determine the exact dates on which the oral versions were recorded; but Abū Salīm assured me that the version recorded for *Min al-Bādiyah* was earlier than the one he had recorded for his own program, *Alwān Shaʿbīyah*. Thus we have three independent instances of transmission or, actually, three versions of a fairly long poem separated from each other by long or short lapses of time; yet the three versions are virtually identical. In other words, each is a faithful reproduction of an original which the poet had composed and memorized.

The Profile and Repertory of a Transmitter: A Case Study

The following is a case study of a transmitter whom I know intimately: my grandfather, Mḥammad as-Slēmān as-Ṣwayyān. My purpose is to show how an illiterate transmitter acquires his repertory of poems and narratives throughout his lifetime. This, I hope, will provide a clearer perspective on the process of oral transmission in Nabaṭi poetry.

My grandfather was born at the close of the last century in al-Shinānah, a flourishing agricultural hamlet near al-Rass in the district of Qaṣīm in central Arabia. He was born into an extended family consisting of "forty souls eating from the same pot," as he puts it. They lived on a big farm called Fōzih with palm trees and fruit trees of all kinds. It should be recalled that at the beginning of this century ʿAbdalʿazīz Ibn Saʿūd had left Kuwait to restore the Saudi rule over Arabia. After recapturing Riyadh and occupying the southern districts, Ibn Saʿūd turned northward and by the end of 1904 had wrested the whole district of Qaṣīm from the control of Ibn Rashīd. After his defeat at the battle of al-Bukairiyah by Ibn Saʿūd and his Qaṣīmī allies, Ibn Rashīd marched against al-Shinānah where he camped for nearly a month. In the struggle between Ibn Rashīd and Ibn Saʿūd over the suzerainty of Qaṣīm, the people of al-Shinānah leaned toward the latter, and one of their poets by the name of Ṣālḥ an-Nāṣr al-Ballāʿ composed a poem cursing Ibn Rashīd and lauding the victories of Ibn Saʿūd. Therefore, Ibn Rashīd was exceptionally cruel in punishing the people of al-Shinānah. His guns reduced the mud houses of the town to rubble and he killed several important men, including two uncles of my grandfather and Nāṣr al-Ballāʿ, killed in place of his son Ṣālḥ, the aforementioned poet, who had fled al-Shinānah before the arrival of Ibn Rashīd. Ibn Rashīd also confiscated all the camels, sheep, and cows of al-Shinānah, distributing them among his troops to slaughter for meat. His troops let loose their horses and camel mounts to graze on the farm crops and, after looting the fruits of the palm gardens, Ibn Rashīd had all the palm trees cut down. In the words of my grandfather, "Not a single frond was left standing."

Like all significant events in the history of Arabia, what Ibn Rashīd did to al-Shinānah and its citizens was woven into a long narrative, usually referred to as *gaṭᶜat aš-šnānih*, "the cutting of [the palm trees of] al-Shinānah." These atrocities were witnessed by my grandfather, who was a young boy at the time, and they left a lasting impression upon him. From what he had seen with his own eyes and from what he heard later from older men and relatives, he created his own version of the narrative, which describes the events that took place with such eloquence, emotion, and historical accuracy that it has always held the attention of his listeners throughout its telling. The narrative is interspersed with poems relating to the various incidents of this saga, such as the poem by Ṣālḥ an-Nāṣr al-Ballāᶜ mentioned above, and the poem composed by Saᶜad Abu Ḥjāb lamenting the destruction of al-Shinānah and expressing satisfaction at the final defeat of Ibn Rashīd by Ibn Saᶜūd. Appended to the story of the "cutting of al-Shinānah" is a constellation of episodes from the wars between Ibn Saᶜūd and the house of Āl Rashīd. My grandfather relates these episodes as background for five poems he knows: three by Xwēlid Ibn Sābil of al-Bukairiyah and two by Ṣāliḥ Ibn ᶜAwaḍ of al-Shinānah. These are panegyrics praising Ibn Saᶜūd and extolling his victories against his foes such as Ibn Rashīd and Fayṣal al-Dawīsh, the paramount chief of the Mṭēr tribe.

Most of my grandfather's narrative repertory consists of factual accounts of things that happened to him personally or that he witnessed with his own eyes, like the story of the cutting down of the palm trees of al-Shinānah. After that catastrophe, the people of al-Shinānah were dispersed in all directions. My grandfather, his father, his brother, and other men from the aṣ-Ṣwayyān family went to al-Madinah on foot, a distance of over five hundred miles. After working on the Hijaz railroad for a few months, he enlisted in the Ottoman army for four years. Then he left the Ottoman army to enlist in the army of Sharīf Ḥusayn of Hijaz, where he served for another four years. All this time, until the outbreak of World War I, he was stationed in or near al-Madinah. After Britain gave Sharīf Ḥusayn promises of Arab independence, he declared the Arab Revolt against Turkey and sent his Arab Army to Palestine and Syria to wrest those regions from Turkish control. The Qaṣīmi contingent (usually called ᶜGēl or ᶜGēlāt) of the Sharifian army, to which my grandfather belonged, was stationed at al-Shōbak just south of the Dead Sea in the push against the Ottoman troops when he decided to desert from the army, and go back home to al-Shinānah. How he made his escape through rugged mountains, desert wastes, Sharifian military posts, and the territories of hostile tribes—not to mention the fact that he was a renegade soldier crossing Sharifian territory into the territory of Ibn Saᶜūd, the arch enemy of Sharīf Ḥusayn—makes up a long adventure story which my grandfather is always proud to tell with zestful eloquence.

The years my grandfather spent in the military were the most carefree in his life and, in his words, "the pay was good." During these years he had plenty of leisure time to sit and listen to older men and poets from Qaṣīm who were his comrades in arms, first with the Ottoman and then with the Sharifian army, narrate anecdotes and recite poems dealing with the affairs of Najd in general and Qaṣīm in particular. During this period he accumulated a large repertory of poems and narratives, and he polished his natural gift for narration and poetic recitation and developed it into a remarkable skill. He is an excellent raconteur with an elegant style, and possesses an exceptional ability to enliven his delivery with vivid metaphors, grand gestures, and dramatic tones. The exotic people, novel customs, and curious incidents he encountered in the lands of Hijaz and Palestine make up a sizable collection of short episodes, some of which are quite hilarious and delightful.

After leaving the military service, my grandfather became a farmer, until he retired about twenty years ago. First he was a farmer in al-Badāyiᶜ, about fifteen miles east of al-Shinānah, his birthplace; later he moved permanently to ᶜUnaizah, about ten miles farther east. Unlike military service, farming was extremely hard work. The only respite farmers in Arabia have is a month or two in the summer, after the wheat harvest. My grandfather is fond of reminiscing about how during that part of the year he and his friends, some of whom were poets of repute, would stay up every night until early dawn talking and reciting poetry. They would also invite poets from neighboring settlements to share with them their compositions. Summer, it should be recalled, is also the time when the nomads congregate around agricultural settlements. My grandfather and his friends would go occasionally to the nomads' camp to enjoy their company and to participate in *al-mzayyan* (also called *al-mṣannaᶜ*), which is a night activity involving singing and poetic competition. The villagers with their poets form one line and the nomads with their poets form another. The two lines face each other standing up and two poets, one from each side, engage in poetic composition. Their verses are sung by the two lines, who accompany their singing with hand clapping. At the same time, a bedouin beauty is chosen to be *ḥāšī* (also called *jilūbih*). The *ḥāšī* unplaits her hair and dances between the lines holding a rattan cane in her hand. Her beauty and graceful steps inspire the poets and fill the hearts of the singers with enthusiasm.

From the time he moved to ᶜUnaizah, my grandfather stopped making any significant additions to his store of poems and narratives. All the poems and narratives he knows he acquired while a young boy at al-Shinānah, a soldier in al-Madinah, and a farmer in al-Badāyiᶜ. As has been mentioned already, most of the narratives are direct reports and firsthand accounts of significant events and unusual incidents which he witnessed or that happened to him personally. But of course his repertory includes other narratives told to him by other narrators, which he thought of sufficient interest to be passed on. The same is true of the poems: some he received directly from their composers, and others he learned through other transmitters. His repertory of poems may not be the most prodigious, but he does know a great deal of poetry. He is a true *rāwī* (transmitter) in the sense that he, and only he, knows the compositions of some poets, who are his relatives and close friends, along with some interesting details about the poets' lives. I asked him repeatedly how he came to know so many poems. His answer was consistently that in his youth his memory was so good that whenever he heard a poem he liked recited a few times it became imprinted in his mind.

Among the poets that my grandfather came into direct contact with were Ṣāliḥ Ibn ᶜAwaḏ and his twin brother, Ḥamad, and Ṣālḥ an-Nāṣr al-Ballāᶜ and Saᶜad Abu Ḥjāb. These four poets were all from al-Shinānah and, like my grandfather, served in the Sharifian and Ottoman armies. While a farmer in al-Badāyiᶜ, my grandfather became a close friend of ᶜĀyid ad-Dimnih. Today, the poetry of ᶜĀyid, I suspect, survives only on the lips of my grandfather and in my notebook. Also while in al-Badāyiᶜ, my grandfather made the acquaintance of ᶜAbdallah Ibn Ḥṣēṣ, the blind poet of ᶜUnaizah, and Xwēlid Ibn Sābil, the blind poet of al-Bukairiyah. Every summer after the wheat harvest, Xwēlid Ibn Sābil would travel from al-Bukairiyah to al-Badāyiᶜ to receive gifts of wheat from his farmer friends there. During his stay in al-Badāyiᶜ, he would spend most of his evenings with my grandfather.

The poems that my grandfather received directly from their composers include: (1) a love poem of thirteen lines by his maternal grandfather, Mḥammad al-Ḥishḥūs, (2) a poem of nine lines by his cousin Mḥammad al-Brāhīm as-Ṣwayyān about his unsuccessful marriage to a bedouin lass called Jōza, (3) a poem of eight lines by another relative by the name of Abu Marwih lamenting the sudden death of his only two sons, (4) a love poem of twelve lines by ᶜĀyid ad-Dimnih, (5) another poem of eight lines by ᶜĀyid, (6) a third poem of nine lines by ᶜĀyid about a humorous incident, (7) a poem of eighteen lines by Xwēlid ibn Sābil recounting the victories of Ibn Saᶜūd against Ibn Rashīd, (8) another poem of seven lines by Xwēlid praising the people of al-Khabra for their courageous stand against Ibn Rashīd, (9) a third poem of three lines by Xwēlid defending the people of al-Bukairiyah who were accused by the people of ᶜUnaizah of siding with Ibn Rashīd, (10) a poem of four lines by Ṣālḥ an-Nāṣr al-Ballāᶜ cursing Ibn Rashīd and praising Ibn Saᶜūd, (11) a love poem of four lines also by Ṣālḥ al-Ballāᶜ, (12) a third poem of nine lines by Ṣālḥ al-Ballāᶜ about a violent incident between some men of al-Shinānah and some men from Shammar tribe, (13) a poem of nine lines by Ṣāliḥ Ibn ᶜAwaḍ praising Ibn Saᶜūd, (14) a poem of six lines by ᶜAbdallah Ibn Ḥṣēṣ about his unsuccessful marriage to Hēlih.

Many of the poems my grandfather knows are not published anywhere, nor have I ever heard them on the lips of other transmitters. These include the poems mentioned above as well as the following poems: two love poems by Mašᶜān al-Htēmi (one of twelve and the other of ten lines); three love poems by Nahār al-Mūržī (of eight, six, and four lines); a love poem of eight lines by an anonymous poet; a love poem of eleven lines by Abu Ršēd; a poem of nine lines composed by Ibn ᶜAskar and addressed to Ibn Sbayyil; and *alfīyah* poem of fifty-six lines by Ibn Mānīᶜ; a poem of six lines composed by Ibn Saᶜūd and addressed to Ibn Rashīd in the form of a threat; a poem of nine lines by an ancient poet describing the encounter of his tribe with the tribe of Bani Ṣaxar; three panegyrics by Ibn Hḏēl of Ṣbēḥ (one of eleven lines in which he praises Ibn Haḏḏāl, the paramount chief of al-ᶜAmārāt tribe, one of nine lines in which he praises Muḥammad Ibn Rashīd, and the third of five lines in which he praises Niga aš-Šṭēr of the Ḥarb tribe).

My grandfather also knows other poems and parts of poems which appear in various printed anthologies, though with occasional divergences between his versions and the printed ones. Included in this category are parts of five love poems by the famous poet ᶜAbdallah Ibn Sbayyil which are published in his *Dīwān* (al-Faraj 1952:I, 205–211, 220–223, 223–225, 253–255, 259–260) and a love poem by Fhēd al-Mijmāj which appears in Ibn Raddās (A.H. 1398:32) and in al-ᶜUtaybi (A.H.1390:56). Five of the poems that my grandfather knows appear in a two-volume published anthology dedicated to the poets from the town of al-Rass and its neighboring settlements, such as al-Shinānah, al-Dulaimiyah, and al-Nabhaniyah (al-Rashīd 1965–1972). The five poems are (1) a love poem by Srūr al-Aṭraš (I:33), (2) a love poem by Mbārak al-Badri (I:36), (3) another love poem by al-Badri (I:38), (4) a love poem by Ḥamad Ibn ᶜAmmār (I:87–89); and (5) a poem by Ḥamad Ibn ᶜAwaḍ in praise of Ibn Saᶜūd (II:27–28).

According to the compiler of this anthology, the poems were collected from oral sources (I:10). Therefore, the published versions of the five poems just mentioned are actually oral versions recorded on paper. In contrast, the versions I collected from my grandfather are other oral versions which I have recorded on tape. It is instructive to compare the printed versions with the taped ones and examine their divergences. In the first poem, there is a slight divergence in wording, and the taped version is five lines longer than the printed one, which consists of only seven lines. With regard to the second poem, there are divergences in the number of lines, wording, and even attribution. The printed version is attributed to al-Badri, but the taped version is attributed to a poet by the name of Šimahlīl. The printed version consists of twelve lines whereas the taped version consists of only eight, but one of these eight lines does not appear in the written version. The third poem is short; therefore the divergence between the two versions is not as great as in the case of the other poems. There is no difference in wording; but although each version consists of four lines, the third line in the taped version does not appear in the printed version, and the fourth line in the printed version does not appear in the taped version. The fourth poem is much longer in print, seventeen lines as opposed to ten lines on tape. There is also a slight difference in wording and in the arrangement of lines, and the taped version is misattributed to Ibn Sbayyil. The fifth poem attributed to Ḥamad Ibn ʿAwaḏ in print is attributed to his twin brother, Ṣāliḥ, on the tape; the printed version consists of only six lines whereas the taped version consists of eight lines, but my grandfather forgot the second hemistichs in lines four and eight.

These observations illustrate the extent and nature of divergences which an orally transmitted poem undergoes in its various versions. These divergences include misattribution, commutation of lines, omission of lines, and replacement of a word or phrase with another one of the same meaning and syllabic structure. Here, however, I must reiterate a point made earlier, namely, that such changes are inevitable in oral transmission. I must also add that the divergences I have just discussed are not so radical when we consider the fact that some of the poets, like Srūr al-Aṭraš, have been dead for nearly two centuries. Furthermore, such divergences may demonstrate the fallibility of human memory, but they do not negate its role in the transmission of Nabaṭi poetry. I taped from my grandfather most of the poems he knows, and the taping was done on various occasions and in different performance contexts at intervals of two and three years. On several occasions he complained to me that he no longer had a chance to exercise his recitation skills because people today are not interested in his type of poetry. Yet, despite this lack of practice and despite the length of time intervening between the various recordings I made, and regardless of the performance context, the texts of the poems he recited never changed—not even with respect to a single word. This clearly shows that although a Nabaṭi poem may in fact exist in several versions, each transmitter will have his own version, which he regards as the correct one, and which is fixed and seldom changes.

VII

PERFORMANCE

Written transmission may be the most certain method to ensure the survival of a poem in its original form for an indefinite period of time, but in other respects it is deficient in comparison to oral transmission. There is a crucial difference between a static written text and the dynamic recitation of a Nabaṭi poem. To the uninitiated, a Nabaṭi poem on the written or printed page is baffling, especially since the Arabic script, though quite adequate for writing literary Arabic, is not quite suitable for writing vernacular Arabic. A person who is not familiar with Nabaṭi poetry is likely to read the written text of a Nabaṭi poem as if it were written in literary—not vernacular—Arabic. As a result of this misreading, and consequent mispronunciation, the verses of the poem become unintelligible and unmetrical. The reader's distress is compounded by the fact that published anthologies rarely provide the exegetical remarks and background information necessary to comprehend this poetry, and many of these anthologies are produced carelessly with abundant typographical errors. In the oral process, however, where every instance of transmission is a living performance governed by a dynamic interaction between the reciter and the audience, the salient features of the poem—rhythm, diction, and rhetorical eloquence—are maintained and preserved.

The Performance Context

Before discussing the performance context of Nabaṭi poetry, it is pertinent to stress once more its important social function and the serious attitude with which it is viewed by the native audience. Just as the form and content of Nabaṭi poetry are governed by culturally circumscribed aesthetic conventions, the poetry itself exercises unrivaled influence on the culture and society of Arabia; this is especially true of premodern times. People quote Nabaṭi verses and compose them on all occasions, and they listen to poetry not merely to be entertained but, more importantly, to be edified and uplifted. Indeed, the popular attitude to poetry in Arabia is very serious. In addition to the names *šiʿir, giṣīd,* and *gāf,* poetic verses are also called *amṯāl* or *miṯāyil* (exempla, guiding principles, parables, allegories). Poetry is held in high esteem, and it is said to provide (the best guide for discerning men) *al-amṯāl l-ar-rjāl ad-ḏhana xyār ad-dalāyil,* since it provides them with a system of values and a model for ideal conduct. Poetry is also called the "driving stick" of men (*al-giṣīd mišāᶜīb ar-rjāl*), because it spurs them to act with manliness in defense of their tribal honor and communal interests.

We have already observed in previous chapters how Nabaṭi poetry played an active role in the political affairs of premodern Arabia. On the whole, and especially among the nomads, poetry was viewed as a vehicle for social and political action over and above being a source of amusement, and its composition and transmission were a public responsibility and obligation. In the desert, every tribesman considered it his duty to memorize and propagate verses that glorified his tribe and recounted the deeds of its heroes. Of course, there were active and passive bearers of poetry; but the poetic tradition was considered a public record and a public trust, which each generation passed on to the next to nurture and cherish. It contained historical and genealogical information recorded in rich poetic language that gave it meaning and permanence and made its recitation an eagerly anticipated, emotionally charged experience.

There is no special time or setting for reciting Nabaṭi poetry. Whenever men gather together, they are likely to engage in such activity. When a poet begins to recite, silence reigns over the assembly and strict attention is paid to the message contained in the poem. Wilfred Thesiger, who lived for some time with the desert Arabs, wrote that "they find it an almost unendurable hardship to keep silent. Yet that evening when someone started to recite poetry, a hush fell over the camp, broken only by the sound of pounding as they crushed *saf* leaves which they had gathered in the wadi, before plaiting the fibre into rope. One after the other they gathered round, silent except when they repeated the final line of each verse" (1959:72).

Before he begins to recite, the poet clears his throat as a signal to the audience to lend him their ears. Then he proceeds to declaim his poem in a loud, full voice, repeating the choicest lines and pausing slightly after some of the lines to give the audience time to savor his words and ponder their meaning. All the verses in one poem end with the same rhyming syllable. To express their appreciation, members of the audience pick up this final rhyming syllable in unison with the poet: ". . . the kassād recites, and it is a pleasant adulation of the friendly audience to take up his last words in every couplet" (Doughty 1921:I, 306). After a verse of particularly appealing content, the audience expresses its approval by shouting "*hū ṣāžž*" ("That is the truth!"). To interfere with the poet or interrupt his recitation is a serious offense. The famous poet Mḥammad al-ᶜŌnī would stop reciting and leave an assembly if he noticed the slightest sign of lack of interest among his listeners (Ibn Khamīs 1958:13).

A Nabaṭi poem that is composed to celebrate a specific event does not give a detailed account of that event, but only makes allusions and cryptic references to it. To illuminate these allusions and put the poem in its proper social and historical context, the reciter provides his listeners with a prose narrative (*sālfih*) outlining the occasion (*mnāsibih*) on which the poem was composed or explaining the motives for its composition. When the poet recites his poem for the first time, the introductory narrative may not be necessary, because the listeners themselves are likely to be well informed about, or active participants in, the events with which the poem deals—the poem may even be addressed to them or to one of them. The more remote the poem becomes in space and time, the more urgent becomes the need for commentary and background information, which is spun into a narrative of flexible structure.

Generally speaking, poetic recitation alternates with prose narration dealing with the lives of various poets and the events celebrated in their poetry. The wording of the poetry is fixed, but the prose narrative is discursive and loosely structured. It usually consists of several episodes which the poet spins together as he goes along with no predetermined order. There is no established sequence in which the episodes must follow one another; even chronological sequence may not be observed. Once the narration begins, it can be developed in any of several directions. An individual narrator may have his own loosely arranged version of a narrative episode, but no two narrators will have identical versions; even a version by the same narrator will exhibit verbal and stylistic divergences from one performance to the next. The listeners contribute to the shaping of the narrative and to some extent direct its development by asking for missing details and by injecting comments and expressions of approval or disapproval. Audience participation in developing the narrative contributes further to the divergence of one version from another. This divergence is made even more pronounced when the narrators are partisans of different characters in the narrative.

The narrative associated with a particular poem is called its *sālfih* (pl. *sawālif*). The noun *sālfih* is dereived from the verb *salaf*, which means to have happened in the past, because the *sālfih* deals with historical events and biographical or social circumstances connected with the immediate or remote past. The telling of *sawālif* and the recitation of poetry are termed the "discourse of real men" (*kalām ar-rjāl*) because only discerning men can grasp their deeper significance, and because the poems deal with the actions of noble men and heroes, which are mainly the domain of adult males, just as folktales (*sibāḥīn*) are the domain of women and children. Although there are accomplished poetesses, and poets whose poetic genius flowers at an early age, the women and children are generally passive but eager and attentive audience whose minds are molded by the poems and narratives recited by men.

The most favored time for telling *sawālif* and reciting poetry is at night, when the men gather around the hearth in the tent of a gallant nomad or in the coffee-chamber of a noble citizen. Behind the hearth sits the host, who is continually busy with the fire and the preparation of coffee, and is usually assisted by another person who sits to his left to hand him wood for the fire, and pound the cardamom and roasted coffee beans for him. A young man, usually the son of the host, stands up with the coffee pot in his left hand and small china cups in his right, pouring coffee for the assembled guests. The guests sit on the floor forming two lines facing each other. Important guests sit closest to the hearth—the more important, the closer. The guest of honor sits right next to the host on his right. Uninvited guests and men of lower rank sit at the end, by the door, near the outside, where guests remove and leave their shoes. (To indicate the low status of a man, one says, "So-and-so sits near the shoes.") Such guests rarely participate in the conversation, and they are the last to be served coffee. The conversation is concentrated around the fire-hearth. The flickering blaze, the smell of roasted coffee beans and crushed cardamom, the rhythmic pounding of the mortar, the rattling of the china cups, and the affability of the host infuse the atmosphere with a spirit of congeniality and comradeship. In a nomadic tent, this assembly of men is separated from the women by only a thin curtain. The wife or daughter of an important chief will feel confident enough to shout her comments and remarks from behind the curtain. The conversation round the coffee-hearth may begin in a desultory fashion, with short moments of silence alternating with tumultuous moments when almost everyone is talking at the same time. New guests may arrive, occasioning the rising of the assembly to greet newcomers and rearrange the seating, whereby each newcomer is given a seat according to his rank.

At the beginning of the evening the conversation is restricted to a discussion of mundane and frivolous matters and to the exchange of greetings and pleasantries with newcomers. But as the evening goes on, the conversation becomes more structured and elevated. The transition may be gradual, or it may be abrupt. After a few rounds of coffee, and after all the important men have been introduced to one another and have chatted for a while, there is a sudden lull in the conversation, followed by a moment of silence. Then, the host or one of the senior guests near the hearth asks a question such as: "By the way, which of you, honored men of this assembly, knows the poem composed by so-and-so on such-and-such occasion?" This prompts one of the guests to recite the poem and the occasion which led to its composition. This recitation may be followed by a discussion of the historical accuracy and artistic merit of the poem. If another poet has composed a response to the first poem, then that poetic response may also be recited by whoever knows it. From there, the discussion may drift to which tribe has the best poets, or who is the poet most esteemed by the people and whose verses are the most appealing. Such questions can split the assembly into different factions which engage in a lively discussion interspersed with choice poetic examples. The conversation may focus on the artistry and beauty of poetry, or it may focus on poetry as the catalyst of noble actions. If a poet happens to be in the group, he will most likely contribute the most to the conversation, reciting not only his own poetry but also that of others. As it grows later in the evening, two or three men dominate the conversation, bouncing words between them like balls and passing the conversation gently from one to another in an orchestrated manner. Only an unpolished churl would talk when it is not his turn, or talk about irrelevant and trivial matters, thus tossing the conversational ball (*yašgil*) out of the field.

People compose and recite poetry all year round, but in the summer there is always an extraordinary flurry of poetic activity. In the rainy season, the farmers are busy plowing their fields and sowing their seed, while the nomads split up and disperse in the desert. Hence there are very few social activities. Summer, however, is the time of reunion when the various lineages congregate at their tribal wells and when the nomads and settlers come together to renew their social and economic relationships. Communication between these groups becomes very intense, and visitation very frequent. The nomads go to visit their friends in the settlements, and settled men go to visit the bedouin camps. Settled poets and nomads arrange for meetings to exchange newly composed and newly acquired poems, and to engage in friendly poetic competitions. Town amirs and bedouin chiefs call upon each other to drink coffee and talk about tribal raids and their own adventures. They recite the poems that they or some other poets may have composed on these occasions. For these men, the composition and recitation of poetry and the spinning of narratives are ways to review and synthesize the events of the past and to conceive future plans. Poetic correspondence between tribal poets and tribal chiefs increases in the summer when each tribe camps for ninety days at one particular spot. By the end of the summer, the nomads break up their camps to go back into the desert. The settled poets lament the departure of the nomads, and the nomadic tribes lament the dispersal of the tribe and the separation of friends and lovers.

The performance context which I have just described is disappearing rapidly. It has already been noted in an earlier chapter that the recent socioeconomic and political changes in Arabia have severely curtailed the social role of Nabaṭi poetry and constrained its function. Interest in Nabaṭi poetry is on the wane, and the number of active bearers of the tradition is becoming ever smaller. Furthermore, radio and television, along with phonographic and tape recording machines, which have reached even the bedouin tents in the desert, have usurped or radically altered the traditional public roles of composers and reciters of Nabaṭi poetry. But in some measure these modern innovations are also contributing to the proper preservation of Nabaṭi poetry. The utility of the tape recorder in this respect cannot be overemphasized. A recorded tape of Nabaṭi poetry is in many ways superior to a printed anthology (inasmuch as oral transmission is superior to written transmission), especially if the poetry is recorded by the poet himself or by a qualified and competent transmitter. In a sense, such a recorded tape is a slice of reality. On it one can capture a fleeting instance of a living performance to enjoy, play over and over again, and reflect upon at leisure. Even more interesting is the videotape, on which one can capture the kinetic and visual, as well as the aural, aspects of the performance. The University of Riyadh in Saudi Arabia, realizing the importance of Nabaṭi poetry and the potentials of the videotape, has for the last two years been sponsoring an annual three-day festival of poetry, with all aspects of the festival recorded on videotape and deposited in the university archives.

The traditional setting for poetic recitation and performance has in recent years gradually become replaced by special programs on Nabaṭi poetry which are broadcast on a weekly basis from the radio and television stations in Saudi Arabia, Kuwait, and Qatar. Monitoring of these programs is a must for anyone interested in Nabaṭi poetry. The programs are very popular among certain segments of the population, and there is usually a close rapport between the program and those who tune in to it. Listeners frequently write the host of the program requesting to hear a certain poet or a certain poem, or asking about the correct version or correct attribution of a particular poem. Some even write to dispute or correct the wording, the attribution, or the occasion of a poem that they heard recited on a previous program. Usually, the hosts of these programs are illiterate or semi-illiterate, with no training whatsoever in public broadcasting, but with those unique abilities which are essential for the success of the program. They are authorities on Nabaṭi poetry who have wide knowledge about and connections with Nabaṭi poets, and some are accomplished poets in their own right.

Production of the above-mentioned programs is quite simple. On a particular day of the week at a certain time, poets and transmitters come to a designated studio in the radio or television station to be recorded for a small compensation (the radio program *Min al-Bādiyah* broadcast from Riyadh pays 100 Saudi riyals for an original composition and 50 riyals to a transmitter reciting the composition of someone else). After recording, the tape is edited for broadcasting. To add a touch of spontaneity to these programs, the host will usually chitchat with the contributors, and the contributors are also allowed to talk with one another informally, as they would under normal circumstances. The setting of one program, *Maḏārib al-Bādiyah,* which is broadcast by the television station in Jidda, is a large tent completely furnished with rugs and pillows and a fire-hearth with all the necessary utensils for making coffee and tea. The host of the program sits by the hearth, while the contributors sit on the floor and line themselves up as they would in a coffee-chamber or a bedouin tent. The program is interspersed with the showing of various scenes from the desert, such as camel herds and droves of sheep grazing in lush desert pastures, or nomads drawing water from deep wells for their thirsty animals. Despite the formal and somewhat artificial setting of these programs, there are occasions when the recording session turns into a truly authentic, living performance, as is illustrated by the following selection which I recorded in the fall of 1978 from the archives of the radio station in Riyadh.

A Poem and Its Narrative by Riḏa Ibn Ṭārif aš-Šammari

The following poem and narrative are told in the voice of the poet himself. Riḏa Ibn Ṭārif aš-Šammari is a good example of the oral poet of the desert who not only composes poetry but also has many poems and historical anecdotes stored in his memory. He is a nomad with a distinctive Shammari accent and a resonant declamatory voice. He is a gifted raconteur of anecdotes and narratives.

In this recorded example Riḏa, prior to reciting one of his poems, relates the events that led to its composition. He has fallen in love with a bedouin lady who expresses her willingness to marry him. But when he sends a messenger to confirm her pledge of marriage, the messenger instead asks for her hand for himself. This leads to complications and misunderstandings; in the end, however, the treacherous messenger is found out. Riḏa and the lady make up, but by now it is time to break up summer camp and disperse into the desert; thus the marriage is postponed.

The recounting of narrative and poem takes up about fourteen minutes of recording time. The prose narrative employs a diction no less polished and a style no less refined than those of the poem. Although both narrative and poem deal with an actual event, each is cast in a traditional style and each constitutes an attempt to comprehend on a general level the impact of tribal migration on individual lives. In that sense, narrative and poem give us an ethnographic portrayal of desert life cast in artistic form.

The difficulty of translating the poem and narrative is compounded by the no less problematic task of transforming a dynamic oral performance into a static written text. The dramatic changes of voice quality and intonation leave no traces on the written text. Unlike the poem, which is composed and memorized prior to delivery, the narrative is composed as it is performed. This is not to say that Riḍa is inventing fictitious episodes. Rather, he is arranging real-life events into a narrative sequence and making sure that the audience is following. Therefore, flashbacks, background information, exegetical remarks, clarifications, graphic details, hesitations, and repetitions are superimposed upon the narrative thread and interwoven with it.

Riḍa addresses his words to Brāhīm al-Yūsif (Abu Yūsif), the host of the radio program *Min al-Bādiyah,* knowing well that he will be heard by the many people who tune in to this popular program. The active participation of Brāhīm adds further complexity to the linear development of the prose narrative. Brāhīm and Riḍa exchange traditional expressions of courtesy which do not really contribute to the story, but which are expected in this situation since they serve to establish rapport between the narrator and the audience. Brāhīm often tries to direct the flow and wording of this recorded version of the narrative, not only because he has heard the story before and wishes to make this version conform to the one he heard previously, but because its traditional format makes it possible to anticipate what is coming next. Moreover, the active participation of an interlocutor is one of the constitutive elements in determining the structure of this type of narrative. Brāhīm interjects comments and expressions of support and encouragement and asks for missing details. At times he becomes so involved that he assumes the character and role of the poet and acts as his voice, and there are occasions when he literally puts words into Riḍa's mouth. By so doing, Brāhīm is acting as a truly interested and genuinely involved audience.

As a result of these conditions, which are characteristic of oral performance, the prose narrative as it is written down may appear somewhat loose in structure and hard to follow. The reader is advised to keep pretending, while reading the text, that he is not looking at it but listening to it—to imagine Riḍa delivering the narrative orally and addressing his words to Brāhīm, an eager and animated listener.

Brāhīm$_1$: May God grant you long life, my friend Riḍa.
Riḍa$_1$: May God preserve you.
B$_2$: There is a poem of yours—may your life be long—of which

I know one verse in which you say, "May God bring no good to a vile man who deceives a trusting Muslim." I believe this poem has an occasion?

R_2: Yes, it has an occasion; this is one of my poems.

B_3: I know it is one of your poems. Your poems are many and, praise God, you have memorized other poems [besides your own].

R_3: By God, such is my duty.

B_4: You are called the just poet. You are not prejudiced either toward Shammar [your own tribe] or toward any other tribe.

R_4: May your life be long—I am proud of the whole history of the desert; I am proud of the history of all the tribes.

B_5: And so you should be, may your life be long. That is why you are called the just poet.

R_5: Yes.

B_6: What is the occasion for it, the poem?

R_6: It has an occasion, and that is a long story. But I will give a brief summary so that it will not exceed the time of the program.

B_7: Yes. I think you dispatched someone as a go-between, or something like that.

R_7: A bedouin lady and I fell in love with each other. As you know, all my life I have lived in the desert with the nomads. I am still a nomad.

B_8: Of course, you are still.

R_8: Yes. When we fell in love it was the rainy season. Summer came—the time for making camp—came and we camped by the same watering place, her people at one well and mine at another; we were not all camped by the same well.

B_9: But you were close to each other.

R_9: Yes. We were close. We were all camped in the same plain.

B_{10}: In other words, you could visit each other.

R_{10}: Yes, we could visit each other. We were camped in one plain, we were all in the same plain which had about ten wells. I sent someone to her; that is, I sent him to ask for her hand.

B_{11}: You wanted to see if she had no objection.

R_{11}: I wanted to see if she held to her word, her promise [made] in the rainy season, or whether she had changed her mind. I had some doubts, because spring love always—it is always the case that a woman who does not love you very dearly, love you madly, I mean, she will most likely change in the summer, because in the summer there are many [other] faces.[1]

B_{12}: True.

R_{12}: There are many faces.

B_{13}: True.

R_{13}: Hah. So I sent a man; and when I sent him to her I told him. Go to her, give her my greetings; if she is still true to the vow we made, then I will ask her family for her hand.

B_{14}: Yes. And if she had changed her mind, then may God keep me and her above reproach.[2]

R_{14}: And if she had changed [it], then may God keep her above reproach. Hah. And there will be no reason [to pursue this affair any further]. He [the go-between] said: I have no objection. It is an honor to me to be of assistance to you; anyway, her family lives right next door to me.

He, you know, is acquainted with them[3] [her family], and visits them frequently. He is even related to them, related to them, to her family. But his relationship to them is not a close one, I mean not so close that I would have any misgivings about him. They are his maternal uncles.

B_{15}: His maternal uncles.

R_{15}: He claims they are his maternal uncles. He also had his tent pitched next to theirs.

B_{16}: He was their neighbor, yes.

R_{16}: He was their neighbor. And he had no wife. At that time such a man was called *ṣimil.* Among the nomads a man who had no wife was called *ṣimil*—a man who has no woman in his tent. He had his tent pitched next to theirs. She [the lady] and her sisters were helping him out, and so on.

B_{17}: You mean they cooked his supper and did his chores.

R_{17}: They cooked his supper, did his chores, fetched him water; his tent was pitched next to theirs.

B_{18}: Observe: in honor and good faith.[4]

R_{18}: Of course, in honor and good faith, yes.

Hah. He went [to the lady]. I do not know what he told her when he went, but the next day when he met me, he said: You there, your lady friend has changed her mind. I said: She has changed her mind? He said: Yes. I said: What did she tell you? He said: She told me that God ordains the going out on raids and the returning from them.[5] I said: Fine, but I am still on my way to the raid, I have not turned back. He said: But she is turning back. I said: Did you not ask her? Did you not say, What are the reasons? He said: Of course I did. I didn't leave anything out. She told me: It is true that I gave him [Riḍa] my word at the time that I was interested—I mean interested in marrying him, nothing else,[6]—but after I inquired about him—I didn't know if he was married—

B_{19}: I see; she found out that you had a wife.

R_{19}: —I found out that he had a wife, and someone who has a wife does not suit me; a married man does not appeal to me. I said: Fine; but she [already] knew I had a wife!

B_{20}: Probably she knew [about] you before you sent this man.

R_{20}: She knew [about] me. I told her that I was married and she said: I do not care about the other wife; she is your responsibility. Even if you had three wives I would become the fourth. That is what she said to me before.

B_{21}: Those were her words then.

R_{21}: Then. But now this man brought me this last report. He said that she said: He [Riḍa] cheated me then. He said: I will marry you, and I have no wife. But when I inquired I found out that he had a wife and children. This does not suit me—I mean, a man with a wife and children! For God's sake, no. May God keep me and him above reproach.[7]

I got angry; you know, an honest man is inclined to believe what others tell him.

B_{22}: True.

R_{22}: I got angry. After I got angry with her I pursued this affair no further. Before, I used to visit her people; I used to go beyond all the tents close to mine and go over to their side of the camp. Love drew me their way.

B_{23}: I see; and then you decided to avoid their neighborhood entirely.

R_{23}: At this point I avoided their whole area completely; I switched wavelengths.[8] I never went in their direction, never. Then time passed and the wells began to dry up.

B_{24}: And perhaps the pasture was not as good as before.

R_{24}: Not as good as before. We, the people who raised camels, began to suffer. Only the people who raised sheep remained in the plain.

B_{25}: People who raised sheep.

R_{25}: Yes; and they [her people] raised sheep.

B_{26}: I see, they raised sheep.

R_{26}: They raised sheep.

B_{27}: And you raised camels.

R_{27}: We raised camels. My clan, who were close to me and to whom I was close, had already left. They had gone; where did they go at that time? They went to Iraq, to the marshes.

B_{28}: Toward Iraq.

R_{28}: Toward Iraq.

B_{29}: To the marshes.

R_{29}: To the marshes, at the beginning of fall, after the appearance of the star Canopus. There is good fall grazing in the marshes and at this time of year, when the weather begins to cool, the evil fever of Iraq, *az-zrēği*, which is dangerous to camels, goes away. So my people left, but I and my family remained behind. One day I went to visit them [the lady's people]. And there was this brother of hers who—like present company[9]—

B_{30}: The like of yourself is praiseworthy.

R_{30}: —is a man whose coffee pots are always brewing [i.e., generous]. I went to see him that day—all the neighbors with whom I used to spend my time before had gone—

B_{31}: And no one remained but you and her people.

R_{31}: And no one remained but myself, her people, and the other sheep herders, for those who raise sheep never go into the desert. So I went to see them. Her brother said: Hail, Abu Ṭārif, may God grant you long life, you've been avoiding us, it's a long time since you came to see us. I said: I am really a busy man, and as the saying goes: Summer camps are crowded; if your tent is not right next to mine, you might as well be dead [i.e., I would not see you].[10] Whenever I decide to come and visit you I am detained by the hundreds of hearths along the way. But today, here I am with you; my people have gone. He said: And you? Where will you go? I said: I really do not know. Maybe I shall follow my people when my camels come back for water, because my camel-herder is beginning to complain that the camels are restless and starving and that the plains are becoming barren. I am sure that I have to follow my people; I have no choice.

We talked for a while like this; then I went back home.

B_{32}: Perhaps she was listening to your conversation.

R_{32}: Of course; she was at home, in the tent—may your life be long—in the women's section, and she overheard our conversation. When I went home I took a nap in my tent, it was nearly noon; but my sister awakened me. "What is it?" She said: Someone is here to see you. At first I thought it was a man; but when I raised my head I saw that it was she who had come to our tent. The entire summer long she had never come to see us, except for this one time; she had never come to our neighborhood before. But after she overheard me say that we would go into the desert when the camels come back to drink, she became upset and was anxious to get in touch with me.

B_{33}: Then the man you had sent to her was not telling the truth.

R_{33}: No, of course not. Had he been telling the truth she would not have come. I greeted her and after I greeted her [I said]: I am surprised by your visit! She said: Believe me, had I not heard today that you were preparing to move into the desert, I would not have come, because I am angry with you. I said: There is a saying, "Meet accusations with accusations and you will be safe."[11] What makes you angry? She said: I am angry because you gave me your word then, and I have been waiting for you until now. But I see that you have been avoiding me, and I do not understand the reason for this. I did not remain faithful to the pledge we made to each other all this time because I thought you were the most handsome of men or the most generous, but because of what you said to me and what I said to you. So now I want to meet with you face to face and clear up this matter. I said: I see; now that you have found out that I am about to go into the desert, you say these fair words to me in hope of rekindling my heart, so that I may compose a poem about you and make you famous.

B_{34}: But, on the contrary, I sent so-and-so to you—

R_{34}: But, on the contrary [i.e., to prove my serious intentions], I sent you, in the first place, I sent you a messenger; but you told him, "So-and-so [Riḍa] lied to me. He said 'I have no wife,' but I found out that he has a wife and children." She said: Your messenger, who is he? I said: My messenger is so-and-so. She said: This is not true. He did come and ask for me—

B_{35}: For himself.

R_{35}: —For himself. He said to me, "If you are not averse to marrying me, my maternal uncles wish me no evil; I shall ask for your hand from my uncles." I said, "May God keep you and me above reproach; but I am not really interested in men right now." As for you, he did not even mention your name—did not even mention your name.

B_{36}: He did not say, "So-and-so sent me."

R_{36}: He did not say, "So-and-so sent me." He did not mention your name, ever.

At that time it happened that my wife was not with me in the tent. She had taken the children and gone to her parents' tent. Her parents had no one to help them with the chores, so I gave her permission to go to her parents.

B_{37}: But your sister was with you.

R_{37}: My sister was with me to take care of household matters. My wife was not with us; she was at a different watering place, not the same one I was camped at. At any rate, the lady and I made up. However, when we made up it was time for me to move to the desert, and I moved. But now the matter had become clear to me.

B_{38}: You said to her that now it was time—

R_{38}: I said that—

B_{39}: That I promised—

R_{39}: I said that now I—

B_{40}: When the camels come back from pasture we will—

R_{40}: That I had made up my mind to move into the desert—

B_{41}: Yes; we shall move—

R_{41}: And when the camels come back I shall leave, I have no choice; but, God willing—

B_{42}: In the future—

R_{42}: In the future we shall meet again, under happy circumstances. She said: God is gracious. Hah. Things had become clear to me. It is a long story, O Abu Yūsif, but I only wanted to tell you the story and what happened. I moved into the desert, and after I moved I composed this poem. In the first part of the poem I castigated the land which had become barren and caused friends to be separated from each other.

B_{43}: Had dispersed you, yes.

R_{43}: Had dispersed us and took me away from my lady love.

1 When passions fill my breast, I say: Bring forth my graceful mount; put on her saddle and her trappings.

2 Put on her saddle and grant me leave [to go]; I must seek relief on the desert roads.

3 It's time to strike camp and move out, on spirited beasts which march on by day and by night.

4 We load up and leave on sturdy camels with great hooves, fleet and enduring.

5 Their ribs are broad, their gait is smooth; they groan and growl in foreign tongues.[12]

6 We quit the barren land and seek the verdant steppe, like a flock of birds in a gusty wind.

7 The barren wastes drive us on; the scanty pastures suffice no more.

8 Oh, so uncertain is fate; many a camp has become deserted; obliterated are the camps where once resided gallant men,

9 The stalwarts who roar on the battlefield like camels of burden, intoxicated by the sight of death so near.[13]

10 O land, why do you drive us so hard? You press upon us as the grass cutters prod their loaded beasts.

11 O land, you dispersed the camps; you scattered the large tents wherein lodge weary guests.

12 The tribesmen moved and left behind the sweet water in the wells; whoever had a wing to fly, took off.

13 The black ravens circle their deserted camps, like the little lambs which roamed there before.

14 Leave that; carry my verses, ye riders on stout mounts which travel the highways of waterless wastes,

15 Thoroughbred camels with muscular thighs whose male progenitor was of a noble line.

16 Hail, well-mounted riders; halt and listen to me, since you are going to her camp—the lady with thick, long hair.

17 When you alight by the camp of the faithful lady, the lady whose love has penetrated my heart,

18 Tell her that even if she were to stay away from me for thirty years, I should not forget her unless the nomads quit migrating,

19 Or unless the Riʿīlih ridge is moved amongst the peaks of the Salma chains.

20 Her love is causing me so much suffering; her red cheeks are painted the [bloody] color of death.

21 Her eyes are the eyes of a falcon swooping over a flock of birds: a hunting bird of reddish color; its talons tear off the feathers and spill the blood of the prey.

22 Its broad wings strike the bustards; when the male bustard sees it, he leaves the sky and seeks the ground.

23 Her legs are seemly, wearing new anklets. She is my choice among all fair maidens when she unplaits her wavy hair.

24 She is the branch of a sweet basil bush nurtured by the dew in the shade of a palm garden,

25 A supple branch with beautiful fragrance; its perfume is spread by the gentle breeze as it grows beside the running water.

26 I sent an emissary to my faithful lady, wishing only to hear from her a word of greeting.

27 My messenger proved useless as an old discarded garment; I found him putting obstacles in my path.

28 He brought me word from the fair maiden of lovely figure; that ill-omened messenger, he closed all doors in my face.

29 May God bring no good to a vile man who deceives a trusting Muslim.

30 The lady told me the truth; I heard it from her own lips, not from mounted couriers.
31 She warned me not to trust that man again; she said: Do not seek flesh from the bones of a starved camel.[14]
32 Thus ends this poem and I conclude the rhymes, my rhymes; precious verses which I did not compose in vain.
33 I close with an offer of prayers on the soul of the Prophet, like the rain which falls from laden clouds.

B_{44}: May your tongue be sound.[15]
R_{44}: May your body be sound.

Singing and Musical Accompaniment

The usual manner of delivering a Nabaṭi poem is to chant it or, most commonly, to declaim it in an elocutionary fashion. Declamation is called *hadd̠* or *had̠b* (*had̠b* refers to the swift pace of a trotting mount) because it is quick and takes less time than chanting. Chanting is called *dēwinih*, a word etymologically related to *dīwān* (a written collection of poems) and to *dīwāniyyah* (a coffee-chamber). Perhaps the etymological connection comes from the fact that in towns and settlements men gather together in the coffee-chamber of one of them and invite a professional reciter to chant poetry to them from a manuscript. However, *dēwinih* means chanting whether the chanter recites from a book or from memory. On rare occasions, especially when the poem is short and the moment of delivery is the moment of composition, the poet sings his verses to the accompaniment of the *ribābih*, alternating between the singing of verses and bowing on the instrument without singing. While bowing, the poet is silently composing in his head, and when he has composed a verse he sings it out to the tune of the *ribābih*.

Such methods of delivery are employed when the primary object of the performance for the reciter and the audience alike is the words and overall content of the poem. So far, this chapter has been dealing with this type of performance. But there are occasions when the focus of performance is singing and music, in addition to the words, and it is such occasions that I wish to discuss now.

Theoretically, any poem can be sung, but generally speaking some poems are sung and others are recited. Sung poems have the same meters as recited poems, but they are always short, on the average seven lines. A section of a long poem may be lifted out of it and sung as an independent piece. Singing may or may not be accompanied by musical instruments: the *ribābih* in the case of an individual performance, or the *ṭbūl* (drums) in the case of a collective performance. I shall first consider the individual performance.

Although the word *rabābah* occurs in classical times (meaning a leather pouch in which the arrows used for drawing lots were deposited), we have no record of when the musical instrument of that name was introduced into Arabia, or who was the first to introduce it. The *ribābih* is a one-stringed instrument made in the shape of a rectangular wooden box covered with skin on both sides (nowadays a gasoline can may be used instead). The size of the box varies, but the one that I have measures 6½ by 10 inches with a depth of 3 inches. The skin used to cover the box is generally that of a goat, or a young camel or cow. Tradition has it that the best skin is that of a wolf; a *ribābih* covered with wolf skin is said to howl (*tʿawi*) like a wolf. Because the wooden box is covered with skin the instrument is also called *šannih*, a word meaning dry skin, which is more generally applied to an old shriveled dry water bag (*žirbih*) made of skin. The instrument and its bow, made of a thin rattan branch, are strung with *hilb* (hair from a horse's tail).

The *ribābih* player is not necessarily himself a poet, and will most likely be singing someone else's composition. While bowing on the *ribābih*, he will sing a verse once or twice, then wait a while and let the *ribābih* take its turn; then he will sing the next line, and so on. The audience may just sit and listen, or they may join the singer in a chorus.

The *ribābih* is played in several modes. To avoid monotony, the player continually shifts from one mode to another. Since different modes usually require different meters, shifting from one mode to the other implies shifting from one poem to another which, in turn, implies that a long poem is never sung on the *ribābih* from beginning to end, but that only a few lines of it are selected for singing.

The most popular modes played on the *ribābih* are the following:

> *Hlāli* This is the *nisbah* (relative adjective) form derived from the Banu Hilāl, an ancient Arabian tribe that migrated to North Africa centuries ago. Strictly speaking, this adjective does not refer to the musical mode itself, but rather to the poetic meter that fits that mode. This meter is ⏑ – – ⏑ – – – ⏑ – – ⏑ – ⏑ –, which is the classical Arabic *ṭawīl* meter. (On the prosody of Nabaṭi poetry and its relationship to classical Arabic prosody, see the next chapter.) This meter is still employed by contemporary Nabaṭi poets, but it is called *hlāli* since it was the most popular meter during the days of Banu Hilāl.
>
> *Masḥūb* or *majrūr* The two verbs *saḥab* and *jarr* are synonyms with several meanings, among them "to pull, to drag, to extend, to

stretch out, to draw out." This mode of singing is very slow, and the singer draws out the last syllable of every verse in a long drone which is sustained for nearly half a minute. The meter for this mode is – – ⏑ – – – ⏑ – – ⏑ – –, which is the most popular meter in Nabaṭi poetry.

Marbūʿ This is similar to *masḥūb* in meter but has a lighter rhythm.

Xmiši Popular among the *al-xmiših*, a large section of the ʿAnazah tribe, this mode shares the same meter with *marbūʿ* and *masḥūb*.

Ṣxari Popular among the northern tribe of Bini Ṣaxar, its meter is ⏑ – – – ⏑ – – – ⏑ – –, which is the classical Arabic *hazaj* meter with one extra foot.

Hjēni This is a very popular mode of singing in the Arabian desert. It is sung not only accompanied on the *ribābih* but also while traveling fast on riding camels called *hijin*, hence its name. (Nowadays, people still sing it when traveling in cars, trains, and even planes). Its rhythm is light and somewhat bouncy, to go with the swift movement of a trotting camel mount. It comprises several meters, the most popular of which are – – ⏑ – – ⏑ – – –; – – ⏑ – – ⏑ – – – ⏑ – – –; – ⏑ – – – ⏑ – – – ⏑ – –; – ⏑ – – – ⏑ – – ⏑ – – –; – ⏑ – – ⏑ – – – ⏑ – – ⏑ – – ⏑ – –. These are all classical meters; the first two are varieties of *basīṭ*, the third *ramal*, the fourth *madīd*, and the last *mumtadd*.

An altogether different type of musical performance is collective singing accompanied by the beating of large round drums (*ṭbūl,* sing. *ṭabil*; also called *dammām* or *ṭār*). The individual *ribābih* performance is a casual affair compared with the collective performance, which is a very complex event, socially and artistically. There are various types of collective performances and various occasions for them; the most important are subsumed under the following categories, which are also used to designate the relevant musical modes.

Sāmri

The verb *sāmar* means to stay up at night talking and singing in a joyous mode, and *sāmri* means singing together at night. The *sāmri* is performed at important social events such as weddings, and on festive occasions such as *yōm al-ʿīd*, or when the king or some high official visits. In ʿUnaizah, my home town, every Thursday evening (because the next day, Friday, is the Muslim sabbath and people do not have to get up early for work), those who know how to play *sāmri*, accompanied by a large crowd of enthusiasts, go out of town to sand dunes to sing and dance till dawn. The singers of the *sāmri* sit on the sand forming two lines facing each other; each line (*ṣaff*)is made up of ten to twenty singers and the lines are separated by a space about ten feet wide. The space between the lines is reserved for the dancers.

The *sāmri* has many melodies but only one basic beat, and any poem in any meter can be sung to fit this beat. Before the drumming begins, the melody is established by singing the first verse of the song four times. One group begins to sing this verse, which is repeated by the second group; then the first group sings the verse again, and the second group repeats it after them. Then the singers move to the next verse and sing it in the same fashion, and so on until the end of the song. Drumming begins with the second verse. Some of the drummers keep a steady beat, while others improvise on this beat.

In addition to the singers, there is always a large number of people socializing and enjoying the music. Anyone among the audience may get up and dance or may join in the singing; but those who have not yet mastered the beat, or the swaying, side-to-side and up and down movement of the upper part of the body which goes with the beat, must stay at the end of the line. Anyone wishing to learn *sāmri* must faithfully attend this performance every Thursday evening for a long time until he masters the beat and body movement. First, he goes out and only watches what the singers do. In a few months he learns the melodies and songs by hearing them repeated over and over again. Then he feels confident enough to sit with the singers at the end of one of the lines, singing, moving his body, and clapping his hands. After doing this for many weeks, the beat, melodies, and songs become ingrained in his mind and he begins to try to handle the drum. For the first few times he loses the beat every now and then, but eventually he becomes able to keep the beat steadily, and in a few months he will be able to improvise on the basic beat. The better he gets, the closer he moves to the center of the line, a place reserved for masters of the art. The singers are hesitant to admit anyone to the line who does not know the beat, because his unmeasured and erratic strokes could destroy the structure of the rhythm and cause everyone to lose the beat. The performance is best when all the singers and drummers are masters of the art.

It must be remembered that in *sāmri* the performance focuses more on the music than on the content of the poem. The *sāmri* songs are short poems, ten to fifteen lines long, and generally deal with erotic themes and physical beauty. Some are so popular that they exist in many versions, and sometimes it is impossible to determine their original versions. They become true folk songs, and the singers feel free to change them or to add to them at will.

ʿArḍih or galṭih

The verb *ʿaraḍ* means to show, to exhibit, and the verb *galaṭ* means to step forward as in a duel or to advance as on a battlefield. The *ʿarḍih* is essentially a war dance, which is an exhibition of strength and determination. Unlike the *sāmri* in which singers sit on the ground, the *ʿarḍih* requires that the singers perform standing up, moving forward steadily with measured steps. Participants in the *ʿarḍih* dress as if they were going to battle; they wear badges and carry weapons. The dancers brandish their swords and spears and execute acrobatic movements indicating strength, agility, and endurance. In the past the *ʿarḍih* was strictly a war dance, but now it is merely a form of entertainment performed on important occasions. The drums used in *ʿarḍih* are the same as those used for *sāmri*, and the singing is done in a similar fashion, but the melodies and the beat are different. The *ʿarḍih* beat is a combination of two beats, one called *taxmīr* and the other *irćāb*. The most popular meters of *ʿarḍih* are: ––⏑– ––⏑– ––⏑–; –⏑–– –⏑– –⏑–– –; –⏑–– –⏑– –⏑–– –⏑–; –⏑– –⏑–– –⏑– –; and –⏑– –⏑–– –⏑– ––. All are classical Arabic meters; the first is *rajaz*, the second and third are varieties of *madīd*, and the fourth and fifth are varieties of *mumtadd*.

The original purpose of the *ʿarḍih* was to incite people and raise their courage on the way to battle. The poems sung on such an occasion usually contained some interesting and reliable historical facts inserted by the poet to add weight to his impassioned appeals to his people to defend their honor and property from aggressors. The songs for *ʿarḍih* were usually composed on the spot and made to fit the occasion; a poet would improvise one verse and the singers would pick it up after him and keep on singing it till he came up with the next verse, and so on till the end. Like the *sāmri* songs, *ʿarḍih* songs are short, but they are regarded with more seriousness; their attribution is always known, and no one dares change their words consciously.

Poetic Dueling

Like *sāmri* and *ʿarḍih*, poetic dueling is a collective performance, and it usually takes place on the same occasions as these other activities. It is called *galṭih* (from *galaṭ*, "to step forward") or *mrādd* (from *radd*, "to answer back"). A poetic duel, called *riddiyyih*, involves two poets, and consists of a few rounds of exchanges between them, each round consisting of two verses.[16] The first poet steps forward and improvises two verses in which he greets the assembled audience-participants and, at the same time, asks for a challenger to come forward and face him. These opening verses are called *wisīmih* (from *wasm*, "brand," "mark") because they mark, or establish, the patterns of rhyme and meter for the entire *riddiyyih*. A second poet answers the challenge with two verses of his own following the rhyme and meter established by the first poet, who in turn retorts with two more verses; these two verses are answered by the second poet, and so on until the end of the *riddiyyih*. A *riddiyyih* is thus actually the work of two poets, but it is viewed as one unit and its verses all have the same rhyme and meter. Although it follows the established patterns of rhyme and meter, it is different from the regular *giṣīdih* in structure and function and it is composed in performance.

The verses of the dueling poets are repeated by the groups of singers who arrange themselves in two lines, standing up and facing each other with some space between them for the dueling poets to move in. Singing is accompanied by hand clapping only, with no drums or other instruments. This makes it easy for anyone present to join in the singing. Dueling poets do not come up with their verses one verse right after the other. It takes a few minutes for a duelist to decipher the meaning of his opponent's verses and form the proper response to them. Each verse, therefore, is repeated several times by the singer, until one of the poets comes up with the next verse. Each new verse is received enthusiastically by the singers with loud cheers or jeers, depending on its content.

Generally speaking, a *riddiyyih* consists of no more than eight or ten rounds (sixteen to twenty verses) of exchanges divided equally between the contesting poets. The pressure of performance and the constraints of rhyme limit the length of the *riddiyyih*. As in a regular *giṣīdih*, the *riddiyyih* has two rhymes, one for the first hemistich and one for the second, and a word cannot be used more than once in a rhyming position. At the same time, it should not take a dueling poet too long to compose his verses; otherwise, he loses. If a poet lingers in composing his verses, the singers shout at him, "*ᶜlēt*," "You have been topped" (i.e., the other poet is above, literally over, you), which signals his defeat.

The topic and general tone of a *riddiyyih* are determined by whether the poets are friends or antagonists. In many cases, the poets are from different tribes or different districts, or one may be from the desert and one from the settled country. In such cases, each poet becomes the champion of his group and expresses pride in belonging to it while attacking the group of his opponent. Each draws on his vast repertory of historical and genealogical information to praise his group and ridicule that of his opponent, and the contest often turns into a match of wits. All of this, however, is taken with good humor by the poets and their audience. If the dueling poets are friends, these exchanges are complimentary, but with occasional humor. Friendly poets may try to work out a misunderstanding between them in their *riddiyyih* or, if they had not seen each other for some time, may inquire of each other about some private affair, or one may ask the other whether a rumor that has been spread about him is true, and so on. This, however, must be done in a veiled and oblique way, almost like riddling, that only a discerning poet can understand. In many cases, although the singers repeat the verses of the dueling poets, only the poets themselves know what the verses really mean.

My purpose in discussing *al-mrādd* is not to give a thorough analysis of its thematic structure or social function, but to examine it as a performance in order to give a complete picture of how Nabaṭi poetry in its varied forms is performed in public. With regard to its structure and function and to the manner of its composition and performance, *al-mrādd* is considered a poetic genre sui generis independent from *giṣīd*, which is the primary topic of the present study. The native audience consider *al-mrādd* and *al-giṣīd* to be separate categories, each with its own enthusiasts, and a poet who excels in one of these categories does not necessarily excel in the other.

In this chapter we have surveyed the various contexts of performance of Nabaṭi poetry. We have seen that long poems are declaimed or chanted either from a book or, in most cases, from memory. Only short poems or selections from long poems are sung, sometimes individually to the accompaniment of the *ribābih*, and sometimes collectively to the accompaniment of drums. Love songs are performed in *sāmri* fashion, while war songs are performed in *ʿarḏih* fashion. In general, composition precedes performance except on rare occasions when the need for composition is urgent and the poet composes a few lines while playing the *ribābih*, or when he composes for the *ʿarḏih* singers. Only in *al-mrādd* does the poet always compose in performance. Here it should be pointed out that, in Nabaṭi poetry, composition in performance is a totally different procedure from that in epic poetry. The epic is an exceedingly long poem composed quickly at the rate of "from ten to twenty ten-syllable lines a minute" (Lord 1960:17). In Nabaṭi poetry the rigid constraints of rhyme and meter make composition in performance a slow labor; it takes a few minutes to compose each verse. Furthermore, these constraints make it impossible for a Nabaṭi poet to compose more than a few verses in performance. Spontaneous and improvised composition is, therefore, an infrequent feature of Nabaṭi poetic performance.

Part Three

COMPARATIVE

VIII

PROSODY AND LANGUAGE: A SYNCHRONIC AND DIACHRONIC OVERVIEW

In this chapter and the next, I shall present a broad view of Nabaṭi poetry in its specific linguistic and literary contexts. No one who has studied Nabaṭi poetry can fail to note its striking resemblance to classical Arabic poetry. Their affinity was remarked upon more than six hundred years ago by Ibn Khaldūn, who asserted that the bedouin poets of his time, though their diction had deviated from that of their ancient predecessors, followed very closely the ancient modes and themes (1967:1125). Socin wrote of the Nabaṭi poetry which he himself had collected from Najdi informants residing in Mesopotamia that it was "a direct continuation of the ancient Arabic art of poetry according to content, form, and language" (1900–1901:III, 46). Ibn Khamīs (1958:94–174) discusses some of the thematic correspondences between Nabaṭi poetry and classical Arabic poetry and points out that these correspondences stem from the fact that, in addition to their historical relationship, the two poetries are products of the same physical and human conditions.

At the same time, it is abundantly clear that Nabaṭi poetry presents many linguistic and prosodic divergences from classical Arabic diction. It is obvious that the language has undergone many changes, which have produced corresponding changes in poetic diction in general, and in prosodic techniques in particular. The prosodic relationship of Nabaṭi poetry to classical Arabic poetry is a critical question which has not hitherto been fully examined. I shall deal with this question in the present chapter, first presenting a synchronic description of the most significant linguistic and prosodic features of Nabaṭi poetry, and then moving to a discussion of the historical process that eventually led to the transformation of poetic diction in Arabia from "classical" to "vernacular."

The Prosodic Characteristics of Nabaṭi Poetry

Before we can discuss the relationship of Nabaṭi prosody to classical prosody, it is necessary to analyze the metrical structure of Nabaṭi poetry itself and to devise a method for its scansion. Such an analysis must, however, be preceded by a preliminary discussion of some phonological aspects of the vernacular diction in which Nabaṭi poetry is composed and recited, and of the ways in which this diction diverges from that of classical Arabic.

Phonological Observations

The diction of Nabaṭi poetry and that of classical Arabic poetry are the two ends of one and the same poetic idiom which is based on, but of course more polished than, the spoken language of Arabia. This poetic idiom has changed slowly and gradually through time as a consequence of changes affecting the phonology, morphology, syntax, and semantics of the spoken language. In the following pages, I shall be mainly concerned with sound changes in the language, specifically those affecting short vowels and the glottal stop, which triggered a realignment in the syllabic structure of the spoken language which, in turn, contributed to the development of the specific prosodic structure of Nabaṭi poetry and its divergence from classical prosody.

Needless to say, there are dialectal differences and variations in pronunciation between the various regions and tribes of Arabia, but for our purposes these variations may be considered negligible since they rarely affect the syllabic structure. In this work, Nabaṭi poetry is transliterated and scanned according to the pronunciation rules of the dialect of ᶜUnaizah,[1] my home town, which is famous for its outstanding Nabaṭi poets. T. M. Johnstone has characterized the dialect of ᶜUnaizah as:

> . . . a stable dialect and therefore particularly well suited to throw light on problems of the phonology of the Nejdi dialects as a whole. This stability results partly from the fact that there has not been, at least until recently, any substantial influence of prestige dialects from outside the area, and partly from the fact that the Nejdi dialects are regarded by their speakers as preserving many important features of Classical Arabic which have not been so preserved in other dialects. A certain pride also is felt in the colloquial poetry, *al-shiᶜr al-nabati*, which is composed in a poetical 'Nejdi' dialect. (1967a:1)

The following is an inventory of the consonants in the dialect of ʿUnaizah:

ʾ = ء	*x* = خ	*š* = ش	*f* = ف	*h* = هـ
b = ب	*d* = د	*ṣ* = ص	*g,ǵ* = ق	*w* = و
t = ت	*ḏ* = ذ	*ṭ* = ط	*k,ć* = ك	*y* = ي
ṯ = ث	*r* = ر	*ḏ̣* = ظ	*l* = ل	
j = ج	*z* = ز	ʿ = ع	*m* = م	
ḥ = ح	*s* = س	*ġ* = غ	*n* = ن	

The classical sound *ḍ* (ض) has merged with *ḏ̣* (ظ), and *q* (ق) has been replaced by *g*. In certain phonetic environments, mainly in the contiguity of the high front vowels *i* and *ī*, the voiced velar stop *g* and its voiceless counterpart *k* are fronted to voiced and voiceless affricates *ǵ* and *ć* respectively.[2]

In addition to the three long vowels *ā, ī, ū* of classical Arabic, the dialect of ʿUnaizah has two or more, *ē* and *ō*, which are reflexes of the classical diphthongs *ay* and *aw*. In the dialect, these two diphthongs appear only as the terminal elements of a final syllable, and in most cases as reflexes of the old *ū* and *ī: gūlaw*, "say (m.p.)!"; *gūlay*, "say (f.s.)!"

Except in some pronominal forms and before a geminate bilabial, the short, high back vowel *u* has been fronted and completely assimilated to the front vowel *i*,[3] which leaves the dialect with primarily two contrastive short vowels: the high vowel *i* and the low vowel *a*. These two vowels behave differently in open syllables, as I will explain below. But first, the syllable must be defined.

A short syllable consists of a consonant followed by a vowel *CV* and a long syllable consists of a consonant followed by a long vowel *CV̄* or a short syllable closed by a consonant *CVC*. A syllable always begins with a consonant. In case the utterance begins with a vowel, a glottal stop which is concomitant of vocalic onset takes the place of an initial consonant.

In an initial open syllable, the high vowel *i* is elided,[4] thus giving rise to initial consonant clusters (a feature not permitted in classical Arabic): *flān* (so and so), *rjāl* (men), *ʿgad* (knots), *ḏbiḥ* (he was slain). In a medial open syllable the vowel *i* is elided only if the initial consonant of this medial syllable is identical with the consonant closing the preceding syllable, which gives rise to a cluster of three consonants. This applies to all the active participles of the second verbal form: *mdarrsīn* (teachers), *mrawwḥāt* (they [f.] are going). But if the aforementioned consonants are not identical, then the medial three-consonant cluster is not permitted and, instead of elision of the vowel *i*, a metathesis takes place whereby the vowel moves forward one consonant: *misilmīn* (Muslims), *takitbīn* (you [f.p.] write).

The low vowel *a* is raised to *i* in an open syllable: *jibal* (mountain), *ǵidam* (foot), *giᶜūd* (young male camel), *giṭaᶜ* (he cut), *d̠ibaḥ* (he slew). The raising of the low vowel does not take effect when it is:

1. Preceded by a guttural (*ḥ x ᶜ ġ h '*): *hadab* (fringes), *ġadīr* (pond), *xarūf* (lamb), *ḥamād* (hard plain), *'akal* (he ate)
2. Followed by a long syllable the initial consonant of which is a guttural or a sonorant (*l m n r w y*) and the vowel of which is *a, ā, ē,* or *ō*:[5] *waᶜad* (he promised), *daxal* (he entered), *walad* (a youth), *d̠ahab* (gold), *salām* (peace), *saḥāb* (clouds), *sahēt* (I forgot), *banāt* (girls), *darā* (he knew)

The vowel *a* is homorganic with gutturals and its behavior is strongly influenced by them. Gutturals not only inhibit the raising of *a* to *i* but also the copy vowel *a* is introduced after the guttural when a guttural closes a nonfinal syllable the vowel of which is *a: laḥam* (meat), *šaᶜar* (hair). The copy vowel is not introduced when:

1. The guttural is followed by a short high vowel which is elided: *taᶜbat* (she became tired)
2. The guttural is the last radical in the stem: *ṭalaᶜnā* (we went out, left)
3. The form is an elative: *aḥlā* (sweeter), *axḍar* (greener)
4. The form is the perfect of verbal form IV: *aġdā* (he lost)
5. The form is the active participle of verbal form I: *taᶜbān* (he is tired)

In addition to the elision of short high vowels in open syllables, the short vowels marking mood and case have also been deleted, giving rise to final consonant clusters. If the last consonant in this final cluster is a sonorant, an epenthetic vowel *i* is introduced to break up the cluster: *ḍ̣abiy* (deer), *ġaziw* (a raid), *šiᶜir* (poetry), *ᶜajil* (swift), *najim* (star), *xašin* (coarse). The anaptyctic vowel is not inserted when the consonants in the cluster are both sonorants: *jirm* (stature), *garn* (horn, century). In continuous speech, the anaptyctic vowel disappears when the final consonant cluster is followed by a vowel or by a word that begins with an initial consonant cluster. Hence the word for foot, *rijil,* becomes *rijlēn* (feet), *rijl al-walad* (the boy's foot), *rijl mḥammad* (Muḥammad's foot).

In other cases, however, the anaptyctic vowel appears even in a nonfinal position: *rijil mūsā* (Mūsā's foot).

In addition to the above-mentioned vowel changes, the glottal stop *hamzah* has also undergone changes that have profoundly affected its syllabic status. In classical Arabic, the glottal stop functions as a consonant that can open or close a syllable anywhere in the utterance. In the vernacular, it has either been assimilated to an adjacent vowel or has been changed to *w* or *y,* or has been deleted altogether, except in a very few restricted positions or in cases of direct lexical borrowings from literary Arabic. All these changes are determined by the phonetic environment; but since the glottal stop, like any other consonant, can occur in a wide variety of environments, it is very difficult to exhaust all the possibilities or to formulate a general rule that would cover all the cases. Here I can only point out the most frequent changes that the glottal stop has undergone in the dialect of ᶜUnaizah.

When it closes a syllable, the glottal stop drops and the preceding vowel is prolonged if it is not already long: *bćā* (crying), *xaṭā* (wrong-doing), *ardā* (worse), *garā* (he read), *birī* (he became cured), *rās* (head), *ḏīb* (wolf), *lūlū* (pearls). If it can be assumed that the long vowels *ī* and *ū* are really *iy* and *uw,* then it can be stated that a glottal stop after a long high vowel or a diphthong drops and the last element of the vowel or the diphthong is geminated: *biriyy* (innocent), *suww* (evil), *šayy* (a thing), *fayy* (shade), *ḓaww* (fire), *xaṭiyyih* (wrong-doing), *mruwwih* (altruism, manliness). When the glottal stop opens a syllable in a noninitial position, it changes to *y* unless the preceding vowel is *u,* in which case it changes to *w: gāyim* (standing up), *ḏyābih* (wolves), *ryih* (lung), *fwād* (heart), *lūlwih* (a pearl).

An initial open short syllable that begins with a glottal stop that is not part of the root is frequently dropped, especially if the following syllable is also open (but see exceptions 1 and 2 below): *gāmih* (staying), *rādih* (will), *ᶜamā* (blind), *xaḏar* (green), *hawaj* (rash). Therefore, the citation form for the word *family* is *ahal,* but when this word is linked to another word following it, causing the second syllable to be open, the first syllable drops: *hal al-bēt* (people of the house). If the initial glottal stop is the first radical of the root, it drops only when the next two syllables are both open in the old form: *klituh* (she ate it [m]). When the initial glottal stop is the first radical of the root it is preserved in a few cases: *akal* (he ate), *axaḏat* (she took), but it usually changes to *w: wilif* (he became used to, fond of), *wimar* (he ordered). The glottal stop always changes to *w* in the passive voice and in the second and third verbal forms: *wćil* (it was eaten), *wakkal* (he gave to eat), *wākal* (he ate with). To avoid the initial glottal stop, the functions of the fourth verbal form have frequently been relegated to the first or the second forms: *dār* (he caused [something] to turn), *ṭāᶜ* (he obeyed), *mawwat* (he put to death), *nawwax* (he caused [a camel] to kneel), *dammā* (he caused to bleed), *dannā* (he brought [something] near).

Short syllable sequences, although permitted in classical diction, are avoided in the vernacular. When two short syllables follow each other and the vowel of the second syllable is *i* (i.e., *CVCi*––), the vowel of the second syllable drops and its consonant closes the preceding syllable and makes it long: *ḏibḥat* (she was slain), *šarbat* (she drank). In case the vowel in both syllables is *a* (i.e., *CaCa*––), the vowel of the first syllable drops while that of the second remains: *ćḏibat* (she lied), *mġarib* (sunset) (this last example illustrates the stability of the copy vowel introduced after a guttural: it is the old *a* which drops while the new one remains). If this type of sequence of two short syllables is in a medial position (i.e., –CaCa–), either vowel may drop: *istaᶜjal/istᶜajal* (he rushed), *ištaġlat/ištġalat* (she worked). A sequence of two short syllables is, however, unavoidable under any of the following phonetic conditions:

1. When the imperfect of the first form of a verb whose first radical is a guttural is conjugated with the first person singular: *aᶜarif* → *a ᶜa rif* (I know)
2. When the imperfect of the fifth and sixth verbal forms is conjugated with the first person singular: *atigallab* → *a ti gal lab* (I toss and turn), *atimēwat* → *a ti mē wat* (I pretend to be dead)
3. When nunation is suffixed to a noun of the form *CaCaC: waladin garm* → *wa la din garm* (a gallant lad)
4. When the definite article *al* is prefixed to a noun that begins with a vowel which is not syllabically linked to the following consonant: *al-aṣāyil* → *a la ṣā yil* (the thoroughbreds), *al-asad* → *a la sad* (the lion).[6]

Scansion

Previous scholars who tackled the prosody of Nabaṭi poetry failed to provide a satisfactory method of scanning this poetry. The long discussion by Socin (1900–1901:II, 52–70) is rather fuzzy and unrevealing. Ibn Khamīs (1958:56–66) and Sh. al-Kamālī (1964:76–104, 156–177) do no more than throw their hands in the air after identifying a few Nabaṭi meters with classical ones. The most interesting observations were made by Wallin (1852:193) and C. de Landberg (1895:17 ff.). They noted that short vowels, which are elided when Nabaṭi poetry is recited, are usually restored to their original positions when the poetry is chanted or sung. Both hinted at the necessity of restoring these vowels to discern metrical regularity, but neither demonstrated in a systematic manner how this was to be done; and the distorted verses in their collections betray their lack of sensitivity to Nabaṭi meter. As I have shown above, the elision of these vowels gives rise to consonant clusters which are permitted in ordinary conversation and poetic declamation. To enunciate the elided vowels while reciting would make the poetry sound stilted, but it is almost impossible to sing or chant Nabaṭi poetry without these vowels. The restoration of these vowels is also necessary for metrical regularity, as I will show below.

The meter of Nabaṭi poetry, like that of classical Arabic poetry, is quantitative. It is determined by the number of short and long syllables to a foot and the manner in which these short and long syllables are concatenated. A Nabaṭi poem consists of anywhere from a few to a few hundred (but on the average from twenty to forty) monorhyming lines, with each line divided into two usually equal hemistichs and all lines having the same meter. In Nabaṭi poetry, the hemistich (not the verse) is the maximum unit of scansion, the syllable the minimum unit. Metrically speaking, the hemistich is not a collection of words but a collocation of short and long syllables. In scanning, word boundaries must be disregarded completely, and the hemistich taken as one unit of continuous utterance. When a word in noninitial position begins with a vowel, this vowel becomes syllabically linked to the final consonant of the preceding word: *rāᶜ al-hawā* → *rā ᶜal ha wā* (the man of passion), *šift al-ġaḏī* → *šif tal ġa ḏī* (I saw my beloved), *rabᶜat al-bēt* → *rab ᶜa tal bēt* (the man's part of the tent). In case the preceding word ends with a long vowel, the long vowel is deleted: *ćimā aḏ-ḏārī* → *ći maḏ ḏā rī* (like a hungry wolf), *ᶜalā al-finjāl* → *ᶜa lal fin jāl* (on the cup).

When Nabaṭi poetry is scanned or chanted, all consonant clusters must be resolved except those at the very beginning or the very end of the hemistich. To resolve these clusters, a metathesized or elided vowel is restored back to its original position to form an independent short syllable with the preceding consonant: *misilmīn* → *mis li mīn* (Muslims), *sarrḥah* → *sar ri ḥah* (take it [f.] to pasture), *al-mdāwī* → *al mi dā wī* (the medicine man), *damᶜ ᶜēnī* → *dam ᶜi ᶜē nī* (the tears of my eyes), *tġannī ṭyūr al-mā* → *ti ġan nī ṭi yū ral mā* (the waterbirds are singing). Restoration of elided vowels cancels out the anaptyctic vowel which is introduced to break up final consonant clusters. The anaptyctic vowel is retained only at the very end of the hemistich. For example, the scansion of the word *al-ᶜaṣir* (the afternoon) is *al ᶜaṣ ri* in medial position but *al ᶜa ṣir* in final position.

The prosodic structure of Nabaṭi poetry, in harmony with that of the spoken language, does not allow short syllable sequences except in those very restricted and phonetically conditioned cases that were specified at the end of the previous section. Otherwise, the short syllables in the hemistich must be separated from one another by no less than two but no more than three long syllables, as we shall see below. Therefore, when the restoration of the elided vowels yields two short syllables, these two short syllables are automatically reduced to one long syllable by dropping the vowel of the second syllable and linking its consonant to the preceding syllable to close it and make it long. For example, the utterance *jibt slāḥī* (I brought my weapon) scans as *jib tis lā ḥī* but not as **jib ti si lā ḥī*. More examples: *jāb ᶜyāluh → jā biᶜ yā luh* (he brought his children), *ḥinnā ᶜnizih → hin naᶜ ni zih* (we are of the ᶜAnazah tribe), *tigl rmikih → tig lir mi kih* (as a grown female horse).

The metrical form of a Nabaṭi poem is a syllabic matrix to which all the verses conform. Therefore, when we come across an utterance that can be scanned in more than one way in an individual hemistich, we choose the one that conforms to the metrical form of the specific poem. For example, an utterance consisting of a word with a final closed syllable followed by a word with an initial consonant cluster, such as *šaggag ṯyābuh* (he tore off his garment [out of extreme passion]), may be scanned in two ways: we can restore the elided vowel after the initial consonant of the second word—*šag gag ṯi yā buh*—or we can reduce the final closed syllable in the first word to a short syllable and link its terminal consonant to the initial of the second word—*šag ga giṯ yā buh*. Another example: when we have an utterance consisting of a word with a final long vowel followed by a word with an initial consonant cluster, such as *ṣirnā frag* (we became divided into small groups), we may scan it either as *ṣir nā fi rag* or as *ṣir naf rag*.

A final consonant cluster is permitted at the very end of a hemistich. An initial consonant cluster is permitted at the very beginning of a hemistich. In this position, a long syllable with an initial consonant cluster may be counted as just one syllable, or the initial consonant may be counted as an independent short syllable; this is determined by whether the first foot of the meter of the poem begins with a short syllable or a long one. A word like *ḥṣānī* (my horse) may thus scan, depending on meter, either as *ḥṣā nī* or as *ḥi ṣā nī*. If the initial syllable with the initial consonant cluster is short, it may be counted, again depending on the meter of the poem, either as short (e.g., *gḏibat → gḏi bat* [she seized]), or as two short syllables reduced to one long syllable (e.g., *mtawallᶜin → mit wal li ᶜin* [burning with passion]).

By observing these scansion techniques, the verses of a poem, from first to last, become arranged into strings of syllables which are collocated in such a way that the short syllables and the long syllables of all the verses align themselves perfectly in vertical columns. By so arranging the verses, we will find that in many instances syllables are unambiguously long or short with each syllable falling into its expected column. The postulated cases will also fall in their expected columns along with the clear-cut cases. For example, consonants that are followed by elided vowels and that are expected to form independent short syllables will always fall in the same columns with consonants that are followed by unelided vowels.

To demonstrate the validity and applicability of the scanning techniques outlined above, here is a short poem composed by ʿGāb Ibn Siʿdūn al-ʿWājī lamenting the departure of Nūt, his sweetheart. First, I shall transliterate the poem with interlinear translation; then I shall transliterate the poem syllabically according to the scansion techniques outlined above. So that the reader can readily see the working of these techniques, elided vowels will not be supplied; their places will be left as blanks which can be filled simply by inserting the vowel *i*.

1 *yā-nūt ʿannā ḏʿūnikum lēh šālat // yāḥēf tamm frāginā yā-ḥabībī.*
O Nūt, why did you load your camels and depart with your tribe? I am sorry to see you leave, my love.

2 *zamlić maʿ al-ḥazm al-mšarrif tikālat // waggaft arāʿīhin w-galbī ġaḏ̣ībī.*
With a broken heart, I stood watching your pack camels climb the high hill.

3 *ʿigbić ʿyūnī b-ad-dmūʿ istaxālat // damʿī ʿalā xaddī niṯar fōg jēbī.*
My eyes became clouded with tears that ran over my cheeks and fell to my lap.

4 *ʿigbik ʿalay yā-zēn al-ayyām mālat // irjaʿ w-ʿālij ḏ̣āmrī ya-ṭibībī.*
Since you have gone, O beautiful lady, my happy days have left me; come back, O my physician, and cure my heart.

5 *wi-diyārinā min ʿigib fargāk sālat // min damʿ ʿēnī gām yidrij šiʿībī.*
Since you have gone, rain has poured upon our territory from my tears, which have flooded the land.

6 *win ćan fargākum ʿala al-galb ṭālat // nanṣāk fōg mnaṯṯrāt as-sibībī.*
Should you stay away much longer, we will come to you on swift mares.

7 *nāṣalk lō min dūnik al-gōm ḥālat // min fōg gibbin yarhajinn al-ḥarībī.*
Even though the men of your tribe come between us, we will reach you on slender mares which will frighten the fleeing foe.

8 *law ćān dūnik girrah al-xēl jālat // lāzim yijībik ḥaḏḏinā min niṣībī.*
Although full-grown horses with riders try to keep me from you, with luck I shall have you to myself.

This poem scans as follows:

	-	-	˘	-	-	-	˘	-	-	˘	-	-
1	*yā*	*nū*	*t*	*ʿan*	*naḏ*	*ʿū*	*ni*	*kum*	*lē*	*h*	*šā*	*lat*
	yā	*ḥē*	*f*	*tam*	*m f*	*rā*	*gi*	*nā*	*yā*	*ḥa*	*bī*	*bī*
2	*zam*	*lić*	*ma*	*ʿal*	*ḥaz*	*mal*	*m*	*šar*	*rif*	*ti*	*kā*	*lat*
	wag	*gaf*	*ta*	*rā*	*ʿī*	*hin*	*w*	*gal*	*bī*	*ġa*	*ḏī*	*bī*
3	*ʿig*	*bić*	*ʿ*	*yū*	*nī*	*bad*	*d*	*mū*	*ʿis*	*ta*	*xā*	*lat*
	dam	*ʿī*	*ʿa*	*lā*	*xad*	*dī*	*ni*	*ṭar*	*fō*	*g*	*jē*	*bī*
4	*ʿig*	*bik*	*ʿa*	*lay*	*yā*	*zē*	*na*	*lay*	*yā*	*m*	*mā*	*lat*
	ir	*jaʿ*	*w*	*ʿā*	*lij*	*ḏā*	*m*	*rī*	*yā*	*ṭi*	*bī*	*bī*
5	*wid*	*yā*	*ri*	*nā*	*min*	*ʿig*	*b*	*far*	*gā*	*k*	*sā*	*lat*
	min	*dam*	*ʿ*	*ē*	*nī*	*gā*	*m*	*yid*	*rij*	*š*	*ʿī*	*bī*
6	*win*	*ćā*	*n*	*far*	*gā*	*kum*	*ʿa*	*lal*	*gal*	*b*	*ṭā*	*lat*
	nan	*ṣā*	*k*	*fō*	*g m*	*naṯ*	*ṯ*	*rā*	*tas*	*si*	*bī*	*bī*
7	*nā*	*ṣal*	*k*	*lō*	*min*	*dū*	*ni*	*kal*	*gō*	*m*	*ḥā*	*lat*
	min	*fō*	*g*	*gib*	*bin*	*yar*	*ha*	*jin*	*nal*	*ḥa*	*rī*	*bī*
8	*law*	*ćā*	*n*	*dū*	*nik*	*gir*	*ra*	*ḥal*	*xē*	*l*	*jā*	*lat*
	lā	*zim*	*yi*	*jī*	*bik*	*haḏ*	*ḏi*	*nā*	*min*	*ni*	*ṣī*	*bī*

The Metrical Structure of Nabaṭi Poetry

The first step in determining the meter of a Nabaṭi hemistich is to divide it into its constituent syllables. Then the syllables are grouped into larger units of metrical measurement called feet. A foot is a unique combination of one short syllable and two or three long syllables.[7] The procedure followed to discover metrical feet is quite simple. First, we find simple meters in each of which only one type of short and long syllable combination repeats itself; this combination is isolated and identified as a foot. After examining all the simple meters and identifying their feet, we then proceed to analyze complex meters as combinations of two or more of the already identified feet.

The following is an inventory of fifty-one metrical patterns (grouped into meter classes) which I have been able to identify in Nabaṭi poetry. Each metrical pattern will be represented by one hemistich illustrating its use.

A. 1. *agūl an-niṣāyiḥ wa-aʿidd al-fiḏāyiḥ*
B. 2. *yā-rjāl al-ḥamiyyih*

3. *ya-llah al-yōm yā-rawwāf*
4. *yā-mjallī tisammaᶜ l-ᶜōdin fiṣīḥ*

C. 5. *ᶜalāmih marr ᶜajlān*
6. *ġarīmin b-al-hawā rūḥī*
7. *sigā ṣōb al-ḥayā miznin tahāma*
8. *anā mā-nīb haḏḏārin miṯil nāsin yahaḏrūn*
9. *salāmin sālmin mihdīh lik yā-gāyd al-ġizlān*

D. 10. *yōm šāf al-ġāwyāt*
11. *fazz galbī fazz galbī*
12. *yā-salāmī yā-salām allah*
13. *kill šayyin ġēr rabbik w-al-ᶜamal*
14. *rawwaḥan miṯl al-giṭā ṣōb aṯ-ṯimīlih*
15. *bint šēxin mā yiḥīd aṭ-ṭēr ᶜan mandātih*
16. *lī ṯalāṯ snīn aᶜaḏḏil fīć y-al-ᶜēn aš-šiġiyyih*
17. *ya-hal al-ᶜērāt bāćir ćān marrētu ṭawārif xillī*

E. 18. *yā-rabbinā mā min miṭīr*
19. *yalᶜab ṭarab w-al-hamm mā jāh*
20. *yā-ḏ-al-ḥamām allī sijaᶜ bi-l-ḥūn*
21. *yā-galb lā tiyyis walā tirtāᶜī*
22. *hāḏī ᶜnēzih mā nibīᶜ ah b-az-zihīd*
23. *ya-dḥēm yā-maškāy šīlaw ᶜadl al-amṯāl*

F. 24. *anā hāḏ̣ mā bī nōḏ̣ barrāg*
25. *al-aᶜmār sifnin w-as-snīn bḥār*
26. *al-ayyām mā xallan ḥadin mā ćawannih*
27. *bidā al-ġīl min jafnih jifā laḏḏat rgādih*
28. *xalūjin tijiḏḏ al-galb b-aᶜlā ᶜwālhā*

G. 29. *gāl min wallaf jawābin ṭarā lih*
30. *lā tikāṯar jayyitī yā-niḏ̣ar ᶜēnī*
31. *yā-hal al-bistān min faḏ̣likum ᶜingūdī*
32. *ya-llah innī ṭālbik ya-mṯīb allī ṣibar*

H. 33. *ᶜaddēt b-al-mistiġillī*
34. *yā-mill galbin ᶜalā mīhāf*
35. *yā-sidritin gāᶜat al-ġirmūl yizzīć*
36. *ḥayy allah allī yiġīb w-yisriᶜ ar-riddih*
37. *in ćān hāḏī miṭālībik gaharnā ar-rḥīl*
38. *yaḥḥōl anā min jrūḥ al-galb w-al-ḥibb yaḥḥōl*

I. 39. *yā-ᶜalī ṣiḥt b-aṣ-ṣōt ar-rifīᶜ*
40. *yā-ḥamāmin ᶜalā al-ġābih yinūḥi*
41. *yōm ᶜaddā ar-riġībih rās mašḏūbih*
42. *yā-ḥamāmih ġarībih ᶜind bāb as-salām*
43. *ams fī sūg m-adrī ᶜarriḏ̣at lī ġazālih*

J. 44. *ḏibaḥnī b-at-tiġillī lih ᶜzūmin giwiyyih*

K. 45. *yā-ᶜēn ya-llī ġilīlin nōmahā min ćamm lēlih*

46. *ᶜayyant kisrā w-gēṣar ᶜazzalaw w-al-kill bāsih šidīd*
L. 47. *yā-ġārᶜ ad-dammām gim w-igriᶜih*
48. *nāḥ al-ḥamām b-ᶜālyāt al-migāṣir*
49. *ᶜādat ᶜalā allī b-al-hawā sabbal al-ḥibbih*
M. 50. *yā-hal al-fāṭr allī fōgahā min kill dašnin jidīdin ġalī*
N. 51. *mānīᶜ xayyālin b-ad-dakkih*

To show the relationship between these metrical patterns, I will convert the above hemistichs into short and long syllables. Each hemistich consists of a string of short and long syllables with the short syllables separated from each other by no less than two but no more than three long syllables. The only exception is hemistich 51 which is made up of long syllables only, thus making it impossible to divide it into feet. The fifty-one hemistichs group themselves into fourteen meters, each having from one to eight variants. The variants of a meter all share the same foot or combination of feet, but they are different in length, that is, in number of syllables. In addition of syllables to the shortest variant may be even, as in class E, or there may be jumps and leaps. The gaps created by these jumps and leaps are accidental and not formal. They may be the result of incomplete sampling or they may represent neglected (*muhmal*) variants. The syllabic breakdown of the meters is shown on the following page.

The scansion techniques explained in the previous section are consistent with the way the poetry is chanted or sung. But the above metrical inventory is a formal classification for which there is no equivalent classification employed by the poets themselves. Nabaṭi poets, except perhaps for those few among them who are literate, are not and need not be consciously aware of the metrical structure of their compositions—even though in many cases, as we shall see shortly, this structure may correspond to that of a classical literary metrical scheme.

The way Nabaṭi poets regulate the rhythm of their compositions is quite different. If a Nabaṭi poet wishes to determine whether his verse is metrically sound (*ᶜādil*) or broken (*maksūr*) by recitation, he can make sure by singing it. The way a verse is sung or chanted is called *ṭarg* (beat rhythm) or *šēlih* (raising of the voice). When one hears a new poem one may ask "*wiššū h-aṭ-targ*" ("What is this rhythm?") or "*wišlōn šēlitah*" ("How is it sung?")

In much the same way as the fifty-one hemistichs given above can be grouped into metrical classes based on syllable arrangement, Nabaṭi poets arrange them into melodic categories. The most famous melodies are *masḥūb, marbūᶜ, hlālī, xmīšī, ṣxarī, hjēnī, sāmrī, ḥōṭī,* and *ᶜarḏih*. The first five categories are usually sung individually to the accompaniment of the *ribābih* (the one-stringed, fiddle-like instrument). The sixth is sung

A.	1.	⏑ – –	⏑ – –	⏑ – –	⏑ – –	
B.	2.	– ⏑ –	– ⏑ –	–		
	3.	– ⏑ –	– ⏑ –	– –		
	4.	– ⏑ –	– ⏑ –	– ⏑ –	– ⏑ –	
C.	5.	⏑ – – –	⏑ – –			
	6.	⏑ – – –	⏑ – – –			
	7.	⏑ – – –	⏑ – – –	⏑ – –		
	8.	⏑ – – –	⏑ – – –	⏑ – – –	⏑ – –	
	9.	⏑ – – –	⏑ – – –	⏑ – – –	⏑ – – –	
D.	10.	– ⏑ – –	– ⏑ –			
	11.	– ⏑ – –	– ⏑ – –			
	12.	– ⏑ – –	– ⏑ – –	–		
	13.	– ⏑ – –	– ⏑ – –	– ⏑ –		
	14.	– ⏑ – –	– ⏑ – –	– ⏑ – –		
	15.	– ⏑ – –	– ⏑ – –	– ⏑ – –	– –	
	16.	– ⏑ – –	– ⏑ – –	– ⏑ – –	– ⏑ – –	
	17.	– ⏑ – –	– ⏑ – –	– ⏑ – –	– ⏑ – –	– –
E.	18.	– – ⏑ –	– – ⏑ –			
	19.	– – ⏑ –	– – ⏑ –	–		
	20.	– – ⏑ –	– – ⏑ –	– –		
	21.	– – ⏑ –	– – ⏑ –	– – –		
	22.	– – ⏑ –	– – ⏑ –	– – ⏑ –		
	23.	– – ⏑ –	– – ⏑ –	– – ⏑ –	–	
F.	24.	⏑ – –	⏑ – – –	⏑ – –		
	25.	⏑ – –	⏑ – – –	⏑ – –	–	
	26.	⏑ – –	⏑ – – –	⏑ – –	⏑ – –	
	27.	⏑ – –	⏑ – – –	⏑ – –	⏑ – – –	
	28.	⏑ – –	⏑ – – –	⏑ – –	⏑ – ⏑ –	
G.	29.	– ⏑ – –	– ⏑ –	– ⏑ – –		
G.	29.	– ⏑ – –	– ⏑ –	– ⏑ – –		
	30.	– ⏑ – –	– ⏑ –	– ⏑ – –	–	
	31.	– ⏑ – –	– ⏑ –	– ⏑ – –	– –	
	32.	– ⏑ – –	– ⏑ –	– ⏑ – –	– ⏑ –	
H.	33.	– – ⏑ –	– ⏑ –	–		
	34.	– – ⏑ –	– ⏑ –	– –		
	35.	– – ⏑ –	– ⏑ –	– – ⏑ –	–	
	36.	– – ⏑ –	– ⏑ –	– – ⏑ –	– –	
	37.	– – ⏑ –	– ⏑ –	– – ⏑ –	– ⏑ –	
	38.	– – ⏑ –	– ⏑ –	– – ⏑/– –	– ⏑ –	–
I.	39.	– ⏑ –	– ⏑ – –	– ⏑		
	40.	– ⏑ –	– ⏑ – –	– ⏑ –	–	
	41.	– ⏑ –	– ⏑ – –	– ⏑ –	– –	
	42.	– ⏑ –	– ⏑ – –	– ⏑ –	– ⏑ –	
	43.	– ⏑ –	– ⏑ – –	– ⏑ –	– ⏑ – –	
J.	44.	⏑ – – – ⏑ – – ⏑ – – – ⏑ – –				
K.	45.	– – ⏑ –	– ⏑ – –	– ⏑ – –	– ⏑ – –	
	46.	– – ⏑ –	– ⏑ – –	– ⏑ – –	– ⏑ – –	⏑ –
L.	47.	– – ⏑ –	– – ⏑ –	– ⏑ –		
	48.	– – ⏑ –	– – ⏑ –	– ⏑ –	–	
	49.	– – ⏑ –	– – ⏑ –	– ⏑ –	– –	
M.	50.	– ⏑ – – ⏑ – – – ⏑ – – – ⏑ – – ⏑ – – – –				
N.	51.	– – – – – – – –				

The syllabic breakdown of meters.

either to the accompaniment of the *ribābih* or while riding on thoroughbred camel mounts (*hijin*). The last three categories are sung collectively to the accompaniment of drums (*ṭbūl*). This melodic classification does not in any way correspond to or accord with the metrical classification worked out above. Poems of different meters are grouped in the same melodic category even though they are sung differently. For example, hemistichs 14, 34, 36, and 43 are all *hjēnī*, and hemistichs 22, 30, 32, 40, and 41 are all *ʿarḏih*. Moreover, an individual poem may belong to several melodic categories although it has only one meter. For example, hemistich 7 is classed both as *ṣxarī* and as *sāmrī*, hemistich 34 as both *hjēnī* and *sāmrī*, and hemistich 46 as *masḥūb, marbūʿ*, and *ḥōṭī*.

Relationship of Nabaṭi Metrics to Classical Prosody

Although the prosody of Nabaṭi poetry exhibits some differences from that of classical Arabic poetry, the two are generically related, and their differences can be explained as the result partly of linguistic changes and partly of a general tendency toward symmetry and simplification of the metrical paradigm.

Al-Khalīl ibn Aḥmad, who lived in the eighth century A.D., was the first to formulate the metrical system of classical Arabic poetry.[8] He posited five metrical circles, each containing from two to nine ideal metrical forms. A metrical circle is a circle consisting of a specific number of long and short syllables combined in a specific manner. The meters of a circle are formally related to each other. By starting to count from one point on a circle, one of its meters is obtained; the others are likewise derived from it by changing the starting point. The total yield of the five metrical circles is twenty-two ideal meters, including six "neglected" (*muhmal*) meters. These six are accidental gaps in the metrical system because they are not employed by classical poets even though there are no formal constraints to prevent their use.

The number of classical meters actually observed is much larger than the number of ideal meters from which they are derived, so to speak, through formal rules. Several variants can be derived from the ideal form of a meter by changing the syllabic structure of the last foot of the first hemistich (*ʿarūḍ*) and the last foot of the second (*ḍarb*). These changes are called *ʿilal* and they are binding: whatever changes the poet introduces in the *ʿarūḍ* and *ḍarb* of the first verse of a poem he must continue to adhere to throughout the remainder of the poem. The verses in a poem are all of the same meter throughout, and the two hemistichs of every verse are metrically similar except for the *ʿarūḍ* and *ḍarb*, which are usually different. Because of this probable difference, it is not possible to identify exactly the meter of a classical verse without knowing both of its hemistichs in order to know its *ʿarūḍ* and *ḍarb*.

In addition to the *ʿilal* there are other syllabic changes called *ziḥāfāt*. Whereas the *ʿilal* are binding and affect only the *ʿarūḍ* and *ḍarb*, the *ziḥāfāt* affect the remainder of the verse, called *ḥašw*, and are optional poetic licenses. Unlike the *ʿilal*, the *ziḥafat* do not affect all the verses of a poem in the same way and are not binding but may be varied.

In Nabaṭi prosody, the general tendency toward symmetry has resulted in eliminating the difference between the last foot of the first hemistich and that of the second; the two hemistichs of a Nabaṭi verse are metrically identical except in those verses which are composed in the classical *ṭawīl* meter. For this reason, I consider the hemistich, rather than the entire verse, to be the maximum unit of metrical measurement in Nabaṭi poetry; the syllable is the minimum unit. No classical poem is free of *ziḥāfāt*, but in Nabaṭi poetry they are rare and affect only the initial syllable of a hemistich, which can be optionally reduced from long to short or, if already short, deleted altogether. As a matter of fact, those *ziḥāfāt* which permit the deletion of one or two short syllables, the substitution of two short syllables by a long one, and the reduction of a long syllable to a short one in the contiguity of another short syllable are all inapplicable to Nabaṭi poetry because they all presume the unconditioned permissibility of a sequence of two short syllables, a feature which is avoided in Nabaṭi vernacular. In cases where the phonetically conditioned sequence of two short syllables discussed in the preceding pages may affect a verse in a Nabaṭi poem, one of these two short syllables will always fall in a column of corresponding short syllables, but the other will fall in an adjacent column of long syllables. But this is a phonetically conditioned, not an optional, syllable substitution, and therefore cannot be considered a *ziḥāf*. The rules of *ziḥāfāt* in classical poetry are based on division of the feet of a classical meter into smaller units of syllable combinations called *asbāb* and *awtād*. But since the *ʿilal* and *ziḥāfāt* rarely apply to Nabaṭi poetry, it suffices to divide the feet of Nabaṭi meters simply into short and long syllables.[9]

The avoidance of sequences of two short syllables has also resulted in the disappearance of two classical meters, *al-wāfir* and *al-kāmil*, from the metrical inventory of Nabaṭi poetry, since two of the feet of these meters, namely *mufāʿalatun* and *mutafāʿilun*, include a sequence of two short syllables. Five more classical meters, all of the *al-muštabih* circle—namely *as-sarīʿ*, *al-munsariḥ*, *al-xafīf*, *al-muḍāriʿ*, and *al-muqtaḍab*—have no correspondences in Nabaṭi poetry. In these matters—uniquely among the classical meters—five short syllables are separated from one another by four long syllables. It is perhaps this anomaly that led to the disappearance of these meters from Nabaṭi poetry, since in Nabaṭi meters short syllables are separated from each other by no more than three but no less than two long syllables.

The meters of the last five hemistichs (47–51) in the metrical inventory presented above do not correspond exactly to any of the classical meters. We may consider the meter of hemistichs 47–49 as an adaptation of the classical *ṭawil* meter, differing from it only by the absence of an initial short syllable. It is not possible to determine the meter of hemistich 50 because there is more than one way in which it can be divided into feet and none of the possible divisions corresponds to any classical meter. Hemistich 51 cannot be divided into feet since its constituent syllables are all long.

Despite these differences between the metrical structures of Nabaṭi and classical Arabic poetry, a cursory examination of the Nabaṭi metrical inventory will show that many classical meters are still being used: *al-mutaqārib* (1), *al-mutadārak* (2–4), *al-hazaj* (5–9), *ar-ramal* (10–17), *ar-rajaz* (18–23), *aṭ-ṭawīl* (24–28), *al-madīd* (29–32), *al-basīṭ* (33–38), and *al-mujtaṯṯ* (45–46). The meters *al-mumtadd* (39–43) and *al-mustaṭīl* (44), which belong to the *al-muxtalif* circle, are used by Nabaṭi poets even though they are neglected (*muhmal*) in classical poetry. Some of the classical meters used in Nabaṭi poetry have been made longer (e.g., *al-hazaj* (8–9) and *ar-ramal* (15–17). A Nabaṭi hemistich can be as long as it is possible for a singer to chant in one breath; and as far as I have been able to determine, breath seems to be the only limiting factor on length. Hemistich 50 has a sum total of twenty syllables; the longest hemistich in classical Arabic poetry is fourteen syllables.

Rhyme

Turning now to the rhyme scheme of Nabaṭi poetry, we also observe both similarities and differences with respect to classical Arabic poetry. In a classical poem, only the second hemistichs of the verses rhyme throughout, never the first, whereas a Nabaṭi poem usually has two rhymes, one for the first hemistichs and a different rhyme for the second. Not infrequently, the rhyming consonant, *ar-rawiyy*, of the first and second hemistichs is the same while the preceding vowel, *ar-ridf*, is different. For example, the first hemistichs may rhyme in *-ūb*/*-ōb* and the second in *-īb*/*-ēb*. As a result of the monophthongization of diphthongs, *ū* and *ō* can serve interchangeably as *ridf*, as can *ī* and *ē*. Certain blemishes, such as *iqwā* and *sinād*, against which medieval prosodists warned post-classical poets, are not applicable to Nabaṭi poetry due to the shedding of case endings and the leveling effect of centralizing high and low vowels.

The Historical Development of Classical Arabic Poetic Diction

The continuity between ancient Arabic poetry and Nabaṭi poetry, and the exact nature of their historical relationship are matters that are obscured by their linguistic differences—the most salient feature, which distinguishes one from the other. The problem is made more complex by the fact that the diction of ancient Arabic poetry was elevated from its origins as a poetic vernacular to a highly esteemed literary language, which continues to the present day to be employed by cultivated poets as a medium of composition. This may lead one to ask how it is that popular poetry composed in the vernacular can be considered the descendant—or even a near relation—of classical Arabic poetry, which is traditionally viewed as the perfect model of literary excellence. And even should we accept the proposition of the descent of Nabaṭi poetry from classical Arabic poetry, does this proposition in any way modify our view of postclassical and neoclassical Arabic poetry composed in "literary" Arabic? To answer these questions it is necessary to take a few steps backwards in history in order to review the development of the Arabic language and to trace briefly the transformation from "classical" to "vernacular" of the poetic diction of Arabia.

As has already been noted, the diction of Nabaṭi poetry and that of classical Arabic poetry may be considered as the two poles of a single poetic idiom deriving from the spoken language of Arabia. This poetic idiom underwent many developments in the course of time—developments that resulted from parallel changes in the phonology, morphology, syntax, and semantics of the spoken language. It may be assumed that originally the degree of difference between the spoken language and the poetic idiom of ancient Arabia was probably no greater than that between the language spoken in Arabia a few decades ago and the diction of vernacular poetry. The diction of ancient Arabic poetry, or what we now in retrospect call "classical" Arabic, was essentially a polished form of the language spoken by the people in their daily intercourse, as is the case today with the vernacular diction of Nabaṭi poetry. It was, as Gibb puts it, a "standardized poetic idiom based on the spoken dialects but distinguished from them by refinements of vocabulary, inflections and syntactical articulation" (1968:10). The poets of ancient Arabia were popular, illiterate poets who did not go to institutions of higher learning in order to learn "classical" or "correct" Arabic, but who acquired their poetic diction in the same way that modern popular poets learn their own poetic idiom: by listening to and interacting with their peers and elders.

It was not until the Arab conquest of neighboring nations and the spread of Islam outside Arabia that the structure of spoken Arabic began to deviate radically from that of classical Arabic, the function of which was by then changing from that of a poetic vernacular to that of a literary language in which fluency was acquired through formal education and rigorous training. After the Arabs took up residence in the newly conquered territories and mingled with the native populations, their speech began, as a result of their exposure to other languages, to diverge significantly from that of the ancients. But this linguistic change did not mean the disappearance of the classical tongue. Because it had been captured at a given moment and utilized as the medium of divine revelation, classical Arabic was destined to sanctity, permanence, and prestige as the language of faith and learning. Early Muslim philologists felt that it was a religious duty to preserve and study classical Arabic as spoken by the Prophet and his companions, and they scrupulously collected and examined examples of it. The resulting corpus consisted chiefly of the poetry of the desert Arabs among whom the classical poetic diction had appeared and flourished in circumstances that promoted its continuity. It was on the basis of this corpus that the philologists systematically formulated the grammatical rules and prosodic principles of classical Arabic. In this way there came to be two varieties of Arabic used in urban centers: the relatively stable and uniform classical language, and the colloquial Arabic, which was subject to local and temporal changes. These structurally and functionally different varieties of Arabic have coexisted side by side up to the present time.[10]

Classical Arabic language and classical Arabic poetry remained throughout the ages the models for literary and poetic expression.[11] The grammatical rules of the classical tongue and the prosodic principles of classical poetry came to be viewed as obligatory in the literary compositions of scholars, scribes, the literate elite, and the court poets whose daily intercourse was in colloquial Arabic. However, in response to the changing life-styles and social milieus of the rapidly developing Muslim civilization, postclassical Arabic poetry began to diverge from the classical tradition in its social function, thematic content, and general outlook.

The heroic spirit and social function of the classical poetic tradition persisted among the desert Arabs, who continued to live under the same socioeconomic conditions that had prevailed in ancient Arabia, and whose relative isolation gave them some immunity from foreign influences. Life in the Arabian desert was but briefly interrupted by Islam and but lightly touched by its developing civilization. Desert knights and tribal poets continued to celebrate their valor and gallantry and the virtues of their tribes in verses which spread swiftly throughout the desert. Long after it had become a literary language among the urban population, classical

Arabic endured as a poetic vernacular and medium of popular artistic expression in Arabia. When the language of the urban masses became "contaminated" by foreign influences, illiterate bedouins served as native informants from whom the early philologists of Basrah and Kufah collected samples of classical poetry and usage.

The Rise of Nabaṭi Poetry

While the grammatical rules and prosodic principles of the classical tradition were being maintained and emulated by the scholars and poets of Muslim capitals, they were undergoing inevitable transformations in their native land, the Arabian desert. Bedouin speech slowly began to yield to some of the changes affecting the speech of city Arabs. The majority of desert poets lacked the education and formal training necessary to master and perpetuate the classical grammar and prosody. They were not aware of, and hence not bound by, the rules formulated by the philologists, and, even if they were aware of these rules, they lacked the scholarly training that would enable them to apply them. Furthermore, unlike postclassical urban poets whose compositions functioned as an elite literature which only the educated upper classes could appreciate, desert poetry continued to be composed on public occasions to fulfill public functions. Desert poets played significant social roles as the agents of public opinion and as the articulators of the social norms and cultural values of their society; therefore, their diction was continually adapting to parallel the changing language of their illiterate audiences.

At the same time that these linguistic developments were taking place, Arabia was becoming more and more cut off from the rest of the Arab-Muslim world. After the Arab conquest of Syria and Mesopotamia, the sway of the Arab-Muslim empire shifted to those ancient centers of civilization and away from Arabia, which came to be neglected by the caliphs. A few centuries after the death of Muḥammad, Arabia had lapsed into political anarchy and was veiled by a second *jāhilīyah*[12] from the rest of the world. Although the northern reaches, coastal fringes, and the *ḥajj* routes remained somewhat familiar because they were well traveled, intractable nomads and the forbidding barrenness of the desert rendered the interior of Arabia virtually inaccessible to outsiders.

These linguistic and sociopolitical factors contributed to the gradual isolation of the poetic tradition of the Arabian desert from the mainstream of Arabic literature. For the philologists, the desert Arabs became unapproachable, and useless as informants because their manners and speech had become "corrupt." The poetic diction of the Arabian desert eventually diverged so much from classical Arabic that it became difficult for the literary pedants in urban centers to understand it. Those pedants shunned this truly authentic poetry; and even when it did reach their ears, they frowned upon it and may even have suppressed it as they did other forms of vernacular lore. As a result of this attitude on the part of medieval Arab scholars, we now have no written sources on the poetic tradition of the Arabian desert at this critical period in its long history, and poetic examples from that period are scarce.

Ibn Khaldūn, with his usual acumen, was the only one among the medieval scholars to write on this topic. He noted that the poetic diction of the Arabian desert was changing because the speech of the desert Arabs itself had changed from what it had been in the ancient past.[13] Despite this linguistic change, the poetry of the desert, wrote Ibn Khaldūn, retained its vigor and eloquence—contrary to the dogmatic claims of the philologists of his time:

> Most of the professed scholars of this age, especially philologists, disapprove of this [vernacular] poetry when they listen to it and shun its composition when they hear it recited, claiming that their taste disdains it because it is not eloquent, since its language has lost case inflections. But the real reason is lack of competence in the dialect in which this poetry is composed. Were they to possess the necessary competence, their taste and natural feeling would testify to the eloquence of this poetry, provided that their disposition and perception be not warped. Case inflections have nothing to do with eloquence. Eloquence is the conformity of expression to the thing expressed and to the situation at hand, no matter how subject and object are marked, since these can be easily deduced through syntactic relation, as is the case in their [the desert Arabs'] dialect today. As for meaning, it is based upon conventions agreed upon by the speakers. If the speaker knows these conventions and if the expression [he uses] conforms to these conventions and is appropriate to the situation at hand, then eloquence is achieved regardless of the grammarians' rules. (1967:1126)

His insightful observations notwithstanding, what Ibn Khaldūn has to say about the poetry of the Arabian desert is too sketchy and too general. The examples he provides are very few and lack both commentary and background information. They suffer from metrical irregularities, which may be attributed in part to typographical inaccuracies and the ignorance of modern editors concerning this poetry. Moreover, since the language of these examples is somewhere between classical Arabic and modern vernacular, we have no clear idea of its actual pronunciation and proper scansion.

After a gap of more than two hundred years, we begin to find more poetic examples in a better state of preservation than those given by Ibn Khaldūn. By the end of the sixteenth century, we begin to hear of poets such as Rashīd al-Khalāwī, Abū Ḥamzih al-ʿĀmrī, Giṭan ibn Giṭan, and others who are still remembered (al-Faraj 1952:I, 6–7). The compositions of these and later poets have survived in manuscripts, and some have been recently published in anthologies.

The paucity of sources makes it difficult to trace the gradual development of the poetic tradition in the Arabian desert. Furthermore, the subtleties of the linguistic process, the accumulative results of which came to be the chief distinguishing feature between the classical diction and the vernacular, make it practically impossible to set a point in time where classical and vernacular diverged. It is perhaps more appropriate to divide the poetic tradition of the Arabian desert into stages. Examples from the sixteenth and seventeenth centuries (i.e., early examples of what is now collectively referred to as Nabaṭi poetry) approximate more recent vernacular poems in morphology and syntax but contain classical idioms and lexical items that are not employed by later Nabaṭi poets. These examples are all in classical meters (*ṭawīl, rajaz, hazaj,* and *basīṭ*), and their rhyme scheme follows the classical pattern in that only the second hemistichs rhyme. They also contain many motifs, themes, and images that have become less popular among later poets.

Thus we see that the formal correspondences between classical Arabic and modern vernacular poetry go beyond accidental similarities or the mere influence of an early tradition on a later one. The roots of the latter can be unmistakably traced back to the former, and the divergences that distinguish the two traditions from one another do not imply any categorical difference between them. Their divergences are the outcome of the slow incremental diachronic changes that are inevitable in any living tradition. These changes do not imply in any way a serious break between classical and vernacular poetry. Vernacular poets inherited the classical tradition and continued to develop it through time. Certain thematic and formal conventions were enriched and made more complex, but others have become less popular or have been replaced by new ones. Employing the same formal principles and compositional devices of their ancient predecessors, vernacular poets continued to discover new themes and explore new compositional techniques without interrupting the continuity between their poetry and that of the ancients.

IX

NABAṬI POETRY AND THE CLASSICAL LITERARY TRADITION

In the previous chapter I examined the prosody of Nabaṭi poetry and its relationship to classical prosody; I then traced the historical process that led eventually to the development of certain differences between the two prosodic systems. The prosodic relationship between Nabaṭi and classical poetry is paralleled by a thematic relationship, already touched upon at the beginning of chapter 2 and implicit throughout this work. Aside from the fact that the two poetic traditions perform the same social functions and deal with the same general topics (e.g., boasting, panegyric, eulogy, satire, love poetry), they also employ many of the same compositional techniques and share many of the same stock themes, motifs, and images. In its thematic development, the Nabaṭi poem follows closely the structural principles employed by the ancient poets. As in classical poetry, a long Nabaṭi poem is usually divided into two principal parts, a prelude and the main topic. The journey (*riḥlah*) remains a very significant component of the prelude in Nabaṭi poetry. In this section, the poet pictures himself or his deputy as riding through the wilderness to deliver the poem. He describes in detail the desert roads and stations as well as the physical qualities of the camel mount. In addition to the journey and description of the camel mount, Nabaṭi poets have preserved in their compositions the classical theme of the deserted encampment and the lamentation over the departed lady. Following the example of their ancient predecessors, many Nabaṭi poets may begin or conclude their poems with a few lines expressing general principles or maxims of conduct.

As I have suggested in the previous chapter, the thematic continuity between ancient Arabic poetry and Nabaṭi poetry is the result of their historical continuity; the two traditions are in fact the two ends of one continuous poetic tradition which extends over a long period and which reflects the same sociocultural realities. This historical continuity is, however, complemented by a more specific literary relationship, which is the subject of the present chapter—a relationship involving direct borrowings by Nabaṭi poets of compositional and thematic elements characteristic of, or originating in, the written literature of classical and postclassical Arabic.

Literacy and Compositional Techniques

The fact that Nabaṭi poetry is composed in the vernacular has led Ibn Khamīs (1958:152–174), Sh. al-Kamālī (1964:283–304), and others to assume that all Nabaṭi poets were illiterate. It is true that most of Nabaṭi poetry is the work of nomads and unlettered folk, but there were certainly, among the urban poets, some who knew how to read and write. It may seem surprising that a literate poet would compose in the vernacular instead of the more prestigious and respected literary language; in this connection, we should remember that the culture of premodern Arabia was predominantly an oral culture and that the poets addressed their compositions to a predominantly illiterate audience. A poet who wanted his verses to circulate among the illiterate masses would have to compose not in the literary but in the vernacular diction. The patrons of professional poets were mostly illiterate personages who wanted to be eulogized not in the literary but in the vernacular language. Moreover, literacy does not necessarily imply proficiency in using literary Arabic, for this is a scholarly and demanding skill which requires studious learning and diligent training. Nevertheless, there were a few literate Nabaṭi poets who clearly borrowed techniques and devices from written literature and employed them in their vernacular poetry.

Biographical evidence is perhaps the most unequivocal evidence of literacy. We possess very little biographical information about Nabaṭi poets, but the exiguous data we do have clearly state that a few of them not only knew how to read and write but were indeed learned men. Ibrāhīm al-Jᶜē̱tin (d. 1943) is said to have been well versed in Arabic literature (Kamāl 1960–1971:VIII, 5). Ḥamad Ibn Liᶜbūn wrote of his son, the famous Nabaṭi poet Mḥammad Ibn Liᶜbūn (1790–1831) that he "memorized the Qurʾān, learned how to read and write, and had beautiful handwriting. He panegyrized ᶜUmar Ibn Saᶜūd ibn ᶜAbdalᶜazīz in many poems. At the age of seventeen he migrated to az-Zubayr and he became a poetic genius" (quoted in al-Jāsir 1971:798). M. al-Qāḍi wrote that his grandfather, the famous Nabaṭi poet Mḥammad al-ᶜAbdallah al-Gāḍ̣ī (1809–1868), had memorized the Qurʾān by the time he was eight years old and had studied Islamic jurisprudence with one of the learned men in his home town, ᶜUnaizah, but later became more inclined toward history and literature. He also had a most beautiful handwriting with which he copied *Ṣaḥīḥ al-Bukhārī*. He was wealthy and famous for his liberal hospitality. When he composed his famous panegyric on ᶜUnaizah and its citizens, the amir of the town asked him, "O Abu ᶜAbdallah, how can we reward you for this truly beautiful poem?" Al-Gāḏī answered, "Whenever guests come to town I would like always to be the next to have the honor of entertaining them, after you; this shall be my reward" (al-Qāḍī, in al-Faraj 1952:II, 10–11).

References to writing and to writing materials constitute a significant motif in the compositions of some Nabaṭi poets. This motif includes description of the ink, pen, and paper that are used in writing the poem. In the following examples (the first two by Silīm ibn ʿAbdalḥayy and the third by Miḥsin al-Hazzānī), it is clear that the poets describe themselves as composing with pen in hand.

1 Write! O pen held between the fingers of my hand; make straight lines of black ink on white paper.
2 I will write with you a beautiful poem, verses no one could afford were they to be sold for money.
3 I want to express my longing for a fair maiden with fluttering eyelashes and a long neck, a young lass who has plucked my heart into small pieces.

* * *

1 I constructed seemly rhymes on a scroll of paper for the sake of a lady with many virtues.
2 Greetings to you, lady: as much as the thunder rumbles in the clouds; as much as the herbage sprouts and covers the sand dunes;
3 As much as travelers saddle their mounts; as much as black ink spells [words] on white paper—
4 From the tip of a reed pen in the hand of a poet constructing the foundation of his poem, composing beautiful verses with a clear head.

* * *

1 O riders, turn the necks of your mounts with the reins! Halt! Let me measure my rhymes.
2 Carry with you verses I have composed and strung on the surface of white paper, written with gallnuts and vitriol,
3 From *m ḥ s n* [Miḥsin]—verses recorded and embellished; they are the best—
4 To *m ḥ m d* [Mḥammad] whom I long to see, I send harmonious verses.

Note that in the last example the poet spells his first name in the third verse, and the first name of the friend to whom he is sending the poem in the fourth verse.

Further evidence of literacy which, like spelling, shows the composer's knowledge of the alphabet, is the poetic form called *al-muhmal*. The Arabic alphabet consists of twenty-eight letters, fifteen of which are dotted (*muᶜjam*), and the rest without dots (*muhmal*). A *muhmal* poem is a poem all the verses of which are free of dotted letters; that is to say, the poet restricts himself to words that have no dotted letters (Ibn Khamīs 1958:366–368). I have a copy of a *muhmal* poem consisting of ten verses by Mḥammad al-ᶜŌnī. Al-Gāḏī and Ibn Liᶜbūn have also composed one *muhmal* poem each (Kamāl 1960–1971:VI, 52; X, 101).

Another poetic form that relates to the alphabet is *al-alfīyah*. This does not mean a poem of a thousand lines, as in some didactic poems composed in the Middle Ages, but an alphabetical poem. This is a compositional technique which was practiced by medieval poets (al-Rāfiᶜī 1954:III, 36), but it is much more developed in Nabaṭi poetry. A poem of this sort generally consists of twenty-eight strophes arranged alphabetically according to their initial letters, each strophe being initiated with a different letter of the alphabet. It seems that this poetic form was borrowed from postclassical poetry and introduced into Nabaṭi poetry by al-Hazzānī, since the earliest Nabaṭi *alfīyah* was composed by him. Furthermore, al-Hazzānī composed his *alfīyah* (published in Kamāl 1960–1971:XIII, 8) after the postclassical model, that is, one verse for each letter of the alphabet. But while the *alfīyah* may have originated as a literary form at the hands of literate Nabaṭi poets, it later became popular among all poets, literate or illiterate. Later Nabaṭi poets developed this form in various ways and changed its rhyme scheme to strophic (see Ibn Khamīs 1958:351–354).

In addition to *al-muhmal* and *al-alfīyah*, literate Nabaṭi poets use other literary contrivances including *al-abjadī, ad-darsiᶜī,* and *ar-rēḥānī.* The first of these refers to the alphabetical arrangement known as *abjad hawwaz*, in which each of the twenty-eight letters of the Arabic alphabet is assigned a fixed numerical value whereby letters can stand for numbers and vice versa. Accordingly, an event can be dated by words the numerical value of the letters of which, when they are added up, gives the year in which the event took place. This chronogrammatic dating is widely used by postclassical Arab poets, who called it *at-taʾrix aš-šiᶜrī* or *ḥisāb al-jumal* (or *jummal*) (al-Rāfiᶜī 1954:III, 396–403; ᶜĀnūtī 1970:64–66; Amīn 1972:171–179). Literate Nabaṭi poets have borrowed this device and used it not only to date specific events but for other purposes as well. For example, in the following verse, Rashīd al-Khalāwī advises his listener to marry a lady whose age equals the numerical value of *w* + *y* (i.e., 6 + 10 = 16 years of age): *fitātin b-ḥarf al-wāw w-al-yā sinnahā // fa'in ḥāl ḥālin yitqin al-kāf ḥāsbah*.

Just as letters can stand for numbers, so numbers can stand for letters. Instead of spelling out the name of his lady, for example, a poet can give numbers which correspond in value to the letters that make up the name. This device is a means of concealment to which a poet can resort in case he does not wish to give outright the name of the lady with whom he is in love and about whom he is composing his poem.

Other methods of concealment include *ad-darsīʿī* and *ar-rēḥānī* (ibid.). In *ad-darsīʿī*, the letters of the alphabet are grouped into fourteen pairs: *ḏġ, tj, nq, tḏ, šx, bz, sʿ, dr, fy, lh, ṣḍ, ḥṭ, 'w, km*. To conceal the name of his lady, the poet replaces each of the letters of her name with the letter with which it is paired. For example, if the lady's real name is Hayā, the poet calls her Lafā.

In *ar-rēḥānī*, each letter of the alphabet is designated by a class of things, and the first radical of the word that denotes this class must be the same as the letter that the class designates: for example, *t* = *tamir* (dates), *ḥ* = *ḥadīd* (iron), *r* = *rēḥān* (aromatics), *z* = *zujāj* (glass), *s* = *simak* (fish), *ṣ* = *ṣīn* (china), *f* = *fawākih* (fruits), *n* = *njūm* (stars), *w* = *wuḥūš* (wild animals), *h* = *hawamm* (dangerous beasts), *y* = *yāgūt* (rubies), and so forth. Instead of spelling out the name of his lady, the poet who employs *ar-rēḥānī* will mention in his verses something about the objects that belong to the classes that designate the letters of her name.

Although they are composed in the vernacular, the verses of literate Nabaṭi poets are marked by syntactic and lexical borrowings from literary Arabic, and are full of Qur'anic allusions and references to religious and historical figures and other topics which point to the familiarity of their composers with written sources on religion, history, and literature. Literate Nabaṭi poets were also influenced by postclassical poets in their preoccupation with verbal brilliance and stylistic ornamentation. They strove to embellish their verses and adorn them with rhetorical figures and literary devices. Kh. al-Faraj, who was the first to compile an anthology of Nabaṭi poetry, wrote that al-Hazzānī, Ibn Liʿbūn, and ʿAbdallah al-Faraj were well versed in, and influenced by, postclassical Arabic poetry, and that some of their compositions were characterized by contrived and excessive use of paronomasia, antithesis, double entendre, and other stylistic devices which were employed by medieval Arab poets (1952:7–9).

Among the literary features developed by postclassical poets and adopted by some literate Nabaṭi poets is that known as *al-laff w-an-našr al-murattab*. This consists of dividing the first hemistich of the verse into a series of nouns and the second hemistich into a series of attributes that correspond in order and application to the preceding nouns, as in the following three verses by al-Hazzānī:

1 Tresses, bosoms, and ankles are flowing, erect, and firm.
2 Buttocks, waists, and bellies are plump, slender, and shapely.
3 With promises, trysts, and lies, they are false, deceptive, and generous.

Another postclassical device introduced by literate composers into Nabaṭi poetry is *at-tašrīᶜ*. Instead of dividing the verse into two hemistichs as usual, in *at-tašrīᶜ* the poet divides every verse in the poem into four parts; each part must rhyme with the corresponding parts in the other verses. Furthermore, the second and fourth parts of every verse can be taken out and there will still remain a meaningful verse. Here is an example from a long poem by Ibn Liᶜbūn:

1 *yā-galb lō habb al-hawā (lik w-nāḥī) // bālik tijībih y-al-ġawī (wēn mā rāḥ).*
2 *kibb as-sifāh w-mā ḥawā (min mzāḥī) // ḏ̣āmī ḏ̣ᶜūnih tirtiwī (damᶜ saffāḥ).*

Some literate Nabaṭi poets may try to emulate even more demanding literary techniques such as that known as *al-insijām al-lafḏ̣ī*, which was invented by Badīᶜ al-Zamān al-Hamadhānī and al-Ḥarīrī in their *Maqāmāt*. With this technique, the poet chooses the words for his verses so that the words in each verse will share at least one sound in common, in an attempt to create a certain acoustic harmony, as in the following two lines from a poem by al-Gāḏ̣ī where we observe that the sound *j* is spread throughout the first verse and the sound *s* is spread throughout the second verse.

1 *fijā mā lijā bī dāj fī lāj mihjitī // rijētih rijā rajwā rijā rāj ṭāyir.*
2 *salāmin tisalsal min salāyil misāyil // b-al-irsāl sāl b-sirr al-asrār sāhir.*

On one hand, Ibn Khamīs (1958:212–232, 350–370) gives a detailed discussion and copious examples of such stylistic devices, yet fails to recognize them as clear signs of literacy. For Ibn Khamīs, these techniques are signs of "luxury and frivolity" (*taraf*) but not of literacy. On the other hand, Sh. al-Kamālī entitles his book on Nabaṭi poetry *al-Shiᶜr ᶜinda al-Badw, Poetry Among the Nomads* (1964), implying that this poetry is composed only by illiterate bedouins. As a matter of fact, al-Kamālī asserts that Nabaṭi poetry is exclusively nomadic. It may have escaped his attention that most of the Nabaṭi poets he discusses in his book, such as al-Hazzānī, Ibn Liᶜbūn, and Ibn ᶜArfaj, are urbane inhabitants of such large towns as az-Zubair, Buraidah, and ᶜUnaizah. It is true that the great majority of Nabaṭi poets are illiterate and that the nomadic outlook pervades the Nabaṭi poetic tradition, but Nabaṭi poetry is composed by both illiterate and literate poets and by nomads as well as settlers. Moreover, the specific devices we are discussing here are not typical of the bulk of Nabaṭi poetry—especially that composed by nomadic poets—but are found only in limited examples and primarily in the works of poets whom other evidence shows to have been literate.

These literate Nabaṭi poets played a significant role in establishing direct links between Nabaṭi poetry and the mainstream of Arabic literature. They were intermediaries who were continually attempting to incorporate into their vernacular compositions formal patterns and thematic features drawn from classical and postclassical poetry. Some of their attempts were so successful and so well received by the general public that they were imitated by illiterate poets and eventually became thoroughly assimilated into the Nabaṭi poetic tradition.

Among the postclassical formal patterns adopted by literate Nabaṭi poets which have been used widely by their illiterate colleagues are the strophic rhyme and the *ramal* meter. In the strophic rhyming scheme, the first three lines of every strophe have their own independent rhyme, while the fourth line of every strophe has the same rhyme, binding all the strophes into one poem. It seems that al-Hazzānī was the first literate Nabaṭi poet to borrow this rhyming scheme from postclassical poetry. It has been pointed out above that al-Hazzānī did not employ the strophic pattern in his *alfīyah*. Nevertheless, he did employ it enthusiastically in many of his other compositions. Ibn Liᶜbūn, who came after al-Hazzānī, also composed strophic poems, but he added the further constraint that the rhyming words in the first three lines of every strophe should not only rhyme with each other but should also be homonyms. In this respect, Ibn Liᶜbūn might have been influenced by the device called *jinās al-qawāfī* (homonymous rhymes) of postclassical Arabic poetry and by the popular Iraqi poetic form *az-zhērī* (as a young man, Ibn Liᶜbūn migrated from Ḥarmih, his home town in Najd, to az-Zubair in southern Iraq). Ibn Ribīᶜih, Ibn ᶜArfaj, and al-Gāḏī composed strophic poems after the pattern set by Ibn Liᶜbūn.

The poetry of al-Hazzānī bears a conspicuous resemblance to the poetry of the celebrated Omayyad poet ᶜUmar Ibn Abī Rabīᶜah. They both dealt explicitly with matters of love, and their compositions included dialogues and flirtations with fair chaste maidens. Also, al-Hazzānī composed in *ramal*, a favorite meter of Ibn Abī Rabīᶜah, and a meter much favored for love lyrics intended for public singing, as in the postclassical poetic genre *al-muwaššaḥ*, the invention of which is closely associated with singing. It is interesting to note, therefore, that after al-Hazzānī introduced the *ramal* meter into Nabaṭi poetry Ibn Liᶜbūn used it in love lyrics which he intoned for singing, thus making it one of the most popular meters in Nabaṭi poetry. The tunes invented by Ibn Liᶜbūn still survive today; they are called *al-alḥān al-liᶜbūniyyah* or, more commonly, *as-sāmrī*. In Kuwait, Bahrain, and the rest of the Gulf area they are sung to the accompaniment of the oud, while in Najd they are sung to the accompaniment of drums.

Just as literate Nabaṭi poets had firsthand knowledge of postclassical Arabic poetry, they were also intimately familiar with classical tradition. In their compositions they allude to ancient poets; moreover, the wording and content of some of their verses clearly indicate that they are direct borrowings from classical Arabic poetry, as is seen in the following three examples by Ibn Liᶜbūn. The first contains a hemistich quoted verbatim from the pre-Islamic poet Zuhayr, and the second and third incorporate hemistichs from the *Muᶜallaqah* of the pre-Islamic poet Imruʾ al-Qays (the relevant hemistichs are underlined).

(1) *tibaṣṣar xalīlī hal tarā min ḍaᶜāyin* // *tigāzan bihum fōg aš-šifā min ḥzūmahā.*

(2) *yanšidninī yōm intawā al-kill bi-rḥīl* // *hal ᶜind rasmin dārsin min mᶜawwal.*

(3) *agfā mṣirrin ćinn jākāt šālih* // *jilmūd ṣaxrin ḥaṭṭih as-sēl min ᶜāl.*

Although the pronunciation of these verses must be changed to comply with Nabaṭi scansion, they are of course completely recognizable; they also point to the adoption in Nabaṭi poetry of the rhetorical device *taḍmin*, a device characteristic of poetry composed by literate poets.

Literacy and Thematic Borrowing: The Muᶜallaqah of Imruʾ al-Qays

Space does not allow for a full treatment of the role played by literacy in establishing direct links between Nabaṭi and classical Arabic poetry. Suffice it here to mention a few examples illustrating the influence of one particular ancient poem, the *Muᶜallaqah* of Imruʾ al-Qays,[1] on the compositions of some Nabaṭi poets. The influence of Imruʾ al-Qays is perhaps nowhere more noticeable than in the compositions of ᶜAbdalᶜazīz al-Mḥammad al-Gāḍī, who in several of his poems borrows from the themes and images of Imruʾ al-Qays. This is shown in the following lines from one poem in which he emulates the famous *Muᶜallaqah* (the lines are numbered according to their sequence in the full text, which is published in Kamāl 1960–1971:VII, 35–37).

1 The loose locks of midnight profusely hang over its ample tail like a surging wave flowing over another surging wave.
2 In the folds of darkness, stars flicker like the distant torches of monks who are expecting visitors.
3 The Pleiades are like the guides of a riding party who turned back to look for some lost riders.
4 To the east of them appears Orion; its belt resembles a glittering girdle adorned with pure pearls.

* * *

6 When will the morning illuminate the darkness of the night, though morning is no more cheerful and will not abate my anguish?

* * *

17 Before you [my beloved] I had enjoyed the company of many a virgin, many a middle-aged woman, barren wench, and pregnant woman whom passion drove to my embrace.
18 And many a nursing mother has slept with me; when her child cries, she gives him her back [and does not turn her face from me] out of respect for me.[2]

Another Nabaṭi poet clearly influenced by Imruʾ al-Qays is al-Hazzānī, as the following two examples will illustrate. In the first, al-Hazzānī describes the effects of rain and compares the drowned gazelles as they float on the water to the plucked ʿ*anṣal* plant—using exactly the same words and image as does Imruʾ al-Qays in the last line of his *Muʿallaqah*: "The wild beasts at evening drowned in the furthest reaches of the wide watercourse lay like drawn bulbs of wild onion" (Arberry 1957:66). Al-Hazzānī's version is:

1 The dust of the parched earth was raised by the first gush of rain, and the gazelles were drowned and carried away by the torrent,
2 Floating on the current like ʿ*anṣal* plants; and low hillocks were covered by rainwater.

In the second example, al-Hazzānī describes how long the night can be for one who is sleepless by saying that the stars seem to be tied to the ground by strong ropes (i.e., they do not move westward), in imitation of Imruʾ al-Qays's words: "Oh, what a night of a night you are! It's as though the stars were tied to the mount of Yadhbul with infinite hempen ropes; as though the Pleiades in their stable were firmly hung by stout flax cables to craggy slabs of granite" (Arberry 1957:64).

Al-Hazzānī writes:

1 On many a night whose terrors turn the hair gray and the stars seemed as if tied to the ground with iron chains
2 I crossed desert wastes with a shining sword of Indian make hanging at my side.

The image of the stars tied with ropes so that they cannot move became a popular one in Nabaṭi poetry.

In the second line of the example quoted above, al-Hazzānī refers to the fact that he has crossed the desert, sword in hand. This is an allusion to an episode in the *Muʿallaqah* of Imruʾ al-Qays in which the poet depicts himself as walking by night defiantly past the guards and relatives of his sweetheart, entering her tent at the time of her taking off her garments in readiness to go to bed, enjoying her company in a leisurely and unhurried manner, fearless of her kinsmen, who would surely slay him there and then did they know of his presence.

> Many's the fair veiled lady, whose tent few would think of seeking,
> I've enjoyed sporting with, and not in a hurry either,
> slipping past packs of watchmen to reach her, with a whole tribe
> hankering after my blood, eager every man-jack to slay me,
> what time the Pleiades showed themselves broadly in heaven
> glittering like the folds of a woman's bejewelled scarf.
> (Arberry 1957:63)

Literate Nabaṭi poets have turned this episode into a favorite theme. The poet's sweetheart and the night spent with her are often described in much sensuous detail; but this is only a poetic background, so to speak, on which are projected the daring, resolution, and other manly qualities which enable the poet to attain his ambitious goals. The unapproachable beautiful maiden symbolizes the aspirations of the poet, and the guardsmen represent the antagonists and obstacles which continually try to frustrate the poet's efforts to achieve his aspirations. With sword in hand, the poet walks on the brink and wrestles with danger in order to reach his lady and enjoy her company.

The following three examples, dealing with the specific theme of the night visit and its implication of the poet's bravery and manliness, illustrate both the attachment of Nabaṭi poets to this theme and the extensive influence of Imruʾ al-Qays upon their treatment of it. The first in particular, by ʿAbdalʿazīz al-Mḥammad al-Gāḍī, employs many images drawn from the *Muʿallaqah*: it emphasizes the poet's courage in seeking out his beloved over all obstacles. (It is worth noting that the beloved here is not a desert maiden but an urban lady protected not only by her kinsmen, but by fortifications as well—a modification of the theme which reflects the poet's own environment.)

1 And how many a night I have stayed awake, passions burning my heart and reflection taking my mind in every direction.
2 The stars seemed as if fixed in place and tied to big boulders with tightly twisted ropes.
3 The dark night had covered the horizons with its black cloak, its darkness resembling the surging waves of the sea, terror upon terror.
4 I have sprung up with a resolute and ambitious spirit which dissipates wealth [to attain its ambitions] and draws a sharp sword upon the guardsmen.
5 To reach the lady with the rosy cheeks, I have trampled over many gallant men, carrying with me a sharp sword of Indian make.
6 She was well guarded in a fortified and lofty palace which was difficult to reach; but for me, nothing is difficult.
7 The ropes of my passion have pulled me up to her, and I have overcome all obstacles; may Allah never put love in the heart of a weakling.

The second example, by Rmēzān Ibn Ġaššām, speaks of the hazards of the desert beasts, and dwells more on the love idyll itself.

1 I slipped away to see her one hour after darkness fell; in my hand I was carrying a sharp sword of Indian make
2 To protect myself against nocturnal beasts that might attack me and try to make me give up my pursuit.
3 My sword was my only true friend—it makes a chuckling sound when it severs the enemy's limb from the rest of his body.
4 After the envious had gone to sleep, the slanderer gone to bed, and lovers closed their eyes,
5 I took my sword and went up to my lady in her bedchamber, and found her lying almost naked but for her nightgown.
6 With the tip of my finger I pinched her on the hip and whispered my name so as not to startle her.
7 I said to her, "Greetings," and she answered, "A thousand welcomes, my beloved."

8 She rested her head on my arm and I rested mine on hers until all the stars descended beyond the western skies.

The third example, by Abū Ḥamzih al-ʿĀmrī, again emphasizes the poet's valor in battle as well as in love.

1 I slipped away to see her at night before the dew fell from the stars, my only companions the carnivorous beasts that followed me, wishing to devour me.
2 Hanging by my side was a sharp, well-made sword; its broad blade glittered in my right hand.
3 My fearless heart routs the enemy with it; it is my best companion on a dark night.
4 I also carry tucked in my belt a crooked dagger that resembles a poisonous snake [for my enemies] or a draught of cool fresh water [for my friends].
5 I am Abū Ḥamzih from the lineage of ʿĀmir; I am the famous knight who is well known on the battlefield.

All of these examples illustrate the borrowing and modification by literate Nabaṭi poets of a specific theme drawn from classical Arabic poetry, and the use of images and motifs strongly influenced by this poetry.

Two Novel Poetic Genres

In addition to imitating stylistic features and compositional forms which were developed by classical and postclassical Arab poets, literate Nabaṭi poets made some novel contributions to the Nabaṭi poetic tradition. The most original of these contributions are the two poetic forms *al-ʿarūs* and *al-murāsalāt aš-šiʿriyyah*.

Al-ʿarūs literally means "the bride." A postclassical or neoclassical poet may metaphorically refer to his poem as *ʿarūs aš-šiʿr* "the bride of poetry," implying that it is a beautiful poem. But in Nabaṭi poetry, *al-ʿarūs* is a panegyric poem addressed to a friend or patron. In this type of poem, the poet chances to meet a beautiful and noble maiden who asks him to find her a worthy husband. The poet first asks her to marry him. This is an important step in the compositional development of the poem. If the poet does not ask the bride to marry him, the audience may conclude that he did not want her because of some fault in her looks or character which he knows about but is concealing. The bride refuses to marry him because he is poor, or because poets are fickle, or some similar excuse. The poet then parades before her, so to speak, several friends or prominent figures one by one, pointing out the merits of each. But the bride refuses each one as he is presented, pointing out that he is not suitable for her because of some fault or shortcoming which she spells out. Every now and then the poet admonishes the bride for being so unreasonable and for causing him such mental anguish. Finally, the name of the man in whose honor the poem is composed comes up, and the poet expatiates upon his bravery, liberal hospitality, and uprightness. The bride picks him as her husband, ending the poem.

This poetic genre is not merely panegyric but also a fascinating social criticism done in a clever way. The poet manages to criticize friends and prominent people without incurring their anger because, after all, it is the bride who points out the shortcomings of these people in her dialogue with the poet, while he mentions only their positive qualities.

Al-Murāsalāt aš-šiʿriyyah refers to a very widespread and interesting poetic genre, that of friendly poetic exchanges between dignitaries and outstanding literary personalities of the various towns and settlements of Arabia. These exchanges should not be confused with poems that are exchanged between town amirs and tribal chiefs for the purpose of delivering threats, declaring war, or suing for peace; nor should they be confused with poems sent by a father to his absent son or by someone seeking assistance from a relative, a friend, or a patron—such poems are composed with a specific and immediate practical end in mind. The poems we are discussing now seem to have no apparent motive aside from the literary exercise and aesthetic pleasure derived from composing and reading them.

This type of poetic correspondence is usually initiated when one poet, upon hearing of the high social standing and good breeding of another who lives in a distant territory, composes a poem which he addresses and sends to that poet, who in turn answers with a *mgāḏ̣āt* (response poem) of the same rhyme and meter. A close inspection of these poetic exchanges can tell us a great deal about the various connections and mutual influences that bound literate Nabaṭi poets together across time and space. We know, for example, that al-Gāḏ̣ī of ʿUnaizah (1809–1868) was the correspondent of Mḥammad al-ʿAlī al-ʿArfaj (d. 1842), the poet-prince of Buraidah, and of Aḥmad Ibn Mḥammad as-Sdērī (d. 1860) who in the course of his long life held various prominent positions in the early Saudi regime. We know, too, that al-ʿArfaj also corresponded with ʿAbdallah Ibn Ribīʿih (d. 1856), just as as-Sdērī corresponded with Ibn Liʿbūn (1790–1831). Ibn Liʿbūn and Ibn Ribīʿih were the rival poets of az-Zubair in southern Iraq. It is no wonder, therefore, that the compositions of these five poets—Ibn Liʿbūn, Ibn Ribīʿih, al-ʿArfaj, al-Gāḏ̣ī, and as-Sdērī—exhibit some similarities in style and share many motifs and formulas.

A close reading of these exchanges soon reveals that their composers were men of culture and high social standing who not only knew how to read and write but were learned men in direct contact with the mainstream of Arabic literature. The content of their compositions exhibits evidence both of wide cultural experience and acquaintance with classical learning. It is not unlikely that some of them read medieval treatises on Arabic poetics and stylistics. They engaged in poetic composition as a literary activity and approached poetry from the point of view of *adab* (belles-lettres). Their compositions are characteristically elaborate in form and show both a cultivated elegance and deliberate literary craftsmanship. Due to their literary nature and the similiarity of their thematic content, *al-murāsalāt aš-šiʿriyyah* constitute a special genre in Nabaṭi poetry.

The writing and delivery of these poems has been worked out into a conventional prelude consisting of an elaborate description of the ink, pen, and paper, as well as of the folding and kissing of the paper on which the poem was written and the placing of this paper on the head before handing it to the emissary. The boldness of the emissary, the strength and beauty of his camel mount, the perilous journey, and the desolate wastes he must traverse are also parts of this conventional prelude. Sometimes, instead of sending an emissary, the poet meets a riding party that is heading for the place he wishes his poetic message to be delivered, whereupon he implores them to stop at his abode for a smoke, a cup of coffee, or some other refreshment, and wait for him to write or bring an already written poetic message to take with them to the gallant, open-handed, and most learned intended recipient. After the prelude, or somewhere in the middle of it, the poet sends his greetings to the person to whom he is sending the poem. By employing the additive style, this greeting can be extended over several lines. The poem may contain a few lines of boasting, and it will certainly include verses praising the person to whom it is addressed. The poet also expresses his friendship and longing for that person in the warmest and most uninhibited terms.

In addition to the conventional prelude, *al-murāsalāt aš-šiʿriyyah* share the same principal topic, which is grief over a past love and complaint about the pains of separation. The poet initiating the correspondence first describes in minute detail the physical beauty of his lady and the joys they once shared together. He then says that, for some reason, they are now separated and he no longer can see her. The poet addressed responds by consoling the grieving poet, counseling him on love, and promising to give whatever assistance is needed to rejoin the grieving poet with his lady. For example, in his response (*mgāḏāt*) he proclaims his readiness to send riders in all directions to look for the lady, or to offer all his wealth and influence to induce the lady's kinsmen to give her to the poet; or, if necessary, to rise up in arms with all his kinsmen to take the lady by force.

These poetic exchanges are essentially a means of forging friendships and alliances between the corresponding poets. The love story in these compositions is merely a convention, the underlying motive of which is the eliciting of support and sympathy from the person to whom the poem is addressed. When the responding poet offers the grieving poet his unconditional and unlimited assistance and promises to reunite him with his lady at any cost, he is actually making a commitment to stand by his side in any adventure or undertaking, whatever the cost to himself.

The genre of poetic correspondence is well known in Arabic literature; in fact, the first to introduce it into Nabaṭi poetry were literate poets such as al-Hazzānī, Ibn Liᶜbūn, al-Gāḏī, and the other poets mentioned above. But once the genre was introduced, it was accepted by literate and illiterate poets alike, and was developed to a brilliance and complexity unparalleled in Arabic literature (see, for examples, the poems sent by Ibn Sbayyil to Feḥān Ibn Zirībān, in al-Faraj 1952:169–211).

The material dealt with in this chapter shows that the historical relationship between Nabaṭi poetry and classical Arabic poetry is complemented by a more specific literary relationship. Literate Nabaṭi poets drew consciously and deliberately from the classical tradition in order to enrich their own vernacular tradition; they also invented new genres which reflect the conditions of their environment. By this constant interplay between the literary and vernacular traditions, Nabaṭi poetry was further expanded and developed.

X

ARABIC POETRY AND THE ORAL-FORMULAIC THEORY

In the preceding chapters we have discussed the social function, performance contexts, and compositional techniques of Nabaṭi poetry. We have seen that, with respect to all these areas, Nabaṭi poetry is a continuation of the tradition of ancient Arabic poetry; and as such, it can provide a valuable model for the elucidation of questions concerning poetry. Chief among such questions is the problem of the supposed "oral-formulaic" nature of ancient Arabic poetry, which has in recent years aroused much discussion and controversy. In this chapter we will take up this topic in an effort to show that ancient Arabic poetry, like Nabaṭi poetry, cannot be considered "oral-formulaic" in the sense that some investigators have assumed, since both, although composed and delivered orally, rely heavily on the role of memory in both composition and transmission, and their use of formulas is a stylistic rather than a generative technique.

In my discussion I shall first examine some theories of oral poetry, in particular the well-known Parry-Lord theory and the controversy it has engendered; I shall then discuss some attempts to apply this theory to ancient Arabic poetry; and lastly I shall demonstrate, using Nabaṭi poetry as a model, that "orality" does not always, or necessarily, imply "oral-formulaic," and that attempts to fit ancient Arabic poetry into this classification are in error.

What Is Oral Poetry?

Ever since Albert B. Lord published *The Singer of Tales* (1960), a landmark in the study of oral literature, many scholars have attempted, with varying degrees of success, to apply his findings to a variety of oral traditions. The dogmatism of many partisans of this theory and the imprecision of its terminology—as well as the fact that Lord's essentially descriptive remarks have been interpreted as prescriptive conditions for all oral poetry—have caused a great deal of confusion and, in many cases, have led to highly doubtful conclusions. Before dealing with specific issues, it is pertinent to give a brief sketch of the main assumptions of the Parry-Lord theory, as it may be designated, as presented in *The Singer of Tales* by Lord, the student of the orginator of the theory, Milman Parry.

Parry was initially interested in explaining the function of formulas in Homeric epics. But since no living representative of the ancient Greek epic tradition survived, he felt that a logical alternative was to turn to the still living tradition of Yugoslav epic poetry. Parry and Lord went into the field and found that textual fluidity and abundance of formulas were the most salient characteristics of this oral epic poetry. The formulas functioned to relieve the epic singer of the task of memorizing his epic songs, each of which might run into thousands of lines. Yugoslav epic singers did not memorize their repertoire; instead, a bard would compose extemporaneously as he sang at a rate of from ten to twenty ten-syllable lines a minute. To facilitate this feat, the bard used formulas which he manipulated to embellish his epic song and to lengthen or shorten it according to the response of his audience and the demands of the performance context. Such formulas could also serve to fill potential gaps in the recitation while the bard was working up the next segment in his head before producing it.

In other words, the epic singer as described by Lord does not recall a previously composed epic; rather, each separate performance entails a re-creation of the epic song. "For the oral poet the moment of composition is the performance. . . . An oral poem is not composed for but *in* performance" (Lord 1960:13). Among the implications of this statement is that questions of origin and attribution in oral epic traditions are irrelevant. The statement also reduces, if not eliminating altogether, the role of memory in the transmission and performance of oral epic poetry.

Despite some basic terminological inadequacies of the Parry-Lord oral-formulaic theory (which I shall touch upon shortly), it describes fairly accurately the situation observed by them in Yugoslavia. It is only when their methods are generalized and mechanically applied to other poetic traditions that the theory begins to lose its credibility. This is a problem that has been noted by many scholars; for example, regarding F. P. Magoun's application of the theory to Old English poetry, Larry D. Benson observes that "so useful has the theory proved and so widely has it been accepted that it is not surprising to find it already hardening into a doctrine that threatens to narrow rather than broaden our approach to Old English poetry" (1966:334). This opinion is echoed by Albert C. Baugh, who writes that "it is a familiar phenomenon in the scholarship on any subject that ideas which begin as opinions become petrified into dogma at the same time that assumptions have a way of taking on the status of fact. In secondary works they are generalized and disseminated"

(1967:1). Similar opinions have been expressed by Michael Curschmann (1967:36), Ruth Finnegan (1976:135), and H. L. Rogers (1966:102).

Proponents of the Parry-Lord theory hold that the presence of formulas in a poem is unequivocal evidence that it is both composed and transmitted orally.[1] "Oral poetry, it may be safely said, is composed entirely of formulas, large and small, while lettered poetry is never formulaic," F. P. Magoun states categorically (1953:447), and concludes on this basis that Anglo-Saxon narrative poetry was orally composed and transmitted. But his conclusion has been challenged by a number of scholars.[2] For example, in two thoroughly documented articles, Baugh (1959, 1967) has shown that the Middle English romance—despite an abundance of formulas and recurrent themes—was the work of literate authors who "wrote with oral presentation in mind" (1967:9). Benson states that "poems which we can be sure were not orally composed use formulas as frequently and sometimes more frequently than supposedly oral compositions such as *Beowulf* or the poems of Cynewulf" (1966:335); he goes on to say that "To prove that an Old English poem is formulaic is only to prove that it is an Old English poem, and to show that such a work has a high or low percentage of formulas reveals nothing about whether or not it is a literate composition, though it may tell us something about the skill with which a particular poet uses the tradition" (ibid., 336). According to Benson, literate poets employ formulas "in the same way any writer observes a literary tradition" (ibid., 337). In other words, a formula might be chosen "not because the demands of the meter or the pressure of oral composition prevent the poet from pausing to select some more suitable phrase but because this phrase *is* suitable, is part of a poetic diction that is clearly oral in origin but that is now just as clearly a literary convention" (ibid., 339). J. J. Campbell concurs with Benson that conventions that are oral in origin—such as various formulas—"could be, and were carried over into written literature" (1960:88), and Michael Curschmann adds that stylistic techniques which are singled out by proponents of the oral-formulaic theory as characteristic of oral composition "may primarily be a more general reflection of popular taste" (1967:49) rather than sure signs of orality.

Such observations are borne out by the example of Nabaṭi poetry. As we noted in our description of this poetry, it does indeed contain many stock phrases and recurrent images; yet these are essentially stylistic conventions used for their appropriateness to the subject rather than to generate segments of a poem. Essentially, it is rarely possible to determine from textual evidence alone whether a Nabaṭi poem was composed by a literate or illiterate poet, as the same conventions will be used indiscriminately by both.

One of the basic problems of the Parry-Lord theory is the rigid distinction it attempts to establish between an "oral" and a "written" mode of composition. Usage of the terms *oral* and *written* literature by proponents of the theory is highly vague and ambiguous. Lord in particular asserts that oral and written techniques of composition are "contradictory and mutually exclusive" (1960:129), an assertion that would deny any essential relationship between poets composing orally and in a written form within the same tradition, or between the "oral" and "written" phases of a given tradition.

But we have already seen how, in Nabaṭi poetry, oral and written composition and transmission coexist and overlap. Among Nabaṭi poets, some are literate and others, the vast majority, are illiterate. A poem composed in written form by a literate poet may circulate by word of mouth, whereas a poem composed orally by an illiterate poet may find its way to the written page and become preserved in this fashion. It is not unusual for an illiterate Nabaṭi poet to seek the assistance of a scribe to write down his poem as he composes it or after it has been composed. Furthermore, an illiterate poet, just like a literate poet composing with pen in hand, will compose his poem slowly with a great deal of reflection and deliberation.

This interaction between "oral" and "written" modes of composition and transmission is not unique to Nabaṭi poetry. Finnegan (1974) discusses the question at length and gives ample references and examples from various traditions from Africa and Asia to show that it is not always possible to draw a clear distinction between "oral" and "written" literature. In another place, Finnegan concludes that "When one looks hard at the detailed circumstances and nature of literary phenomena in a wide comparative context, historically as well as geographically, the concept of 'oral literature' *does* cease to be a very clear one, because of the varying ways in which a literature piece can be oral (or written): 'orality' is a relative thing" (1976:141). Finnegan also writes that oral composition is "a useful term that roughly conveys a general emphasis on composition without reliance on writing, but cannot provide any absolute criterion for definitively differentiating oral poetry as a single category clearly separable from written poetry" (1977:19).

Not only is it difficult, therefore, to draw a clear-cut boundary between "oral" and "written" poetry in terms of form and content, but it is equally difficult to make a meaningful and true distinction between an "oral" and a "written" mode of composition. A Yugoslav *guslar* may compose during performance, but not all oral poets follow his example. In the case of Nabaṭi poetry, I have already explained in detail the effort a Nabaṭi poet goes through in order to compose a relatively short lyric. In fact, slow and deliberate composition prior to delivery is characteristic of oral traditions of diverse cultures (Finnegan 1976:145–159, 1977:73–87). Space does not allow for consideration of all possible cases here, but two examples will suffice. B. W. Andrzejewski and I. M. Lewis explain that Somali poets "spend many hours, sometimes even days, composing their work" (1964:45). J. W. Johnson also stresses that "Somali poets rarely perform their work until composition is completely finished in private" (quoted in Finnegan 1976:146 and 1977:74). Among the Eskimos, poetic composition is equally painstaking. In the words of K. Rasmussen, "a man who wants to compose a song may long walk to and fro in some solitary place, arranging his words while humming a melody which he has also made up himself" (1931:321). In the following lines an Eskimo poet draws a parallel between the labor of composition and that of fishing:

> . . . Why, I wonder
> My song-to-be that I wish to use
> My song-to-be that I wish to put together
> I wonder why it will not come to me?
> At Sioraq it was, at a fishing hole in the ice,
> A little trout I could feel on the line
> And then it was gone,
> I stood jigging,
> But why is that so difficult, I wonder? . . . (Ibid., 517–518)

Once we accept the fact that in oral poetry composition can, and often does, precede performance, it becomes necessary to suppose that memorization plays an important role. John D. Smith has observed that even performers of oral epic in western India rely on memory to a very great extent (1977). Moreover, it is possible to assume that portions of epic poems of especial historical or genealogical significance—such as the catalogue of ships in the *Iliad*—were of necessity memorized and inserted at the proper point.

Furthermore, it frequently occurs that composer and performer are in fact two different individuals. This is certainly the case in Nabaṭi poetry, as was shown earlier. Baugh has convincingly argued that the Middle English romances were composed by learned authors to be memorized and performed publicly by minstrels (1967). He goes on to say:

> It is not necessary to argue whether a jongleur or minstrel could have learned by heart a chanson de geste or a romance. It was his business to do so, just as it is the business of actors at the Old Vic to learn their parts in a variety of Shakespearean plays. As Tatlock

> long ago remarked, "To recite from more or less perfect memory a poem of a thousand short couplets was no more a feat for a minstrel than for a modern actor." (Ibid., 28–29)

E. Knott and G. Murphy (1967:64) have shown that, in medieval Gaelic court poetry, poet and performer were usually separate individuals. The poet composed his poem slowly in a dark room; subsequently he taught it to a bard who memorized it in order to recite it or chant it in the court. Such minstrels or jongleurs were also responsible for transmitting poems over a wide geographical area, traveling from place to place and earning their livings in this manner.

Andrzejewski and Lewis emphasize the role of memory in the performance and transmission of Somali poetry and point out that the concept of a "correct" version is locally recognized. The compositions of each poet are preserved under his name, and a reciter will always inform his audience whether he is reciting his own or someone else's composition. Andrzejewski and Lewis speak of:

> . . . [impressive] feats of memory on the part of the poetry reciters, some of whom are poets themselves. Unaided by writing they learn long poems by heart and some have repertoires which are too great to be exhausted even by several evenings of continuous recitation. Moreover, some of them are endowed with such powers of memory that they can learn a poem by heart after hearing it only once. . . . The reciters are not only capable of acquiring a wide repertoire but can store it in their memories for many years, sometimes for their lifetime. . . .
>
> A poem passes from mouth to mouth. Between a young Somali who listens today to a poem composed fifty years ago, five hundred miles away, and its first audience there is a long chain of reciters who passed it one to another. It is only natural that in this process of transmission some distortion occurs, but comparison of different versions of the same poem usually shows a surprisingly high degree of fidelity to the original. This is due to a large extent to the formal rigidity of Somali poetry. . . .
>
> Another factor also plays an important role: the audience who listen to the poem would soon detect any gross departure from the style of the particular poet; moreover among the audience there are often people who already know by heart the particular poem, having learnt it from another source. Heated disputes sometimes arise between a reciter and his audience concerning the purity of his version. It may even happen that the authorship of a poem is questioned by the audience, who carefully listen to the introductory

> phrases in which the reciter gives the name of the poet, and, if he is dead, says a prayer formula for his soul. (1964:45–46)

As can be clearly seen, this situation virtually duplicates what we have already observed about Nabaṭi poetry.

In the case of the Yugoslav epics described by Parry and Lord, their extraordinary length makes memorization difficult, whereas laxity of meter and absence of rhyme facilitate improvisation. Short poems such as the ballad, however, are easily memorized (Friedman 1961). Moreover, the demanding formal and stylistic features of some poetic traditions, such as alliteration in Somali poetry and strict rhyme and meter in Nabaṭi poetry, inhibit improvisation and put a premium on prior composition and memorization.

In addition to form and content, the social function of poetry determines to a great extent whether it is memorized or improvised. "As a general rule it may be said that the more a tradition is associated with a vested interest, and the more this interest is a concern with the public as a whole and is functionally important, the more exacting will be the control over its recital, and the better the guarantee against distortion through failure of memory" (Vansina 1961:42). As indicated above, such a consideration could apply to specific segments of individual poems that were considered of special community importance; it applies even more specifically to traditions such as that of Nabaṭi poetry, where poetry has a highly significant social and political function.

After surveying a variety of oral poetic traditions, H. M. and N. K. Chadwick come to the conclusion that:

> Both memorization and improvisation are employed in the preservation of oral literature. Sometimes the exact words of a poem may be remembered for hundreds of years, even when the language has become more or less obsolete and unintelligible. Sometimes only the barest outline of a theme or story may be preserved. All possible varieties between these two examples are found. (1940:III, 867)

The Chadwicks give examples of four types of poetry in which strict memorization is the rule. These are: (1) poetry intended for collective singing, (2) sacred poetry (e.g., *Rigveda*), (3) poems of carefully studied diction (e.g., *mele inoa* of Hawaii), and (4) poetry with complicated meters (e.g., Norse ["Scaldic"] poetry) (ibid., 868).

The final point I wish to discuss in this section concerns the instability of the orally transmitted text. Lord has emphasized the fluidity of the epic song. Since in his view every performance of the epic song is a new creation of that song, it follows that "In oral tradition the idea of an original is illogical" (1960:101). Lord goes on to stress that in oral tradition "we cannot correctly speak of a 'variant,' since there is no 'original' to be varied" (ibid.). Many advocates of the Parry-Lord theory have dogmatically adhered to this principle, assuming that *any* textual variation in *any* oral poetic tradition provides incontestable evidence that the poems constituting the tradition were composed, performed, and transmitted in substantially the same manner as the Yugoslav epics; I refer particularly to Zwettler's application of the oral-formulaic theory to ancient Arabic poetry (1978:10–11, 189 ff.). The basic problem with this assumption is that it not only confuses composition *for* oral performance (a typical feature of Arabic poetry) with composition *during* performance (which is much more doubtful), but ignores the historical and technical problems that affected the *transmission* of pre-Islamic poetry during the first centuries of Islam.

Many of the general problems arising from oral transmission were treated in the earlier discussion of the transmission of Nabaṭi poetry. In this discussion we saw that each poem has an original version composed by a specific poet prior to delivery, and that each instance of performance or transmission is never a recomposition but rather a conscious attempt to reproduce the memorized original faithfully. It is obvious that any orally transmitted poem is bound to become subject to various changes which are due mainly to the failure of human memory and the vulnerability of this manner of transmission. Yet a qualified transmitter will retain one version of any given poem which is fixed and seldom changes. The stability of a Nabaṭi poem is influenced by various factors, including its length, beauty, subject matter, public interest, and remoteness in space and time; notwithstanding these factors, however, in the minds of poet, transmitter and audience there always remains the conception of an inviolable entity which is *the* poem.

Applications of the Parry-Lord Theory to Ancient Arabic Poetry

D. S. Margoliouth (1925) and Ṭāhā Ḥusayn (1926) were the first to challenge the traditional views of the ancient Arab philologists regarding the authenticity of Jāhilī (pre-Islamic) Arabic poetry. Through independent efforts and for different but sometimes parallel reasons, Margoliouth and Ḥusayn concluded that the corpus of Jāhilī poetry, which the philologists claimed to have collected from transmitters who received it from past generations, was largely forged. The swift response to the arguments of Margoliouth and Ḥusayn by both Arab and European scholars was effective in laying them to rest.[3] The forgery hypothesis was largely abandoned and the issue was resolved in favor of the genuineness of Jāhilī poetry and the general reliability of the ancient Arab philologists.

More recently, James Monroe (1972) and Michael Zwettler (1976, 1978) have put forth their own assumptions concerning the nature of Jāhilī poetry, which again raise the question of its "authenticity," although in a somewhat different sense. Prompted by the work of Parry and Lord, Monroe and Zwettler concluded, through statistical analysis of texts and the mechanical application of the Parry-Lord methodology, that Jāhilī poetry is oral-formulaic in the same way that Yugoslav and Homeric epic poetry are. Monroe—who entitles his article "Oral Composition in Pre-Islamic Poetry: The Problem of Authenticity"—proposes that the whole controversy concerning the authenticity and forgery of Jāhilī poetry becomes irrelevant once it is realized that this poetry is oral-formulaic. After presenting a statistical survey of formulas in the first ten lines of four Jāhilī poems, he concludes: "It follows that pre-Islamic poets, who were oral-formulaic artists, composed during the course of improvisation rather than relying upon memory" (1972:37). This means that the poetic corpus collected by the early Arab philologists, though not necessarily forged, cannot be, as the philologists assumed, the genuine production of Jāhilī poets. For, in Monroe's view, the oral-formulaic process of composition and transmission obliges us to reject the traditional views of the philologists, who assumed that every poem they collected had an original version by an original composer (ibid., 41).

Zwettler, for his part, confidently claims that in Jāhilī poetry "the dual poetic operation of oral composition and oral transmission is a single act of oral rendition" (1976:199).[4] Later he asserts that "many—perhaps most—poems acquired named composers only considerably later than the time of their presumed composition or actual recording" (ibid., 204). Thus he implicitly denies the importance of deliberation prior to composition and subsequent delivery, and of memorization both in the transmission of poems and in their correct attribution—all aspects of the poetic process to which Arab poets and philologists alike accorded great significance.

The conclusions of both Monroe and Zwettler are based on the assumption that any poetry which is delivered and transmitted orally is necessarily composed orally as well, and is oral-formulaic in the same way as the Yugoslav tradition described by Parry and Lord; and that the mere presence of formulaic expression (or any sort of phrase or even word which is frequently repeated in similar contexts or positions) or any degree of textual variation automatically support this conclusion.

In my opinion, an important methodological shortcoming in the work of Monroe and Zwettler is their failure to consider Nabaṭi poetry and its relevance to the understanding of ancient Arabic poetry. They have thus missed a crucial lesson of the work of Parry and Lord, which is to study the closest living representative of an extinct poetic tradition in order to understand that tradition better. Just as the Yugoslav epic tradition could shed light on some questions relating to Homeric poetry, so Nabaṭi poetry can illuminate many of the problems that have arisen in connection with pre-Islamic poetry, more particularly since it is the direct inheritor and continuator of that tradition. It is surprising, therefore, that scholars who have speculated on the authenticity of Jāhilī poetry, as well as on the manner of its composition, performance, and transmission, have not examined the contemporary oral poetry of Arabia in order to shed some light on these problems, since the formal and thematic relationship of the two traditions, as has been established in the previous chapters of this study, is readily apparent. Nabaṭi poetry fulfills the same sociopolitical function as its ancient predecessor, and Nabaṭi poets occupy the same social position and exercise the same influence as did the ancient poets. It would seem obvious, therefore, that questions relating to the composition, performance, and transmission of pre-Islamic poetry could best be answered by reference to its living continuator, Nabaṭi poetry, rather than to an alien tradition such as Yugoslav or Greek poetry—not least because the Arabic tradition is *not* an epic, but a lyric, tradition, and thus both the cultural and literary contexts of Arabic and Yugoslav poetry are quite different. The close relationship between ancient Arabic poetry and Nabaṭi poetry would lead one to the conclusion that the ancient poets, like Nabaṭi poets, composed slowly prior to performance and relied to a very considerable degree on memory for the propagation and preservation of their poems.

Moreover, Monroe and Zwettler fail to note that the social and political role of poetry in ancient Arabia distinguishes it from epic traditions like that of Yugoslavia. As R. A. Nicholson puts it, "Poetry is at once the promulgation and record of the moral ideals of ancient Arabia" (1969: 82). A poet was considered a tribal asset, and his tribesmen regarded him as "their guide in peace and champion in war" (ibid., 63). In ancient Arabia, there was no legal code or religious sanction to enforce law and order. Poetry was the most effective means of encouraging conformity to proper and accepted standards of social behavior. The poet was the spokesman of his group, the custodian of its honor, and the guardian of its most cherished traditions. He was honored and respected, and he exercised unrivaled influence in his community. It was his duty to praise the worthy and castigate the villain. "By the use of carefully selected epithets," Gibb observes, "he unfolds to his audience a series of idealized portraits of tribal life, a scene of revel, or a desert thunderstorm; he extols his own bravery or defiantly proclaims the glorious deeds of his tribe and the disgrace of its rivals or enemies; he sings the praises of his patron and lauds his generosity; in exultant tones he describes a battle or a successful raid; or he sums up the ethics of the desert in a vein of didactic pessimism" (1963:17–18). Outstanding men were praised and their deeds immortalized as evidence of tribal nobility and as examples to be emulated by later generations. Misers, cowards, the fraudulent, the treacherous, all those who failed to live up to the desert ideals, were ridiculed and derided by the poets, who warned others against mixing their blood with that of such people in marriage.

The poet defended his tribe against antagonist poets and reviled its enemies. Poets of hostile tribes taunted each other in poetic exchanges of boasts and satire—exchanges that were not necessarily conducted face to face; poetic challenges and responses were memorized and transmitted by travelers and migrating tribes who passed them on to others they met until they finally reached the person or tribe to whom they were addressed. It is obvious that such poems must be passed on substantially unchanged, for to respond in kind to an antagonist a poet must know exactly what the other poet said. Moreover, the effect of such boastful, eulogistic, and satiric poems depended on their wide distribution and survival over the years as testimony for or against the individuals or tribes mentioned in them.

Gibb sums up the role and function of pre-Islamic poetry as follows:

> Among the pre-Islamic Arabs, words in themselves seem to have retained something of their ancient mystical and magical power; the man who, by skillful ordering of vivid imagery in taut, rightly nuanced phrases, could play upon the emotions of his hearers, was not merely lauded as an artist but venerated as the protector and guarantor of the honour of the tribe and a potent weapon against its enemies. Tribal contests were fought out as much, or more, in the taunts of their respective poets as on the field of battle, and so deeply rooted was the custom that even Muḥammad, although in general hostile to the influence of the poets, himself conformed to it in his later years at Madina.
>
> In view of such a universal veneration of the poetic art, it is not after all surprising that the productions of the great *qaṣīd*-poets were handed down from generation to generation. It was, again, not merely that they set the linguistic and aesthetic standards which were to dominate almost all Arabic poetry (and much of its prose as well) down to the modern age; but they fulfilled also another function, by no means less important. Poetry, said the later philologists, was 'the *dīwān* of the Arabs'; it preserved the collective memory of the past, and so gave an element of continuity and

> meaning to the otherwise fleeting and insubstantial realities of the present. In the two major themes of eulogy and satire the poets pressed home the moral antitheses and sanctions by which this collective existence was regulated and sustained. With relatively few exceptions, the pre-Islamic poets express, and even prescribe, a high standard of tribal morality, and noticeably avoid any reference to the humbler and ruder features of bedouin life and its environment. (1963:29–30)

In most epic traditions, the singer draws his material mainly from mythical, legendary, and pseudohistorical sources. The epic poet, moreover, usually attempts to reconstruct the history of a nation, or at least a significant portion of that history, and thus unifies his varied materials to that end. Ancient Arabic poetry, by contrast, is in the main a record of local events, tribal feuds, and actual episodes; it is oriented toward the individual and the tribe rather than the nation, which had in any case no meaning in Arabia at that time. Ancient Arabic poetry was called *dīwān al-ᶜArab*, "the register of the Arabs," because it was a repository of genealogical and historical knowledge handed down from generation to generation: "It is this historical character, even more than its high poetic interest, which gives its unique value to that which has survived to us of the compositions of the ancient Arab poets" (Lyall 1885:xv).

Unlike epic singers, who constitute a professional class of entertainers, the poets of ancient Arabia included tribal chiefs and heroes whose pronouncements were treated with the utmost respect and gravity. These poets of high status employed their poetry to achieve social and political ends, and presented their verses as serious statements and carefully contemplated utterances. A tribal hero felt no embarrassment at celebrating his chivalry and noble birth in boastful verses; this was, in a sense, his most gratifying reward for endangering his life in defense of his tribe and for dispensing his wealth in hospitality for the hungry and the wayfarer. The reputation of a poet was measured by the felicity and fidelity of his words. A boasting poet must live up to his claims and match his words to his actions, or else lay himself open to satire. By the same token, a panegyrist or a satirist must measure his praise or blame to the real virtues or vices of the subject. Thus accurate transmission was essential to convey the message—whether boast, praise, or blame—exactly as stated, and any alteration of the original poem would be considered highly undesirable. In the Arabian desert, praise and blame were institutions of social and moral control that had to be employed scrupulously less they lose their effect.

In ancient Arabia, poetry was an integral part, if not the most important part, of daily life. Anything that touched human existence provided a proper topic for poetic composition, and the recitation of poetry required no special setting or occasion. However, an aspiring poet anxious to make a name for himself would most likely seek a public occasion when multitudes of people came together to exhibit his poetic skill. The poets of ancient Arabia took their compositions to annual fairs, such as that of ʿUkāẓ, to recite them before a large audience which included seasoned master poets who judged the poetry (al-Iṣfahānī 1868:IV, 35; VIII, 79–80, 194–195; IX, 163, 182–183; XIV, 41–42; XIX, 73–78).

> Great fairs were held, the most famous being that of ʿUkáẓ, which lasted for twenty days. These fairs were in some sort the centre of old Arabian social, political, and literary life. It was the only occasion on which free and fearless intercourse was possible between the members of different clans.
>
> Plenty of excitement was provided by poetical and oratorical displays—not by athletic sports, as in ancient Greece and modern England. Here rival poets declaimed their verses and submitted them to the judgement of an acknowledged master. Nowhere else had rising talents such an opportunity of gaining wide reputation: what ʿUkáẓ said to-day all Arabia would repeat to-morrow. (Nicholson 1969:135)

The poets who attended ʿUkāẓ or any of the regularly held annual fairs did not improvise, but recited poems that had been prepared well in advance and composed with extreme care and deliberation in order to impress the judges and the audience.

By examining the historical and sociopolitical role of ancient Arabic poetry, we can see that it is a tradition associated with a vested public interest, of the same type that Vansina describes (1961:42; vide supra); control over the recital of such a tradition is very exacting, so as to guarantee against distortion caused by failure of memory. Furthermore, as the Chadwicks observe (1940:III, 868), in a poetic tradition with great formal complexity, such as that of ancient Arabic poetry, strict memorization is the rule. The demanding rules of rhyme and meter in Arabic poetry make spontaneous composition in performance a highly difficult task; on the other hand, this strict prosody and the relative brevity of the Arabic poem make it much more reasonable to assume that prior composition and memorization are the norms, as is the case in most nonepic traditions. It is of interest now to turn to evidence from the ancient tradition itself, which is supportive of this conclusion.

The Views of Ancient Arab Poets and Writers on Composition and Transmission

In the following pages I shall present evidence from two independent sources—first, direct reports and firsthand observations recorded in ancient Arabic sources and, second, references in the poetry itself—to show that in ancient Arabia the composition of poetry was a slow and deliberate process which took place prior to and separate from performance and transmission. These two sources of evidence corroborate each other and provide us with a vista from which we can gain a better view not only of the native scholarship but also of the native perceptions, conceptions, and intuitions concerning poetic creation. The ancient poets were in the best position to tell us, through their verses, how their poems were composed, performed, and transmitted. The ancient Arab philologists, of course, were not so very remote in space and time from the ancient poetic tradition as we are today. The earlier among them were not only perceptive critics but, in fact, part of the general audience who interacted with that poetry and observed its performance in its proper social setting.

Although no one has written on Arabic poetry more than Arab authors, ancient and modern, it is unfortunate that the references cited by Monroe and Zwettler—at least those which they treat seriously—are predominantly Western, and that they fail to take sufficient account of the views of ancient Arab poets and writers on composition and transmission. Of medieval Arab authorities on poetry Monroe writes: "The idea that the poets of pre-Islamic times were illiterate is not a new one. Medieval Arab critics relied on oral transmission by Bedouin informants in writing down and collecting their poems. But although the orality of the transmission they were recording was quite obvious to them, their literate habits of mind blinded them to the significance of this fact, nor were they aware of the techniques of oral composition" (1972:10). Later in the same article he states: "Given the overwhelming importance of the formulaic technique for the production of oral poetry in Arabic, it is curious to note that, as far as I know, medieval Arab critics were not aware of it. This must be attributed to their literate habits of mind, nor should they be blamed for something about which not even modern scholars have been aware" (ibid., 31). Monroe's assumptions are echoed by Zwettler, who writes: "We have good reason . . . to revise substantially our idea of the early *rāwī* and of the manner of composition and transmission of early Arabic poetry. We have too long allowed our judgement in these matters to be swayed by the unintentionally biased reports of medieval literary scholars steeped in a bookish tradition and by our own literarily grounded biases and expectations" (1978:88).

Quite apart from the fact that these assumptions concerning the "literate habits of mind" of medieval Arab scholars—who were living in a society where *oral* habits of transmission with respect not only to literary but to other sorts of texts still prevailed, and where one of the standards of literary excellence was the effect of the work in *oral* performance—seemed derived from more contemporary "literarily grounded biases and expectations," it is, to say the least, ungenerous of Monroe and Zwettler to characterize in this way and call "bookish" those ancient philologists who endured the hardships of the desert in order to collect poetry from its most authentic source, the nomadic reciters. More bookish are Monroe and Zwettler themselves, whose work is based on an analysis of text which they themselves consider unreliable, and on theoretical speculation based on material from totally different traditions, rather than on work in the field. The works of the ancient philologists were the result of firsthand observation of the ancient Arabic poetic tradition and familiarity with its sociocultural setting. Some traveled to the desert to collect poetry from the nomadic inheritors of the Jāhilī poetic tradition, while others drew on the nomads who came to the towns of Basrah and Kufah for barter and various other purposes (Dhayf n.d.:148–149, 160–161; al-Asad 1966:155, 193–194, 482). The early philologists were also contemporary with early Islamic poets who continued to compose in the same language and in the same fashion as their Jāhilī predecessors; thus they were dealing with a living tradition, and were not attempting to fit it into any preconceived theoretical mold.

Although these philologists sought to determine the exact attribution and exact original version of every poem they collected, they were aware of the vagaries of oral transmission. Ancient collections of pre- and early Islamic poetry abound in references to variants in addition to the lexical, genealogical, historical, geographical, and other relevant notes accompanying the poems. Moreover, the basic linguistic conservatism characteristic of Arab poets and philologists alike, and their commitment to the preservation of the language—which holds a near-sacred position in their view—and its literary monuments in their original form, provided additional incentive to record poems just as they were heard from their informants. Given the problems of oral transmission, this may well have been a contributing factor in the appearance of variant versions of the same text, since each investigator would record from each informant precisely what he heard; however, these same philologists were in general quite concerned with questions of authenticity and correct attribution. The failure of Monroe and Zwettler to take seriously the views of ancient Arab writers and to examine more carefully the ancient poetry itself (in more than a merely statistical fashion) constitutes a serious methodological flaw in their work.

Anyone familiar with the history, nature, and function of ancient Arabic poetry is aware that the poets composed their poems slowly and carefully. The ancient poets of Arabia had no exact parallel to the English verb *to compose*; instead, they referred to this creative process with such terms as *naqqaḥa, thaqqafa, ḥakkaka, naẓama, ḥāka, tanakhkhala*, all of which signify the careful selection of words and polishing of verses. The sobriquets of many ancient poets allude to their careful method of composition: al-Muhalhil, "he who refines his poetry"; al-Muraqqish, "he who adorns his poetry"; al-Muḥabbir, "he who embroiders his poetry"; al-Muthaqqib, "he who ornaments his poetry"; al-Mutanakhkhil, "he who sieves his poetry." Some pre-Islamic poets like Zuhayr, al-Ḥuṭayʾah, and al-Nābighah were called *ʿabīd al-shiʿr*, "the slaves of poetry," because they spent much time and effort in polishing their poems (al-Jāḥiẓ 1968:II, 12; Ibn Qutaybah 1966:I, 78; Ibn Rashīq 1963:I, 133). The poems of Zuhayr Ibn Abī Sulmā are called *al-ḥawlīyāt* (the annuals) because it would take him a whole year to compose one poem (al-Jāḥiẓ 1968:II, 12; Ibn Qutaybah 1966:I, 78; Ibn Jinnī 1952:I, 324; Ibn Rashīq 1963:I, 129). When al-Ḥuṭayʾah was asked to give his opinion of poetry, he said, "*khayr al-shiʿr al-ḥawlī al-munaqqaḥ al-muḥakkak*," "the best poetry is the polished and refined poetry which is composed over a long period of time" (Ibn Qutaybah 1966:I, 78; al-Jāḥiẓ 1968:I, 13). A lengthy anecdote about al-Ḥuṭayʾah, which is recorded in several ancient sources, closes with his describing to his audience his method of composition: "I lie on my back, put one leg over the other, and growl after rhymes like a thirsty young camel," "*fa-ḥasbuka wa-llāhi bi ʿinda raghbatin aw rahbatin idha rafaʿtu iḥdā rijlayya ʿalā al-ukhrā thumma ʿawaytu ʿuwāʾa al-faṣīl fī ithri al-qawāfī*" (Ibn Qutaybah 1966:I, 144,326; al-Iṣfahānī 1868:II, 47). In *al-Aghānī*, we read that it took Labīd a whole night to compose a short poem, which he delivered the next morning at the court of al-Nuʿmān, the king of Hirah. Labīd stayed up all night riding a camel saddle, biting it and kicking it (al-Iṣfahānī 1868:XIV, 94–95).

Ancient Arabic sources on the lives and works of early Islamic poets, who continued the oral poetic tradition of their pre-Islamic predecessors, provide direct evidence that these poets approached poetic creation as a difficult and serious labor. The famous poet al-Farazdaq once said, "I am the most eminent poet of Tamīm [tribe]; yet there come times when I feel that the pulling of a tooth would be easier for me than composing just one verse" (Ibn Qutaybah 1966:I, 81; al-Iṣfahānī 1868:XIX, 36). When composition became difficult for him, al-Farazdaq would mount his camel and ride alone through the valleys and mountains (Ibn Rashīq 1963:I, 207). His contemporary, Kuthayyir, preferred to ride in green pastures and deserted encampments when composing (ibid., 206; Ibn

Qutaybah 1966:I, 79). Al-Aḥwaṣ, another early Islamic poet, would seek solitude on the ledge of a lofty escarpment (ibid.).

In his famous book *al-Aghānī*, an indispensable source for every student of classical Arabic poetry, Abū al-Faraj al-Iṣfahānī, a literary historian who died in A.D. 967, discourses in detail on the lives and works of all prominent pre- and early Islamic poets and provides well-documented anecdotes which are highly relevant to the proper understanding of poetic composition in ancient Arabia. Combined with poetic testimonies, these anecdotes, more than tenuous formulas, give us solid evidence on how ancient poets went about composing. The following story concerning Jarīr is recorded by al-Iṣfahānī and translated by Nicholson.

> There was a poet of repute, well known by the name of Ráʿí ʿl-ibil (Camel-herd), who loudly published his opinion that Farazdaq was superior to Jarír, although the latter had lauded his tribe, the Banú Numayr, whereas Farazdaq had made verses against them. One day Jarír met him and expostulated with him but got no reply. Ráʿí was riding a mule and was accompanied by his son, Jandal, who said to his father: "Why do you halt before this dog of the Banú Kulayb, as though you had anything to hope or fear from him?" At the same time he gave the mule a lash with his whip. The animal started violently and kicked Jarír, who was standing by, so that his cap fell to the ground. Ráʿí took no heed and went on his way. Jarír picked up the cap, brushed it, and replaced it on his head. Then exclaimed in verse:—
>
> *"O Jandal! what will say Numayr of you*
> *When my dishonouring shaft has pierced thy sire?"*
>
> He returned home full of indignation, and after the evening prayer, having called for a jar of date-wine and a lamp, he set about his work. An old woman in the house heard him muttering, and mounted the stairs to see what ailed him. She found him crawling naked on his bed, by reason of that which was within him; so she ran down, crying "He is mad," and described what she had seen to the people of the house. "Get thee gone," they said, "we know what he is at." By daybreak Jarír had composed a satire of eighty verses against the Banú Numayr. When he finished the poem, he shouted triumphantly, "*Allah Akbar*!" and rode away to the place where he expected to find Ráʿí ʿl-ibil and Farazdaq and their friends. He did not salute Ráʿí but immediately began to recite. While he was speaking Farazdaq and Ráʿí bowed their heads, and the rest

of the company sat listening in silent mortification. When Jarír uttered the final words—

"Cast down thine eyes for shame! for thou are of
Numayr—no peer of Ka'b nor yet Kiláb"—

Rá'í rose and hastened to his lodging as fast as his mule could carry him. "Saddle! Saddle!" he cried to his comrades; "you cannot stay here longer, Jarír has disgraced you all." They left Baṣra without delay to rejoin their tribe, who bitterly reproached Rá'í for the ignominy which he had brought upon Numayr; and hundreds of years afterwards his name was still a byword among his people. (Nicholson 1969:245–246)

Another anecdote concerning Jarīr— who, along with his rivals al-Farazdaq and al-Akhṭal, were the most eminent poets of their age—is related by ʿUbayd Allāh, the *rāwī* (transmitter) of Jarīr and al-Farazdaq.

One day al-Farazdaq summoned me and said to me, "I have composed a line of poetry, and [since I am convinced that it is matchless] I have vowed to divorce my wife, al-Nawwar, should Ibn al-Marāghah [i.e., Jarīr][5] come up with a retort to it." I asked, "What did you say?" [He recited:] "I shall descend upon you [Jarīr] and annihilate you like death, surely you cannot escape death.—Journey to him with this line!"

So I travelled to al-Yamāmah and found Jarīr in his courtyard, playing in the sand. I told him: "al-Farazdaq has composed a line of poetry; and he has sworn on pain of divorcing al-Nawwar that you could not respond to it." —"Surely his wife will be soon divorced! What is the line? Woe to thee!" After I recited the line to him, he started rolling in the dust and throwing it on his head and chest, till nearly sunset; then he said, "I am the father of Ḥarzah.[6] The wife of the rascal shall be divorced." He came up with this line: "I am Time which nothing can destroy; Time defies death and endures forever. —Journey to the scoundrel [with this line]!"

I went to al-Farazdaq and recited the line to him, and told him all that Jarīr had told me. He said to me, "I beg you to keep this incident secret" [thus conceding that he had lost but not wishing to divorce his wife]. (al-Iṣfahānī 1868:XIX, 32)

Another story concerning al-Farazdaq is related on the authority of a tribesman from Quraysh. Al-Farazdaq and the poet Kuthayyir were seated in the mosque at Medina when a strange youth entered and inquired roughly which was al-Farazdaq. When asked to explain his rude behavior, he answered that he was from the tribe of Banū al-Anṣār and that he wished to challenge al-Farazdaq's claim to poetic eminence by reciting verses by the poet Ḥassān Ibn Thābit, and then allowing al-Farazdaq a year in which to match them. After he recited the poem and left, al-Farazdaq arose in confusion and left the group, which remained discussing the excellence of the poem. On the following day, they reassembled in the same place, and were wondering what had become of al-Farazdaq when he appeared and sat down in the same place.

> He inquired, "What became of the Anṣārī lad?" We responded by railing at the lad and heaping curses upon him. Al-Farazdaq said, "May God's wrath descend upon him; not in my whole life have I been afflicted with the like of him, and I have never heard more beautiful verses than those he recited. When I left you yesterday, I went to my house and started going up and down in every path of poetry, but I could not say one verse; it was as if I had never composed poetry before. I stayed up all night in this state, until I heard the call for the dawn prayer; then I saddled my camel, grasped its halter, rode it to the valley of Dhubāb and cried as loudly as I could, 'Help your brother, O Abū Lubnā!'[7] Then my breast began to stir like a boiling cauldron. I tethered my camel, laid my head on my arm, and did not rise until I had composed a poem of one hundred and thirteen verses."
>
> Just as he began to recite the poem, the Anṣarī youth appeared and came toward us. After saluting us he said [to al-Farazdaq], "I do not mean to rush you and I do not expect anything from you prior to the deadline I gave you; but whenever I see you I shall ask you what you have done." Al-Farazdaq replied, "Be seated," and recited [his poem] to him. When he finished, the Anṣārī lad rose and left downcast.

After the youth had gone, his father and several other tribesmen of al-Anṣār came and apologized for his audacious behavior and begged al-Farazdaq not to visit his satires upon their tribe, which he agreed not to do (al-Iṣfahānī 1868:VIII, 193–194; XIX, 38–39).

A final anecdote from *al-Aghānī* concerns al-Akhṭal when he was at the court of the early Umayyad caliph ʿAbdalmalik Ibn Marwān.

> Al-Akhṭal said to ʿAbdalmalik, "O Commander of the Faithful, Ibn al-Marāghah [Jarīr] claims that he can finish composing a panegyric in your honor in three days; whereas it took me a whole year to finish [a certain] panegyric which I composed in your

> honor . . . and I am still not satisfied with it." ʿAbdalmalik said, "Let us hear it, Akhṭal." Al-Akhṭal began to recite the poem, and ʿAbdalmalik began to swell with pride. At the end he said, "Bravo, Akhṭal; do you wish me to write to the corners of the earth saying that you are the most eminent poet of the Arabs?" "No," said al-Akhṭal; "your word suffices me." ʿAbdalmalik rewarded him with a bowl full of coins and robes of honor. A servant of ʿAbdalmalik took al-Akhṭal to a public place, crying: "Here is the poet of the Commander of the Faithful; here is the most eminent poet of the Arabs!" (al-Iṣfahānī 1868:VII, 172–173)

In addition to the complexity of rhyme and meter in Arabic poetry, which would make it impossible to compose a poem of moderate length on the spot, the poet, even before starting to compose, might need some time to collect relevant information to include in his poem, especially if it happened to be satirical or panegyric. Ḥassān Ibn Thābit, the poet of the prophet Muḥammad, who composed poems in defense of the prophet and satirized his enemies, the people of Mecca, gathered his genealogical information from Abū Bakr, who was considered an authority on such genealogies (al-Asad 1966:209). Jarīr and al-Farazdaq were famous for seeking out historical and genealogical facts to include in their poems (ibid., 227). It is related that, when ʿUmar ibn Lajaʾ al-Taymī arrived in Basra, al-Farazdaq and his *rāwī* (transmitter), Ibn Mattawayh, went to see him. Al-Farazdaq said to Ibn Lajaʾ, "Oh Abū Hafṣ, my cousin Shabbah Ibn ʿUqāl wrote to me that the poets of the Banū Jaʿfar tribe had defamed him in their poetry, and he could not answer them; he asked for my help; but I do not know how to disgrace them because I do not know their defects and blemishes." ʿUmar replied, "I know a great deal about them. I have pitched my tent amongst their tents, I have accompanied them in their migrations, I have been with them at their summer camps and deep in the desert." Al-Farazdaq called for someone to bring a piece of paper and caused the information to be written down for him, and used it in a subsequent poem (ibid., 228).

The anecdotes illustrating the seriousness with which the poets approached composition are supplemented by evidence from the poetry itself. Although the ancient poets were apparently not as preoccupied with the poetic process as are Nabaṭi poets, we sometimes come across lines describing the difficulty and slow pace of composition.[8] Ancient authors such as al-Jāḥiẓ (1968:II, 6–13), Ibn Qutaybah (1966:I, 78–81), and Ibn Jinnī (1952:I, 324) give detailed discussions of this matter, with ample illustrations.[9]

Transmission is another aspect of ancient Arabic poetry that distinguishes it from epic poetry. In Arabic poetry, composition and transmission are two distinct fields of specialization. In most cases, the compositions of a poet (*shāʿir*) were recited and spread not so much by the poet himself as by his transmitter (*rāwī*) (Nicholson 1969:131–134; Gibb 1968:19–21). In reality, transmission was a diffuse activity in that anyone might know a few poems or a few lines of poetry;[10] but some individuals who were endowed with prodigious memories and exceptional gifts of delivery made names for themselves as transmitters. Transmission and composition were not, however, mutually exclusive activities. A poet could very well be the transmitter of the work of an older poet, who was most likely his relative or kinsman.

In their application of the oral-formulaic theory to classical Arabic poetry, Monroe and Zwettler disagree as to the significance of the distinction between *shāʿir* and *rāwī*. Monroe concedes that "the tradition of the *rāwī* points in the direction of memorization" (1972:41); Zwettler, however, chooses to blur this distinction by thinking of the *rāwī* as primarily the apprentice of the *shāʿir*: "The similarity is self-evident between what we know about the activity of the early *rāwī*, his 'apprenticeship' to an older poet within the tribe, and his own emergence as an accomplished poet in his own right, and between Lord's description of the training of an oral poet" (1978:87).

When we examine the etymology of the word *rāwī* we find nothing to suggest that the *rāwī* was the poet's apprentice. In its original sense, the word *rāwī* with its various derivatives refers to the act of carrying water on a camel in large containers made of skin from the water source to the camp. Metaphorically its meaning was extended to signify one who carries in his memory poetry from the poet (the source) to the audience. It is true that many an ancient Arabian poet was also a transmitter; yet some outstanding transmitters were bad poets or could not compose at all. A good poet would, of course, know a great deal about poetry and poets in general, but he would always keep his own compositions separate from those of other poets which he had stored in his memory. Thus, the fact that the same person might be both a poet and a transmitter does not contradict the fact that in ancient Arabia composition and transmission were two independent activities, and that memorization played a crucial role in the latter.[11]

As a matter of fact, it was considered a mark of poetic genius to compose elegant and memorable verses to be memorized and spread by the transmitters. When al-Farazdaq was asked why he preferred to compose short poems, he answered, "Because I have found that they stick longer in the memories of men and spread wider in the assemblies," "*li-annī raʾaytuhā fī ʿṣ-ṣudūri athbat wa-fī ʿl-maḥāfili ajwal*" (al-Iṣfahānī 1868:XIX, 33). To a similar question, al-Ḥuṭayʾah answered, "Because they are absorbed easier by the ears and they stick longer in the mouths of transmitters," "*li-annahā fī 'l-adhāni awlaj wa-fī afwāhi 'r-ruwāti aʿlaq*" (ibid.). It was al-Ḥuṭay'ah who coined the famous phrase, "*waylun li- sh-shiʿri min ruwāti 's-sūʾ*," "Woe to poetry [which is spread] by bad transmitters," which indicates that poets were quite annoyed by bad transmitters whose memories did not serve them well and who mangled verses and distorted poems.

As the following excerpts show (the first from a poem by al-Muzarrid and the second from one by al-Musayyab Ibn ʿAlas, both translated by Lyall), poets would boast that their verses would spread fast and wide through camps and watering places and would be sung by night travelers and caravans.

> (58) I warrant to him with whom I contend that my words shall be so striking that the night-traveller shall sing them as he fares along, and the caravans be urged forward by them on their road;
> (59) Well remembered are they, cast forth with multitudes to bear them about: their sound is gone forth in full sunshine into every land;
> (60) They are repeated again and again, and only increase in brilliancy, when the diligent lips of men test my verse by repetition.
> (61) And he whom I attack with a couplet, it sticks to him and is conspicuous like a mole on his face—and there is nothing that can wash out a mole!
> (62) Thus is my requital for the gifts men bring; and if I speak, the sea is not exhausted, nor is my voice hoarse with too much use. (Lyall 1918:II, 61)
>
> * * *
>
> (15) So shall I surely bring as an offering, on the wings of the winds, an ode of mine that shall pass into every land, until it reaches al-Qaʾqāʾ;
> (16) It shall come down to the watering-places, ever as something fresh and new, and it shall be quoted as a proverb among men, and sung by the singers. (Ibid., 31)

In the following lines, Ḥamīd Ibn Thawr pictures himself in a vast plain singing out his verses to multitudes of eager transmitters who relish them, and singers who sing over and over:

1 *la-aʿtariḍan bi-'s-sahli thumma la-aḥduwan // qaṣāʾida fīhā li'l-maʿādhiri zājiru.*

2 *qaṣāʾida tastaḥlī 'r-ruwātu nashīduhā // wa-yalhū bihā min lāʿibi 'l-ḥayyi sāmiru.*

Once a poet composed and publicized his poem and it was spread widely by transmitters, he no longer had control over its circulation, and could neither change any part of it nor deny its attribution to him. In the following lines, ʿAmīrah Ibn Juʿal expresses his regrets for having defamed his tribe in his poetry; but now it is too late to apologize, since his verses have already been imprinted on the lips of reciters: it is as impossible for him to take back his words as it is to put milk back into the udder.

1 *nadimtu ʿala shatmi ʾl-ʿashīrati baʿdamā // maḍat wa-ʾstatabbat li-ʾr-ruwāti madhāhibuh.*
2 *fa-aṣbaḥtu la asṭīʿu dafʿan limā maḍā // kamā lā yaruddu ʾd-darra fī ʾḍ-ḍarʿi ḥālibuh.*

Jarīr describes how his verses travel swiftly on the lips of reciters to strike his poetic rivals and shed their blood like the sharp edge of a fine sword which quivers in the hand of an expert fighter:

1 *wa-ʿāwin ʿawā min ghayri shayʾin ramaytuhu // bi-qāfiyatin anfadhtuhā taqṭuru ʾdi-damā.*
2 *kharūjin bi-afwāhi ʾr-ruwāti ka-annahā // qara hunduwānīyin idhā huzza ṣammama.*

In another excerpt, Jarīr is addressed by al-Farazdaq, who asks him, "How can you eradicate the satirical verses I have composed against you, which have been spread by reciters from Oman to Egypt?"

1 *taghannā yā jarīru li-ghayri shayʾin // wa-qad dhahaba ʾl-qaṣāʾidu liʾr-ruwāti.*
2 *fa-kayfa taruddu mā bi-ʿumāni minhā // wa-mā bi-jibali miṣra mushahharāti.*

Such verses clearly show that poets took pride in the fact that their verses were memorized, spread widely, and passed on from one generation to the next. Even after a poem became popular among reciters, it remained the property of its original composer, and it would be considered a theft if a reciter were to claim another poet's work as his own. This provides further evidence that in ancient Arabia, composition and transmission were viewed as two separate and independent activities. An aspiring poet might begin his career as a *rāwī*, but once he acquired sufficient compositional skills he would compose his own poems bearing his own name. For example, al-Farazdaq was the transmitter of the poetry of

Imruʾ al-Qays, but he also made a name for himself as a great poet; al-Ḥuṭayʾah was the transmitter of Zuhayr, as well as being himself a poet of great repute.

Such evidence from ancient sources clearly shows that the poets of ancient Arabia approached the composition of poems seriously and deliberately, that they spent considerable time and effort revising and polishing their poems before considering them worthy of delivery, and that it was common practice for a poet to entrust his poems to a transmitter for memorization and publication. This refutes the view that composition and performance were the same event; although there are examples of spontaneously composed poems, these were generally quite brief, and more lengthy compositions were preceded by much thought and deliberation. Moreover, even spontaneously composed verses would subsequently be entrusted to transmitters who were responsible for both their correct attribution and transmission, which demonstrates that composition and transmission were separate activities and that the latter relied heavily on memory. All of this is paralleled by the Nabaṭi poetic tradition which we have already described at length; and investigation of this tradition would surely assist in clearing up some of the misconceptions that exist concerning the oral nature of Jāhilī poetry.

Conclusion

To say that ancient Arabic poetry is not oral-formulaic according to the criteria of Parry and Lord as applied by Monroe and Zwettler is not to deny either its orality or its verbal and thematic conventionality. With regard to the latter, the statement made about Nabaṭi poetry in the introduction to chapter 2 is equally applicable to ancient Arabic poetry insofar as it too is a reflection of a conventional world view, an articulation of collective sentiments, a register of recurring events, and, in short, the product of a traditional society in which all art forms and cultural artifacts are highly conventionalized. As regards verbal formulas, they do indeed appear with high frequency in ancient Arabic—as in Nabaṭi—poetry; but they do not function in the same way as they do in Yugoslav epic poetry, nor are they as abundant. The two poetic traditions, as has been discussed above, are quite different in form, social function, performance context, and modes of composition and transmission.

There is no doubt that, in ancient Arabic poetry, formulas do, to a certain extent, serve a generative function in poetic production; but this function is not primarily to make possible spontaneous composition during performance. Sometimes formulas aid in speeding up composition if the poet has had very little time to prepare his poem before its delivery; and even when the occasion of delivery is not so pressing, an oral poet who does not have recourse to writing down his verses as he composes them cannot allow a long time to elapse between the composition of individual verses lest he forget the opening of his poem before coming to its end. In such cases conventional formulaic language is used to speed up composition as well as to mark the different sections of the poem. Formulas also facilitate memorization, hence enhancing the transmission of the poem in an oral society, and they also serve to fill gaps created by occasional lapses of memory by reciters as the poem travels in time and space.

But the most important function of formulas is not generative but stylistic. As Monroe himself has observed (without fully analyzing the reasons for this), "the most common formulas appear in the earlier parts of the poem" (1972:26); they function to inform the audience—in a context of oral *delivery*—what to expect, what *kind* of poem they are going to hear, what the poetic context is, and obviate the necessity of establishing the latter in lengthy introductory verses. For example, a formula such as *li-man ṭalalun*, "whose are the traces?" (see ibid., 1972:29) immediately alerts the audience to the fact that, in the imaginative context of the poem, the poet and his friends have halted in the course of a desert journey to contemplate the ruined encampment of the tribe of the poet's beloved, and that he will continue by lamenting the pains of separation and perhaps recount episodes of love from the past. In other words, the formula provides important generic and thematic clues to the members of the audience, who, in the context of oral delivery, receive the poem in a strictly linear fashion, but are nevertheless enabled to anticipate what will follow. Such formulas were retained even when the poetry came to be written down more and more, first of all because delivery remained primarily oral even though transmission might be through writing, and second, because of the highly conventional character of Arabic poetry throughout its development. The occurrence of formulas thus reflects the traditional nature of ancient Arabic poetry, the orality of which continued to be a pronounced feature because poems continued to be read or recited aloud; silent reading—as was the case in Western literary traditions as well—was a habit acquired very late in the development of the tradition, and was never of great importance.

In short, although in ancient Arabic poetry formulas have a significant function in performance, this function is different from that of formulas in epic poetry. In the ancient Arabic tradition, a poem's aesthetic quality was measured by its overall impact on a wide audience, its function as a record of, and model for, collective action and individual conduct, and its utility as a cognitive chart to organize the social and physical universe. Given these functions, striving for creativity and originality as they are understood in modern literary traditions has no meaning, and would (even if considered possible or desirable) encumber the poetic message and comprise the role of the poet as a voice of public opinion. Each poet must, it is true, develop his own individual style; yet he must not depart too much from established conventions lest he alienate himself from his audience. Formulaic expressions are artistic conventions and stylistic devices that serve to alert the audience to the thematic movement of the poem and establish the necessary rapport and feeling of familiarity that attract the audience to the poem without jeopardizing its individual quality. It is therefore necessary to reevaluate such terms as *orality* and *formulaic* in order to understand their true importance and function in the Arabic poetic tradition as a whole; and the study of Nabaṭi poetry as the continuator of the classical tradition plays an important role in the achievement of this goal.

NOTES

I: Introduction

1. A Nabaṭi poet is called by his peers simply a poet (*šāᶜir* or *gassād*), and his work is called poetry (*šiᶜir* or *giṣīd*). The poet usually introduces his composition as *giṣīdih* (ode), *abyāt* (verses), *gāf* or *ǵīfān* (rhymes), *gōl* or *ǵīl* (contemplated utterance), *kalām* (solemn address), *amṯāl* or *miṯāyil* (allegories), or *jawāb* (response). (Many a poem is composed as a response to the composition of another poet; such a response is also called *mǵāḍāt*—paying in kind.) A short poem is called *byētāt* (a few verses) or *mšēxītih*, pl., *mšēxītāt, mišāxīt* (ditty, ditties).

2. H. St. John B. Philby casts some doubt on whether Palgrave actually did make the journey to Arabia (see Philby 1922:II, 117–156).

3. For example, *Dīwān al-Nabaṭ* (1952) by Kh. M. al-Faraj; *Shuᶜarā al-Rass al-Nabaṭīyūn* (1965, 1972) by F. al-Rashīd; *Khiyār mā Yultaqat min al-Shiᶜr al-Nabaṭ* (1968) by A. Kh. al-Ḥatam; *al-Tuḥfah al-Rashīdīyah fī al-Ashᶜār al-Nabaṭīyah* (1965, 1969) by M. S. ibn Sayḥān; *al-Majmūᶜah al-Bahīyah min al-Ashᶜār al-Nabaṭīyah* (1969) by A. Bābuṭayn; *Dīwān al-Nabaṭ al-Ḥadīth* (A.H. 1374) by S. Ḥ. ibn Ḥuraywil; *Dīwān al-Shaykh Qāsim ibn Muḥammad Āl Thānī wa-Qaṣāʾid Ukhrā Nabaṭīyah* (A.H. 1984), and *Mukhtārāt min al-Shiᶜr al-Nabaṭī al-Muᶜāṣir* (A.H. 1392) by ᶜA. ᶜI. al-Hadhdhāl.

III. Poetry in the Desert

1. The content and function of poetry in the Arabian desert can be compared to Somali nomadic poetry, of which B. W. Andrzejewski wrote: "Somalis often say that a good poet can sow peace and also hatred; he can win friendship by praise and appreciation, deepen an existing feud, or lead to a new one. In the pastoral interior, poets often act as spokesmen for their clans in disputes, and one can even find interclan treaties in poetic form; it is not unusual for a poet to rise to the rank of a clan leader, if he is not one already.

"The amount of local history enshrined in Somali poetry is enormous, though the historian is to be pitied who tries to find his way through the labyrinthine clan feuds and alliances, obscured as they are by poetic imagery and hyperbole. In the almost total lack of documentation of clan history, however, poetry is the only source of such information apart from the memories, admittedly prodigious, of the Somalis themselves" (1963:23).

Andrzejewski also observed: "When a poem is first composed and recited it is always topical and related to some true life situation of the poet or his clan: it is composed for a particular purpose, at a particular moment of time, and these circumstances are an integral part of the poem. If it achieves popularity in the areas where the happenings would not be common knowledge, the reciter takes care to explain them. With the passage of time the memory of the particular event is likely to fade even among the poet's clansmen, and the reciter will then use his judgment as to whether they need a history lesson or not. The topicality of a poem does not detract from its continued popularity, if it is good enough. One might think of it as a news commentary in poetic form: one is interested today in both news and poetry, and tomorrow the news has turned into history and the poetry is still there" (ibid.).

IV: Poetry and Regional Politics

1. Examples of ʿAbdallah's poetry appear in Ibn Rashīd (1966:94–101), al-Mārik (1963–1965:I, 181–182), and Musil (1928:301–304). Some of ʿUbayd's poetry is published by al-Ḥātam (1968:II, 79–91), Kamāl (1960–1971:III, 57–78), and Musil (1928:300–302).

2. In this incident, ʿAbdallah demonstrated his extraordinary courage and intelligence; but he was badly wounded in the scuffle between himself and the slave of Mishārī. For a detailed account of this incident, see Winder (1965:97–99).

3. At one point Doughty admits, "In this poetical eloquence I might not very well, or hardly at all, distinguish what they had to say; it is a strange language" (1921:306). Winder (1965:155) errs in thinking that this verse cited by Doughty comes from a poem composed by ʿUbayd celebrating his triumphant military expedition against ʿUnaizah in 1845.

4. It has been a common practice in Arabia since ancient times that when a hero charges against his opponent in the field of battle he utters his war cry loudly (as explained in chapter 2). It is not unusual for a hero to utter as his war cry the name of the male relative of whom he is most proud. For example, the war cry of ʿAbdallah Ibn Rashīd was *ana axu ʿbēd*, "I am the brother of ʿUbayd," and that of ʿAbdalʿazīz Ibn Saʿūd, the late king of Saudi Arabia, was *ana bin miǵrin*, "I am the son of Miǵrin" (Miǵrin being the apical ancestor of the house of Āl Saʿūd).

5. Some of the poetry of al-ʿŌnī is published by al-Faraj (1952:II) and by al-Ḥātam (1968:II, 234–243). Aside from the meager biographical information that appears in al-Faraj (ibid.) and al-Mārik (1963–1965:III, 280–298), oral tradition remains the only source on the life and activities of al-ʿŌnī. Most of the information presented here was given me by Brāhīm al-Ḥsēn (see Introduction).

VII: Performance

1. In the rainy season, the members of each nomadic tribe disperse in small groups to forage in their tribal territory. During this period there are so few people around that one cannot be choosy about whom one makes friends with. But in summer, tribal sections congregate around their tribal wells in large numbers, and then one can be discriminating in choosing friends.

2. Brāhīm assumes the role of Riḏa and acts as his voice.

3. Riḏa suspends the narrative to embed some personal information about the go-between.

4. Brāhīm is commenting upon an admirable bedouin trait. Unlike townspeople, the nomads allow people of opposite sexes to mix freely, although men and women must both make sure that such free mixing does not lead to illicit sex and the besmirching of tribal honor. The severe punishment accorded violators ensures conformity to this desert code.

5. This is an idiomatic expression used by someone who changes his or her mind about something. It means that everything is in the hands of God; hence, it should be no surprise that someone may think one way now and an altogether different way later.

6. That is, although she considered marrying him, she was not particularly in love with him.

7. This expression is related to the concept of *sitir*, a concept lacking in English, which is related to honor and reputation. In using this expression, one asks God to protect the honor and reputation of someone and guard him from disgrace. The expression is used to indicate that the speaker, though he may not have harmonious relations with a particular person, wishes him no harm.

8. This expression is borrowed from radio parlance; the radio is very popular among the nomads and has a considerable influence on their speech.

9. This expression is used by the narrator of a story whenever he pays a compliment to a character in the story. It is an expression of courtesy and means that the assembled audience is no less worthy of praise than the character mentioned. The proper response to this expression is "The like of you is praiseworthy."

10. Summer is the time when the nomadic tribes congregate around tribal wells in large multitudes. Because there are so many people camped together, friends may not see each other for a long time, especially if their tents are separated by other tents.

11. According to this proverbial advice, if someone comes to you and starts shouting complaints, abuse, or accusations against you, you must hurl back at him similar shouts. By doing so, it is likely that you will come out exonerated and unscathed.

12. That is, the growling of camels is as incomprehensible as a foreign tongue.

13. Men of the tribe are compared to strong male camels which are specially bred to carry heavy loads and are famous for their stamina and endurance. Such men attack the enemy on the battlefield as courageously and recklessly as madmen who fear not death.

14. This idiom means that nothing can be expected of a certain person or thing; here it means, "Do not expect any good from such a base man."

15. This is said to a reciter after he finishes reciting a poem. The proper response is "May your body be sound."

16. Examples of *mrādd* appear in Abu Mājid (1963:143 ff.), Ibn Sayḥān (1965–1969:II, 292 ff.), and al-Badhdhāl (1975).

VIII: Prosody and Language: A Synchronic and Diachronic Overview

1. For more information on the phonology and syllabic structure of the dialect of ʿUnaizah the reader is urged to consult Johnstone (1967*a*). Other relevant works include Cantineau (1936–1937), Johnstone (1967*b*), Blank (1953, 1970), and Palva (1976).

2. On rare occasions, these affricates are realized by native speakers as independent phonemes contrasting with *g* and *k* as shown in the following minimal pairs: *galb* (heart) /*ǵalb* (upside down, inside out); *gadd* (worthy, equal, fit) /*ǵadd* (aim [m.s.]!, it is fit); *šigg* (tear) /*šiǵǵ* (side); *digg* (beat, pound [m.s.]!) /*diǵǵ* (tiny, insignificant—opposite of *jill*); *ḥigg* (a tin can) /*ḥiǵǵ* (an adult male camel); *ragg* (it [m.] softened) /*raǵǵ* (bring up [m.s.] to the roof!); *sāgi* (my leg) /*sāǵi* (an irrigation canal); *kabb* (he spilt) /*ćabb* (fumigate [m.s.]!); *kaff* (he refrained from; he went blind) /*ćaff* (palm of the hand); *ʿakk* (he carried on his back) /*ʿaćć* (hard); *ḏakk* (it [m.] became tight) /*ḏaćć* (it [m.] is tight). But generally native speakers realize *ǵ* and *ć* simply as variants of *g* and *k*. This is borne out by inconsistent pronunciation and by the rhymes of Nabaṭi poetry. It seemed that *g* and *k* were about to disappear and *ǵ* and *ć* were going to take over completely, but the recent rise in literacy has reversed the process, and now it is *ǵ* and *ć* that are rapidly disappearing. Young people today use *g* and *k* in place of *ǵ* and *ć*, and although they realize that these are merely variants, they are beginning to lose their intuitive ability to make the right choice—so much so that when they try to imitate the speech of their elders, they overdo it and use *ǵ* and *ć* indiscriminately, even in places where *g* and *k* are expected.

3. It seems that the affrication of *g* and *k* into *ǵ* and *ć* in the contiguity of *i* may have taken place before the assimilation of *u* to *i*, because this affrication does not take place when the adjacent *i* is historically *u*. This creates contrastive pairs of the following sort: *girr* (be quiet [m.s.]!) /*ǵirr* (confess [m.s.]!); *kil* (eat [m.s.]!) /*ćil* (measure, load [m.s.] the gun!). The initial consonants of *girr* and *kil* are not affricated because their vowel is historically *u*.

4. When the short high vowel *i* which is not historically *u* is elided, its fronting and affricating effect on the adjacent *g* and *k* remains after its elision: *ǵlādih* (necklace), *ćlābih* (dogs).

5. In the case of *ē* and *ō*, this is probably a lingering effect of the initial *a* of the old diphthongs *ay* and *aw*, of which *ē* and *ō* are reflexes.

6. In Nabaṭi poetry a sequence of two, but no more, short syllables is permitted under these specified conditions; but in ordinary speech one may encounter, in

extremely rare and very circumscribed cases, sequences of three short syllables: *šif al-asad* → *ši fa la sad* (look [m.s.] at the lion!).

7. By combining a short syllable with two long ones we get three feet, – – ⏑, – ⏑ –, and ⏑ – –; and by combining a short syllable with three long ones we get four feet, – – – ⏑, – – ⏑ –, – ⏑ – –, and ⏑ – – –. The number of simple and complex meters and their variants that can be formally derived by combining these basic feet is almost infinite, but the Nabaṭi poets employ only a small and manageable number of these possibilities.

8. On the prosody of classical Arabic poetry and on the prosodic terms discussed in this chapter, consult Wright (1971), Weil (1913, 1960), Ben-Cheneb (1924), and Bonebakker (1974).

9. It should be noted that we have been using syllabic analysis throughout for the sake of convenience; the ancient Arab grammarians and prosodists never developed the concept of the syllable, but spoke in terms of combinations of *mutaḥarrik* (CV) and *sākin* (CVC or CV̄) into the larger elements of *sabab* (pl. *asbāb*) and *watad* (pl. *awtād*) which, in general, represent units larger than a syllable.

10. On the relationship of city to desert and colloquial to classical Arabic, see Blau (1963, 1965).

11. Bedouin life had become associated in the minds of the urban masses with the egalitarian and free life of the desert and was idealized by city Arabs as the pristine cultural stage at its most authentic and genuine. In his discussion of the continued fascination of the Arab masses with the desert, Gibb writes: "There is by now a growing body of sociological observations which throws light on the perennial fascination which the old bedouin life and traditions have exercised upon the thought and imagination of the Arabs at all stages of evolution. It is not merely a matter of historical reminiscence but a genuine nostalgia. The bedouin furnished—and throughout all changes continued to furnish—the living models for two characteristics which were felt to be fundamental to the Arab way of life. One was the cult of the Arabic language, the fountain-head of all Arabic artistic sensibility and emotion. The dogma of the philologists, however much it may have been exaggerated in detail, was founded on the undisputed fact that the most satisfying of Arabic speech in its aesthetic quality, and the most uncorrupted in terms of morphological structure, was that of the desert—always excepting the Qurʿān. In the second place, the heroic virtues of the desert supplied the human and social ideals which were held to be those of the Arabs *par excellence*" (1948:577).

12. This term refers to the pre-Islamic period of paganism in Arabia.

13. Ibn Khaldūn wrote: "The nomads of this age, whose language has deviated from that of their predecessors, still compose poetry in all known (Arabic) meters, exactly like their ancestors did. They compose long poems following the established themes and topics such as love, panegyric, elegy, and satire. The poet may interweave in his composition several themes or he may start with his main theme right away. Many a poem begins with the name of the poet followed by the amatory prelude" (1967:1125).

IX: Nabaṭi Poetry and the Classical Literary Tradition

1. For a translation of the *Muᶜallaqah* of Imruᵓ al-Qays see Arberry (1957:61–66).

2. The lines by al-Gāḏī cited in the example are based on or derived from the following lines from the *Muᶜallaqah* of Imruᵓ al-Qays (numbered according to Arberry's translation): line 1 from *Muᶜallaqah*, lines 44–45 (comparison of the night to the sea and to a horse, condensed into one line by al-Gāḏī); line 2 from *Muᶜallaqah*, lines 71–72 (where it is the lightning which is compared to the anchorite's lamp); lines 3–4 from *Muᶜallaqah*, lines 25–26 (a verbal borrowing lost in translation: al-Gāḏī uses the same expressions in his description of Orion as does Imruᵓ al-Qays in describing the Pleiades. Al-Gāḏī's line is *taᶜarraḏ lah al-jōzā niḏīmah lacinnih // wšāḥin tikāšaḥ fāṣlih lūlwin ṣāfī*, echoing Imruᵓ al-Qays's line *idhā mā 'th-thurayyā fī 's-samāᵓi taᶜarraḍat // taᶜarruḍa 'thnāᵓi 'l-wishāḥi 'l-mufaṣṣali*); line 6 from *Muᶜallaqah*, line 45 (morning is no more cheerful than night); lines 17–18 from *Muᶜallaqah*, 16–17 (Imruᵓ al-Qays describes his night visit to a nursing mother).

X: Arabic Poetry and the Oral-Formulaic Theory

1. The formula itself as an operational concept has come under severe attack, particularly by H. L. Rogers (1966), Bennison Gray (1971), and Ruth Finnegan (1977:71–72).

2. See especially Albert C. Baugh (1959, 1967), Larry D. Benson (1966), Jackson J. Campbell (1960), Michael Curschmann (1967), Robert D. Stevick (1962), and Ann Chalmers Watts (1969), to name only a few.

3. For a rebuttal of the forgery hypothesis, see Muḥammad al-Khiḍr Ḥusayn (1927), al-Ghamrāwī (1970), al-Asad (1966), Lyall (1918:I, xvi–xxi), Arberry (1957:228–254), and Blachère (1952:166–186).

4. In his book *The Oral Tradition of Classical Arabic Poetry* (1978), Zwettler criticizes Monroe's approach on several grounds, pointing out that his work is marred by "inconsistencies and imprecisions." Zwettler calls attention to the fact that the size and choice of the samples that Monroe takes for analysis are too random to reflect the true characteristics of each poem as a whole. Zwettler himself limits his own analysis to only one poem, the *Muᶜallaqah* of Imruᵓ al-Qays, but in its entirety. Zwettler also disagrees with Monroe's claim that it is the order of formulas that determines the meters of Arabic poetry. In Zwettler's view, formulas can never be considered as prior to the meters in which they function. With regard to the mechanics of the techniques of formulaic analysis, Zwettler chastises Monroe for choosing not to differentiate between phrases repeated wholly or almost wholly verbatim and those which are related structurally but share only a single common lexical item (Zwettler 1978:43–50).

5. Ibn al-Marāghah ("the son of a she-donkey") is the name given to Jarīr by al-Akhṭal and al-Farazdaq, his rivals.

6. Ḥarzah is the son of Jarīr.

7. Abū Lubnā is the *shayṭān* of al-Farazdaq. The Arabs believe that every poet has a *shayṭān*, a demon or familiar spirit, which inspires him to compose his poetry.

8. The following examples are illustrative.

(a) (al-Iṣfahānī 1868:XV, 147):

أتى الحُطيئة كعبَ بنَ زهَير، وكان الحُطيئة راويةَ زُهَير وآل زُهير، فقال له: يا كعبُ، قد عَلِمْتَ روايتي لكم أهلَ البيت، وانْقطاعي إليكم، وقد ذَهب الفحول غيري وغيْرَك؛ فلو قلتَ شِعْرًا تَذْكُر فيه نَفسك وتَضعني موضعًا بَعْدك؟ – وقال أبو عُبيدة في خبره: تَبدأُ بِنفسك فيه وتُثنّي بي – فإنّ الناس لأشعاركم أرْوَى، وإليها أسْرع؛ فقال كعبٌ:

فمَن للقوافي شانَها من يَحُوكها   إذا ما ثَوَى كَعْبٌ وفَوَّزَ جَرْوَلُ

يَقول فلا يَعْيَا بشيء يَقُــوله   ومِنْ قائِليها من يُسيءُ ويَعْجَل

كَفَيْتُك لا تَلْقَى مِن النّاس واحدًا   تَنَخَّلَ منها مِثْلَ ما يتَنَخَّل

يُثقّفها حتى تَلينَ مُتُونُهــا   فيَقْصُرُ عنها كلّ ما يُتَمَثّـــل

(b) By Suwayd Ibn Kirā[c] al-Iklī (al-Jāḥiẓ 1968:II, 12–13):

أَبِيتُ بأبوابِ القوافي كأنّمـــا   أُصادِي بها سِرْبًا من الوَحشِ نُزَّعا

أُكالِئُها حتى أُعَرِّسَ بعد ما   يكون سُحَيرًا أو بُعَيدًا فأهجعا

عَواصِيَ إلّا ما جعلتُ أمامَها   عَصا مِرْبَدٍ تغشى نُحورًا وأذرُعا

أهَبْتُ بغُرِّ الآبدات فراجعت   طريقًا أمَلّتهُ القصــائدُ مَهْيَعا

بعيــدةَ شأوٍ، لا يكادُ يَرُدُّها   لها طالبٌ حتى يَكِلَّ ويَظلَعا

إذا خِفتُ أن تُروى عَلَيّ رددتُها   وراءَ التراقي خشــيةَ أن تَطَلَّعا

وجشّمني خوفُ ابن عَفّان رَدَّها   فثقّفتُهـــا حَولًا جَرِيدًا ومَرْبَعا

(c) By Imru' al-Qays (Ibn Rashīq 1963:I, 200):

أذود القوافَ عَنَّى ذِيَاداً ‏'' ‏'' ذِيادَ غلامٍ جَرى، جَرَادَا

فلما كَثُرْنَ وَعَنَّيْنَهُ تَخَيَّرَ مِنْهُنَّ شَتَّى جِيادا

فأعزِلُ مَرْجَانَهَا جَانِباً وآخُذُ من دُرِّها المُسْتَجادا

(d) By al-Ḥuṭay'ah (ibid.: 116)

الشعرُ صَعْبٌ وطَويلٌ سُلَّمه والشعرُ لا يَسْطِيعه من يَظْلِمُهْ

إذا ارْتَقَى فيه الذى لا يعلمه زَلَّتْ به إلى الحضيض قَدَمُهْ

يُرِيدُ أن يُعرِبَ به فيعجمه

9. See also Ḍayf (1965:9–19).

10. Tribesmen were fond of memorizing poems by their own tribal poets, especially those poems which praised their own tribe and defamed its enemies. One poet poked fun at the tribesmen of Banū Taghlib, who were so preoccupied with reciting a boastful poem by their chief, 'Amr Ibn Kalthūm, that they forgot to perform the glorious deeds which the poem claimed for them:

> alhā banī taghlibin 'an kulli makrumatin // qaṣīdatun qālahā
> 'amru bnu kalthūmu,
> yarwūnahā abadan mudh kāna awwaluhum // yā la 'r-rijali la-shi'rin
> ghayri mas'ūmi.

11. For a full discussion of the transmission process in ancient Arabic poetry, see al-Asad (1966:188–255).

BIBLIOGRAPHY

Note: Transliteration of Arabic names, titles, etc., follows the system of the Library of Congress. The definite article *al-* is disregarded for purposes of alphabetization; other particles, such as *Abū, Ibn,* which form part of names, are treated as such for alphabetization purposes. Dates given as A.H. (anno Hegirae) refer to the Muslim lunar calendar (e.g., A.H. 1374 = A.D. 1953/54); for conversion to the corresponding Gregorian dates, consult Lt. Col. Sir Wolseley Haig, *Comparative Tables of Muhammadan and Christian Dates* (Lahore: Ashraf Press, n.d.).

List of Abbreviations

AIEO = *Annales de l'Institut d'Études Orientales d'Alger*
BSOAS = *Bulletin of the School of Oriental and African Studies, University of London*
JAF = *Journal of American Folklore*
JAL = *Journal of Arabic Literature*
JAOS = *Journal of the American Oriental Society*
JRAS = *Journal of the Royal Asiatic Society of Great Britain and Ireland*
JRCAS = *Journal of the Royal Central Asian Society*
JRGS = *Journal of the Royal Geographic Society*
JSS = *Journal of Semitic Studies*
Proc. Amer. Philos. Soc. = *Proceedings of the American Philosophical Society*
PMLA = *Publications of the Modern Language Association of America*
ZDMG = *Zeitschrift der Deutschen Morgenländischen Gesellschaft*
ZS = *Zeitschrift für Semitistik*

Abboud, P. F.
1965 The Syntax of Najdi Arabic. Ph.D. dissertation, Linguistics Department, University of Texas at Austin.

Abū Mājid, ʿAlī
1963 *Maẓlūm; dīwān shiʿr.* Damascus: Maṭbaʿat Dimashq.

Āl-Thānī, Qāsim Ibn Muḥammad
A.H. 1384 *Dīwān al-shaykh Qāsim ibn Muḥammad Āl Thānī wa-qaṣāʾid ukhrā nabaṭīyah.* Qatar: Maṭābiʿ Qatar al-Waṭanīyah.

Alwaya, S.
1977 Formulas and Themes in Contemporary Bedouin Oral Poetry. *JAL* 8:47–76.

Amīn, B. S.
1972 *Muṭālaʿāt fī al-shiʿr al-Mamlūkī wa-al-ʿUthmānī.* Beirut: Dār al-Sharq.

Andrzejewski, B. W.
1963 Poetry in Somali Society. *New Society* 25 (21 March):22–24.

Andrzejewski, B. W., and I. M. Lewis
1964 *Somali Poetry: An Introduction.* Oxford: The Clarendon Press.

ʿĀnūtī, U.
1970 *al-Ḥarakah al-adabīyah fī bilād al-Shām khilāl al-qarn al-thānī ʿashar.* Beirut: al-Jāmiʿah al-Lubnānīyah, Qism al-Dirāsāt al-Adabīyah, Manshūrāt, 6.

Arberry, Arthur John
1957 *The Seven Odes: The First Chapter in Arabic Literature.* London: George Allen & Unwin.

al-Asad, N.
1966 *Maṣādir al-shiʿr al-Jāhilī wa-qīmatuhā al-tārīkhīyah.* 3d ed. Cairo: Dār al-Maʿārif.

el-Azma, Nazeer
1980 The Qurʾan and Poetry. *Al-ʿArabiyyah* 13:65–79.

Bābuṭayn, A.
1969 *al-Majmūʿah al-bahīyah min al-ashʿār al-nabaṭīyah.* Riyadh: Maktabat al-Riyāḍ al-Ḥadīthah.

al-Badhdhāl, Mirshid
1975 *Dīwān al-shāʿir Mirshid al-Badhdhāl.* A. N. al-Ṣāniʿ, ed. Kuwait: Maṭbaʿat Ḥukūmat al-Kuwayt.

Bailey, C.
1972 The Narrative Context of the Bedouin Qaṣīdah-Poem. *The Hebrew University, Jerusalem, Folklore Research Studies* 3: 67–105.

Bateson, Mary Catherine
1970 *Structural Continuity in Poetry: A Linguistic Study of Five Pre-Islamic Arabic Odes.* The Hague: Mouton.

Baugh, Albert C.
1959 Improvisation in the Middle English Romance. *Proc. Amer. Philos. Soc.* 103:418–454.
1967 The Middle English Romance; Some Questions of Creation, Presentation, and Preservation. *Speculum* 42:1–31.
Ben-Cheneb, Mohammad.
1924 Ḳāfiya. *The Encyclopaedia of Islam* II:621–622.
Benson, Larry D.
1966 The Literary Character of Anglo-Saxon Formulaic Poetry. *PMLA* 81:334–341.
Blachère, René
1952–1956 *Histoire de la Littérature Arabe.* 3 vols. Paris: Adrien-Maisonneuve.
Blank, H.
1953 *Studies in North Palestinian Arabic.* Israel Oriental Society, Oriental Notes and Studies, No. 4.
1970 The Arab Dialects of Negev Bedouins. *Proc. Israel Acad. of Science and Humanities* 4(7):112–150.
Blau, J.
1963 The Role of the Bedouins as Arbiters in Linguistic Questions and the Masʾala Zunburiyyah. *JSS* 81:42–51.
1965 *The Emergence and Linguistic Background of Judaeo-Arabic.* Oxford: Oxford University Press.
Blunt, Lady A. I. N.
1879 *Bedouin Tribes of the Euphrates.* 2 vols. London: J. Murray.
1881 *A Pilgrimage to Najd.* 2 vols. London: J. Murray.
Bonebakker, S. A.
1974 Ḳāfiya. *The Encyclopaedia of Islam.* New ed. IV:411–414.
Burckhardt, J. L.
1831 *Notes on the Bedouins and Wahabys.* 2 vols. London: H. Colburn and R. Bentley.
Burton, Sir Richard
1964 *Personal Narrative of a Pilgrimage to al-Madinah and Meccah.* New York: Dover Publications Inc.
Campbell, Jackson J.
1960 Oral Poetry in the *Seafarer*. *Speculum* 35:87–96.
Cantineau, J.
1936–1937 Etudes sur Quelques Parlers de Nomades Arabes d'Orient. *AIEO* 2:1–118; 3:119–237
Chadwick H. M., and N. K. Chadwick
1940 *The Growth of Literature.* 3 vols. Cambridge: Cambridge University Press.

Crosby, R.
1936 Oral Delivery in the Middle Ages. *Speculum* 11:88–110.
Curschmann, Michael
1967 Oral Poetry in Mediaeval English, French, and German Literature; Some Notes on Recent Research. *Speculum* 42:36–52.
Ḍayf, Shawqī
1965 *al-Balāghah, taṭawwur wa-tārīkh*. Cairo: Dār al-Maᶜārif.
Dickson, H. R. P.
1949 *The Arab of the Desert*. London: George Allen & Unwin.
Doughty, Charles
1921 *Travels in Arabia Deserta*. 2 vols. New York: Random House.
Dundes, A.
1966 Metafolklore and Oral Literary Criticism. *The Monist* 50:505–516.
al-Faraj, Kh. M.
1952 *Dīwān al-Nabaᶜt*. 2 vols. Damascus: Maṭbaᶜat al-Taraqqī.
Finnegan, Ruth
1974 How Oral Is Oral Literature? *BSOAS* 37:52–64.
1976 What Is Oral Literature Anyway? Comments in the Light of Some African and Other Comparative Material. In *Oral Literature and the Formula*, B. A. Stolz and R. S. Shanon, eds., pp. 127–166. Ann Arbor: University of Michigan, Center for the Coordination of Ancient and Modern Studies.
1977 *Oral Poetry*. London: Cambridge University Press.
al-Firdaws, F. M.
n.d. *Dīwān Ibn Firdaws*. Kuwait: Dār al-Siyāsah.
Friedman, A. B.
1961 The Formulaic Improvisation Theory of Ballad Tradition—A Counterstatement. *JAF* 74:113–115.
al-Fuhayd, Mandīl
1978 *Min ādābinā al-shaᶜbīyah*. Riyadh: Dār al-Yamāmah lil-Baḥth wa-al-Tarjumah wa-al-Nashr.
al-Ghamrāwī, Muḥammad Aḥmad
1970 *al-Naqd al-taḥlīlī li-kitāb Fī al-adab al-Jāhilī*. Beirut: Dār al-Ḥikmah.
Gibb, Sir H. A. R.
1948 Arab Poet and Arabic Philologist. *BSOAS* 12:574–578.
1968 *Arabic Literature*. London: Oxford University Press.
Glubb, Sir John Bagot
1935 The Bedouins of Northern Iraq. *JRCAS* 22(1):13–31.
1937 Arab Chivalry. *JRCAS* 24(1):5–26.
1960 *War in the Desert*. New York: W. W. Norton & Company.

Goldziher, Ignaz
1966 *A Short History of Classical Arabic Literature*. J. de Somogyi, trans. Hildesheim: Georg Olms Verlagsbuchhandlung.
Gray, Bennison
1971 Repetition in Oral Literature. *JAF* 84:289–303.
Guarmani, C.
1938 *Northern Najd*. Lady Capel-Cure, trans. London: The Argonaut Press.
Gyger, A.
1969 The Old English *Soul and Body* as an Example of Oral Transmission. *Medium Aevum* 38:239–249.
al-Hadhdhāl, ʿA. ʿI.
A.H. 1392 *Mukhtārāt min al-shiʿr al-nabaṭī al-muʿāṣir*. Riyadh: Maṭābiʿ al-Shihrī.
Harris, L.
1962 *Swahili Poetry*. Oxford: The Clarendon Press.
al-Ḥātam, A. Kh.
1968 *Khiyār mā yultaqaṭ min al-shiʿr al-Nabaṭ*. Damascus: al-Maṭbaʿah al-ʿUmūmīyah.
Ḥusayn, Muḥammad al-Khiḍr
1927 *Naqd kitāb Fī al-shiʿr al-Jāhilī*. Cairo: al-Maṭbaʿah al-Salafīyah.
Ḥusayn, Ṭāhā
1926 *Fī al-shiʿr al-Jāhilī*. Cairo: Dār al-Kutub al-Miṣrīyah.
Ibn Ḥuraywil, S. Ḥ.
A.H. 1374 *Dīwān al-Nabaṭ al-ḥadīth*. Beirut: Maṭābiʿ al-Wafāʾ.
Ibn Jinnī, Abū al-Fatḥ ʿUthmān
1952–1956 *al-Khaṣāʾiṣ*. Muḥammad ʿAlī Najjār, ed. 2d ed. 3 vols. Cairo: Dār al-Kutub al-Miṣrīyah.
Ibn Khaldūn
1967 *al-Muqaddimah*. 3rd ed. Beirut: Dar al-Kitāb al-Lubnānī.
Ibn Khamīs, A.
1958 *al-Adab al-shaʿbī fī Jazīrat al-ʿArab*. Riyadh: Maṭābiʿ al-Riyāḍ.
1972 *Rāshid al-Khalāwī*. Riyadh: Dār al-Yamāmah lil-Baḥth wa-al-Tarjumah wa-al-Nashr.
1978 *Min aḥādīth al-samar*. Riyadh: Maṭābiʿ Sharikat Ḥanīfah lil-Ofset.
Ibn Qutayban, ʿAbd Allāh Ibn Muslim
1966 *al-Shiʿr wa-al-shuʿarāʾ*. Aḥmad Muḥammad Shākir, ed. 2 vols. Cairo: Dār al-Maʿārif.
Ibn Raddās, A. M.
n.d.–1976 *Shāʿirāt min al-bādiyah*. 2 vols. Riyadh: Dār al-Yamāmah lil-Baḥth wa-al-Tarjumah wa-al-Nashr.

A.H. 1398 *Shuʿarāʾ min al-bādiyah*. Riyadh: Maṭābiʿ al-Bādiyah lil-Ofsit.

Ibn Rashīd, D.
1966 *Nubdhah tārīkhīyah ʿan Najd*. As told to Wadīʿ al-Bustānī. Riyadh: Dār al-Yamāmah lil-Baḥth wa-al-Tarjumah wa-al-Nashr.

Ibn Rashīq, Abū ʿAli al-Ḥasan
1963 *al-ʿumdah fī mahāsin al-shiʿr wa-ʾādābih wa-naqdih* (Muḥammad Muḥyiddīn ʿAbdulḥamīd, ed.). 2 vols. Cairo: Maṭbaʿat al-Saʿadah.

Ibn Sayḥān, M. S.
1965–1969 *al-Tuḥfah al-rashīdīyah fī al-ashʿār al-nabaṭīyah*. 2 vols. Kuwait: Maṭbaʿat al-Risālah.

al-Iṣfahānī, Abū al-Faraj
1868 *Kitāb al-Aghānī*. I. Guidi, ed. 21 vols. Leiden: E. J. Brill.

al-Jāḥiẓ, Abū ʿUthmān ʿAmr Ibn Baḥr
1968 *al-Bayān wa-al-tabyīn*. ʿAbd al-Salām Muḥammad Hārūn, ed. 3d ed. 4 vols. Cairo: Maktabat al-Khānjī.

al-Jāsir, Ḥ.
1971 Muʾarrikhū Najd min ahlihā. *al-ʿArab* 5:785–801.

Johnson, J. W.
1971 *The Development of the Genre heello in Modern Somali*. Master's Thesis (philosophy), University of London.

Johnstone, T. M.
1967*a* Aspects of Syllabication in the Spoken Arabic of Anaizah. *BSOAS* 40:1–16.
1967*b* *East Arabian Dialect Studies*. London: Oxford University Press.

Jones, J. H.
1961 Commonplace and Memorization in the Oral Tradition of English and Scottish Popular Ballads. *JAF* 74:97–112.

al-Jumaḥī, Muhammad Ibn Sallām
n.d. *Ṭabaqāt al-shuʿarāʾ*. Beirut: Dār al-Nahḍah al-ʿArabīyah.

Kamāl, M. S.
1960–1971 *al-Azhār al-nādiyah min ashʿār al-bādiyah*. 13 vols. Cairo: Maṭbaʿat al-Madanī.

al-Kamālī, Sh.
1964 *al-shiʿr ʿinda al-Badw*. Baghdād: Maṭbaʿat al-ʾIrshād.

Knott, E., and G. Murphy
1967 *Early Irish Literature*. London: Routledge & Kegan Paul.

Landberg, C. de
1895 *Critica arabica* 3. Leiden: E. J. Brill.

1919 *Langue des Bédouins Anazeh*. Leiden: E. J. Brill.
1940 *Glossaire de la Langue des Bédouins Anazeh*. K. V. Zetterstéen, ed. Uppsala: Almqvist & Wiksells Boktryckeri.

Lord, Albert B.
1960 *The Singer of Tales*. New York: Atheneum.

Lyall, Sir Charles James
1885 *Translations of Ancient Arabian Poetry*. London: Williams and Norgate.
1918–1921 *The Mufaḍḍalīyāt, an Anthology of Ancient Arabian Odes. Translation and Notes*. 2 vols. Oxford: The Clarendon Press.

Magoun, F. P.
1953 Oral Formulaic Character of Anglo-Saxon Narrative Poetry. *Speculum* 28:446–467.
1955 Bede's Story of Caedmon: The Case History of an Anglo-Saxon Oral Singer. *Speculum* 30:49–63.

Margoliouth, D. S.
1925 The Origins of Arabic Poetry. *JRAS*, 417–449.

al-Mārik, Fahad
1963–1965 *Min shiyam al-ᶜArab*. 4 vols. Beirut: al-Maktabah al-Ahlīyah.

Monroe, James
1972 Oral Composition in Pre-Islamic Poetry: The Problem of Authenticity. *JAL* 3:1–53.

Musil, Alois
1927 *Arabia Deserta*. New York: The Czech Academy of Sciences and Arts & C. R. Crane.
1928 *The Manners and Customs of the Rwala Bedouins*. New York: The Czech Academy of Sciences and Arts & C. R. Crane.

Nicholson, Reynold Alleyne
1969 *A Literary History of the Arabs*. Cambridge: Cambridge University Press.

O'Neil, W. A.
1960 Another Look at Oral Poetry in the *Seafarer*. *Speculum* 35:596–600.

Palgrave, W. G.
1865–1866 *Narrative of a Year's Journey through Central and Eastern Arabia*. 2 vols. London: Macmillan and Co.

Palva, H.
1976 *Studies in the Arabic Dialect of the Semi-Nomadic ǝl-ʕAǧārma Tribe (al-Balqā District, Jordan)*. Acta Universitatis Gothoburgensis, Orientalia Gothoburgensia, No. 2.

Paredes, A.
1964 *Some Aspects of Folk Poetry.* Texas Studies in Literature and Language, 6.
Philby, H. St. John B.
1922 *The Heart of Arabia.* 2 vols. London: Constable.
1928 *Arabia of the Wahabis.* London: Constable.
1955 *Saudi Arabia.* New York: Frederick A. Praeger.
al-Qurashī, Abū Zayd Muḥammad
1967 *Jamharat ashʿār al-ʿArab.* ʿAlī Muḥammad al-Bajjāwī, ed. Cairo: Dār Nahḍat Miṣr.
al-Rāfiʿī, Muṣṭafā Ṣādiq
1953–1954 *Tārīkh ʾadāb al-ʿArab.* 3 vols. Cairo: Maṭbaʿat al-Istiqāmah.
1956 *Taḥta rāyat al-Qurʾān.* Cairo: Maṭbaʿat al-Istiqāmah.
al-Rashīd, F.
1965–1972 *Shuʿarāʾ al-rass al-Nabaṭīyūn.* 2 vols. Damascus: al-Maṭbaʿah al-Hāshimīyah.
Rasmussen, K.
1931 *The Netsilik Eskimos: Social and Spiritual Culture.* Report of the Fifth Thule Expedition 1921–1924, vol. 8 (1–2). Copenhagen: Gyldendalske Boghandel, Nordisk Forlag.
Rogers, H. L.
1966 The Crypto-Psychological Character of Anglo-Saxon Poetry. *English Studies* 47:89–102.
Smith, John D.
1977 The Singer or the Song? A Reassessment of Lord's Oral Theory. *Man* (new series) 12:141–153.
Socin, Albert
1900–1901 *Diwan aus Centralarabien.* H. Stumme, ed. 3 parts. Leipzig: Abhandlungen der philologisch-historischen classe der Koniglich sachsischen Gesellschaft der Wissenschaften, No. 19.
Spoer, H. H.
1912 Four Poems by Nimr ibn Adwān, as Sung by Ōde Abū Slīmān. *ZDMG* 66:189–203.
Spoer, H. H., and E. N. Ḥaddād
1929 Poems by Nimr ibn Adwān. *ZS* 7:29–62, 274–294.
1933–1934 Poems by Nimr ibn Adwān. *ZS* 9:93–133.
Stevick, Robert D.
1962 The Oral Formulaic Analysis of Old English Verse. *Speculum* 37:282–289.
Stolz, B. A., and R. S. Shanon, eds.
1976 *Oral Literature and the Formula.* Ann Arbor: University of

Michigan, Center for the Coordination of Ancient and Modern Studies.
al-Sudayrī, M. A.
1968 *Abṭāl min al-ṣaḥrā'*. Beirut: Dār al-Kutub.
Thesiger, Wilfred
1959 *Arabian Sands*. New York: E. P. Dutton & Company.
al-Thumayrī, M. A.
1972 *al-Funūn al-shaʿbīyah fī al-Jazīrah al-ʿArabīyah*. Damascus: al-Maṭbaʿah al-ʿUmūmīyah.
al-ʿUbayyid, A. A.
1971 *Qabīlat al-ʿAwāzim*. Beirut: Maṭbaʿat al-Mutanabbī.
al-ʿUtaybī, Muṭlaq Ibn Muḥammad Ibn Bādi
A.H. 1390 *Dīwān Ibn Bādi*. Dammam (Saudi Arabia): Maṭābiʿ al-Muṭawwaʿ.
al-ʿUthaymīn, A.
1977 al-Shiʿr al-nabaṭī ka-maṣdar li-tārīkh Najd. *al-ʿArab* 11:839–863.
1978 Najd mundhu al-qarn al-ʿāshir al-Hijrī ḥattā ẓuhūr al-Shaykh Muḥammad Ibn ʿAbdalwahhāb; al-ḥālah al-dīnīyah. *Addārah* 4(3):32–46.
Vansina, Jan
1961 *Oral Tradition; A Study in Historical Methodology*. H. M. Wright, trans. London: Routledge & Kegan Paul.
Wallin, G. A.
1851 Probe aus einer Anthologie neuarabischer Gesänge in der Wüste gesammelt. *ZDMG* 5:1–23.
1852 Probe aus einer Anthologie neuarabischer Gesänge in der Wüste gesammelt. *ZDMG* 6:190–218, 369–378.
1854 Narrative of a Journey from Cairo to Medina and Mecca, by Suez, Arabá, Tawilá, al-Jauf, Jubbé, Háil, and Nejd, in 1845. *JRGS* 25:260–290.
1858 Bemerkungen über die Sprache der Beduinen. *ZDMG* 12:656–675.
Watts, A. C.
1969 *The Lyre and the Harp: A Comparative Reconsideration of Oral Tradition in Homer and Old English Epic Poetry*. New Haven: Yale University Press.
Weil, G.
1913 ʿArūḍ. *The Encyclopaedia of Islam* I:463–471.
1960 ʿArūḍ. *The Encyclopaedia of Islam*. New ed. I:67–77.
Weil, G., and G. S. Colin
1960 Abdjad. *The Encyclopaedia of Islam*. New ed. I:97–98.

Wetzstein, I. G.
1868 Sprachliches aus den Zeltlagern der syrischen Wüste. *ZDMG* 22:69–194.

Winder, R. B.
1965 *Saudi Arabia in the Nineteenth Century*. London: Macmillan.

Wright. W.
1971 *A Grammar of the Arabic Language*. 3d. ed. 2 vols. Cambridge: The Cambridge University Press.

Zwettler, Michael
1976 Classical Arabic Poetry between Folk and Oral Tradition. *JAOS* 96(2):198–212.
1978 *The Oral Tradition of Classical Arabic Poetry: Its Character and Implications*. Columbus: Ohio State University Press.

INDEX

Ab-al-Xēl, ᶜAbdal ᶜazīz Ibn ᶜAbdallāh al-Mhannā, 78
Ab-al-Xēl, Ḥasan al-Mhannā, 76, 77, 84
Ab-al-Xēl, Mḥammad Ibn ᶜAbdallāh al-Mhannā, 78, 83, 84
Ab-al-Xēl family, 75, 76, 78, 81, 84. *See also* al-Mhannā family
Abū Bakr, 202
Abu Dhabi, 102
Abu Ḥjāb, Saᶜad, 118, 120
Abu Ršēd, 121
al-ᶜAǵil, A., 12
al-Aḥwaṣ, 199
al-Akhṭal, 200, 201–202
Alphanumeric devices, 171–172
Alwān Shaᶜbīyah, 116, 117
Amēlāḥ, 38
al-ᶜĀmrī, Abū Ḥamzih, 1, 167, 179
ᶜAnazah tribe, 9, 41, 53, 57, 58–59, 60, 61, 62, 63, 65, 140; v. Shammar, 68, 70
Andrzejewski, B. W., 187, 188
Arabia: agriculture of, 19; alphabet of, 171; authority in, 67; caliphs of, 20; conformity in, 18; isolated, 165; kinship in, 23; language of, 148, 149, 150, 151–152; literacy in, 105; migration in, 1; nomads of, 19, 20—23, 24–27; oil in, 19; peoples of, 19–27; politics in, 1, 2–3, 20, 75–87, 118; premodern, 67; rain in, 19, 35; regionalism in, 67; settlers of, 19, 20, 21, 22, 23–24, 25; statehood in, 87; subsistence patterns in, 19–20; war in, 20–21
Arberry, Arthur J., 176
al-ᶜArfaj, Mḥammad al-ᶜAlī, 180
al-Aṭraš, Srūr, 97, 121, 122
al-ᶜAwāzim tribe, 9

al-ᶜBād, Ali as-Sālm, 12
al-Badri, Mbārak, 121, 122
Bagᶜa, battle of, 70–71, 72
Bahrain, 102
Bailey, C., 8
al-Ballāᶜ, Ṣālḥ an-Nāṣr, 117, 118, 120, 121
Banu Hilāl tribe, 139
Baugh, Albert C., 184, 185, 187
Bedouins. *See* Nomads
Benson, Larry D., 184, 185
Bini Ṣaxar tribe, 140
Biography, 53–66
Blunt, Lady A. I. N., 8
al-Brāziyyih, Mwēḏi, 107
Buraidah, 69, 75, 76, 84
Burckhardt, J. L., 39, 41
Burton, Richard F., 2
al-Bustānī, Wadīᶜ, 8

Camel: 27, 29; defended, 34, 38, 44; herds, 28, 31, 34–35; ideal, 33–34; importance of, 33; in nomadism, 33; pack, 34, 137; in raiding, 35; riding, 34; speed of, 58; as theme in poetry, 32, 33, 57–58, 81–82, 168
Camp, breaking of, 28, 168; as theme in poetry, 25, 26–27, 29, 30, 114, 136, 155

Designer:	U.C. Press Staff
Compositor:	Prestige Typography
Printer:	Thomson-Shore, Inc.
Binder:	John H. Dekker & Sons
Text:	10/12 Sabon Roman
Display:	Sabon